HARNESS-MAKING

SADDLERY
AND
HARNESS-MAKING

WITH NUMEROUS ENGRAVINGS AND DIAGRAMS

EDITED BY

PAUL N. HASLUCK

J. A. ALLEN AND COMPANY, LTD.
1 LOWER GROSVENOR PLACE, LONDON, S.W.1.

© J. A. ALLEN & CO. LTD. 1962

Reprinted by
J. A. Allen & Co. Ltd.
1 Lower Grosvenor Place
London SW1W 0EL

1971, 1972, 1973, 1975, 1979, 1994

SBN 85131 148 2

(reproduced from the original edition of 1904
by permission of Messrs. Cassell and Company, Limited)

Printed in Hong Kong

FOREWORD

By R. E. WHITING

*Past Master of the Worshipful Company
of Saddlers*

WHEN I was asked to write a foreword on the conditions of the Saddlery Trade for the reprint of those instructive books, Hasluck's Saddle and Harness Making, I realised that I should have to rely greatly on my memory of the conditions in our trade for the last 56 years, as most of those who were employed in one capacity or the other previous to 1905, have passed away, and many interesting records of my own firm were destroyed in the " Blitz ".

Perhaps I should say that the date of the previous publication of the above books, viz. 1904, was the peak in the Harness trade. Practically all road transport was horse drawn, the Omnibus Companies had hardly begun to mechanise, as I see that, according to the records of the L.G.O.C., they had only 20 motor vehicles at the beginning of 1905, but 200 at the end of that year.

Employment was fairly constant at that date, wages for Harness makers varied between 7d. and 8d. per hour for a week of 50 hours or more, overtime was at the same rates, and there were no deductions made, nor any payment for holidays or lost time, unless the employer thought fit to do so, but conditions were much the same in all shops. Brown saddlers, or riding saddle makers, were probably paid a little more than above.

It was my impression in those days that the men were quite satisfied with their jobs, and they certainly took pride in their craft. It was not unusual for one man or the other to try and beat the time for a certain job, and to my knowledge, there were claimants who stated they had lined and flocked a collar in the London style, in 20 minutes, and a record of that description was passed from mouth to mouth throughout the shops in Town. To illustrate the speed of that claim, I should mention that 30 minutes was considered to be very fast indeed, and unlikely to be maintained over a long period in any day.

Not only was speed a matter of pride, but also neatness of sewing and workmanship, which even today can be seen on some of the old coach or state harnesses, where 14 or 16 to the inch in sewing was quite common, and the work beautifully executed. Apprenticeships were the usual method of learning the trade, up to the early part of this century it was 7 years, and is now 5.

In Greater London, the Worshipful Company of Saddlers has for a great many years indentured apprentices, and outside of that area our trade Association, the Retail Leather Goods and Saddlers, also assists in bringing youths into our trade. Many country craftsmen at one time apprenticed their own sons, and many still follow the trade today, although their interests lie largely with riding saddlery, and not harness making.

I have mentioned what I consider to be the peak in the harness trade. There was without a doubt, a gradual reduction from 1905 to the beginning of the first world war, although conditions and rates of pay remained fairly static. In August 1914 the Government commandeered a great number of horses, also their civilian pattern harness, for use with the Expeditionary Force, and it was from then onward that trade became really hectic.

Large orders for universal saddles, pole draft harness, and equipment, were pouring in, and some firms soon found themselves employing ten or more times their usual number of workmen. This demand was fairly constant throughout the war, as when the call for heavy harness was satisfied, there were quantities of pack saddlery for Egypt and the East, and equipment for Russia in 1917, also harness for use on farms, in the great food production drive in 1918.

I cannot be explicit about trade conditions after 1916, as I was in the Army until early in 1919, but I do know that my firm had a strike during that period, something about making shoe pockets at 2/8 each. They went to arbitration and lost the day!

After 1918 there was, as some people will remember, a period of prosperity which raised all wages and other costs, but in 1921, for the harness trade at least, came the slump. Wages dropped back to 1/4 or 1/6 per hour, employment was very difficult, and competition for what orders there were about was extremely keen. This continued into the '30's, but when you realise what the miners and other trades had to put up with, we were not too badly placed, although there was little or no scope for expansion. In fact it was not until 1938 and 1939 that, with the rumours, and later, the inevitability, of war, that the riding and racing really collapsed. It was then that some West End firms shut down, the workmen going into other sections of the Leather trade, or joining the few firms which at that time had Government orders.

There was never anything like the same demand for saddlery and leather equipment during the last war, some firms found themselves with a certain amount of work, but others found the bombing more than disruptive, and labour in London was not easy to obtain.

From 1945 to date, we have perhaps had the

greatest changes that have come over industry in all trades. Saddlers and Harness makers now earning twice as much as they did 15 years ago, and the younger men are asking for, and getting, anything from £12 to £16 per week, with full employment. Are they more satisfied with the conditions of 1961 than their predecessors were in 1911—I doubt it!

I trust the reprint of these two useful manuals will be of invaluable help in maintaining the standard of our craft and the appreciation of good workmanship for which the saddlers and harness makers in this country have been so justly famed.

London, 1961.

CONTENTS.

LIST OF ILLUSTRATIONS.

8   SADDLERY.

SADDLERY.

CHAPTER I.

GENTLEMAN'S RIDING SADDLE.

THIS handbook will treat on practical saddlery as more or less distinct from the making and repairing of harness, which is discussed in a companion volume on "Harness Making," where, however, will be found full descriptions of all tools, appliances, and materials necessary for the work. The elementary processes of cutting up hides, stitching, etc., are also explained in the volume on "Harness Making," and bits, spurs, stirrups, and furniture of all kinds fully described and illustrated. It is assumed here that the worker has a general acquaintance with the craft of the harness-maker.

In making a gentleman's riding saddle, the first article needed is a tree (Fig. 1), which can be bought with a round cantle (the back rising part) or with a square one rounded at the corners, and running in a straight line at the top.

The gullet or fore part of the tree is made in many styles; it may be straight or slanting backwards towards the seat, and it can be obtained full, half, or quarter cut. The tree may be measured along the centre, but the trade method is to measure it at the sides; the seat is measured across the widest part.

There are different styles of saddles both as regards work and material—namely, full shafts, covered all over with hogskin, with knee-pads or flaps ; all hogskin without knee-pads, a style which is called all over hogskin plain flaps ; or full shafts, top and solid flaps—that is, the seat and skirts are hogskin, and the flap is of solid single-stamped leather, plain without knee-pads.

Another style is called shafts top demi-flap, the seat and skirts being covered with hogskin and a knee-pad with hogskin on a plain flap. Another variety is the half shafts with only solid skirts, the seat and flaps being covered with hogskin and having knee-pads on flaps. The commonest style, however, is a hogskin seat with solid leather skirts and flaps and without knee-pads on the flaps.

The saddle bars to which the stirrup leathers

Fig. 1.—Saddle Tree.

are fastened also vary in make and pattern ; there is the ordinary spring bar and numerous patent bars, the attempt being to obtain a secure fastening for the strap and at the same time a loosening of it, in case of accident, to prevent the rider being dragged along by the foot.

The hanging or setting of the flaps is a mere matter of taste ; sometimes the bottom slopes forward, and sometimes the flap is in a straight line with the front of the saddle (see Fig. 2).

To make a saddle, begin by preparing enough straining web to run along the centre twice its length and once over, with 4 in. hanging down below the tree just outside the saddle bars and towards the back. Having damped the web, nail each end firmly to a board—unless a web strainer

is used—and then push something underneath it
to stretch it to the utmost.

After letting it dry, damp it once or twice
according to the stretching necessary, but let it dry
before being again damped. When stretched, cut
it in two and nail two ends of it at the head of
the tree in front, just outside the iron plate, one
end slanting slightly to one side and the other to
the opposite side.

Having pulled them together tight, nail them
at the back of the tree low down below the cantle
on the flat part. This slanting position throws

Fig. 2.—Gentleman's Riding Saddle.

them from 5 in. to 6 in. apart at the back as they
are required ; with headed saddle tacks nail them
down closely, and tack the other piece of web
across close to the saddle bar, bringing it a little
under the point where the bar is riveted to the
trees. Let 4 in. hang down on each side, and pull
it very tightly over the web at the top, nailing it
down with saddle tacks.

Next take another piece of web (any diaper
web will do) and lay it close to the other web
behind, then nail it down tightly ; but it need not
hang over. Run a stitch from one web to the

other, joining them across the top. A piece of
strong linen, large enough to run from the web
all round the seat behind, is stitched across to the
web; nail it round the sides and back of the seat,
covering the points of the web nailed behind.

Having pulled it tight, nail it in a position
which gives the seat when stuffed a suitable rise
towards the cantle, as this is the ground for the
stuffing. Now stitch another piece of linen to
the web in front to cover this part, and nail it
firmly all round, and the seat will then be covered
over without hollow but with a foundation for
stuffing.

Take a piece of basil leather about 6 in. long
or a little less, double it together along the centre,
making it pointed at one end and rather full at
the other. When stuffed it should be a little
thicker than the middle finger at the full end,
tapering away to a fine point at the other. Stitch
the edges together from one side to the other,
but not over, and leave a small opening at one
end, through which the pad can then be stuffed
smoothly and tightly with flock. The hole must
now be closed and flattened slightly with the
mallet. This raises each side of the seat near the
root of the cantle, the thick end being close to
the cantle and the fine end running forward. Put
the pads in their places on each side, flush with
the edge of the tree, and, after rounding them to
follow the shape, nail them on the inside, putting
a nail in the thick end to fasten it to the cantle
at the bottom.

The seat must be covered all over with white
serge; nail it over the edge of the cantle and over
the gullet underneath in front, and underneath
the sides as far as where the web hangs down by
the bar. From this point towards the front, back-
stitch it coarsely to just the shape of the skirt
and seat; thus the seat is gradually narrowed

from the bottom to near the front part of the tree, but just in the front it widens slightly. The shape must be studied and the stitching done accordingly, of course through the foundation and cover at this part.

Now back-stitch the cover through the tree for exactly the length of the leather pads placed at the sides, in order to draw the cover in a little under the side of the pads and allow the seat and skirts at the joint of each to enter the hollow when the seat is adjusted.

Rub a patch, about 2½ in. by 1 in., in the centre of the cover with a lump of black wax, so that it will not unravel when a hole is cut there for stuffing. In the centre of this patch cut a slit 1¼ in. long, and, after passing a pound of white flock through the carding machine three or four times and clipping the wool, if long, with scissors, put it through the opening in small quantities. Use the seat iron for this work, moving the flock about to the sides to prevent lumps; continue stuffing until all is firm and level. Pass the left hand over the seat to ascertain that there is no unevenness, and level it with the seat awl held in the right hand; great care is needed to perform this operation properly. When the stuffing is finished a stitch must be run in the opening.

The seat, which should be cut from a piece of good hogskin large enough to cover the seat well and be nailed underneath, can now be adjusted. Damp and nail it on firmly, taking care that it is quite smooth in all parts; nail it underneath over the sides and at the back in such a manner that the nails can easily be pulled out with a claw, and that no mark will be left when the saddle is finished. Any mark would be visible and would stain the leather, thus completely spoiling the work. Pull it together behind the cantle so as to make all the small pleats form two large ones,

one on each side of the crupper staple ; thus they
can be cut and the edges stitched neatly together
when dry.

After letting the seat dry, cut the skirts (Fig. 3)
from a flat piece of brown skirt leather, and cover
them with hogskin, which must be pasted over
them before stitching and then allowed to dry ;
or paste a piece of serge on them, running to
within ¼ in. from the edge all round, and, when
dry, cover them with hogskin and stitch without
pasting.

Before either covering or stitching, cut a piece
of hogskin belly to run at a distance of 1 in. from
the edge along the under part of the skirt to
within 4 in. from the narrow point and 1½ in. beyond in front, but low enough down to be nailed
under the tree when the skirt is in place. Paste
some linen on the flesh side of this for lining, and
when it has dried put it in position on the skirt
and cut holes through the skirt over the edge with
a shoemaker's bent awl. The holes must not go
through, but only be raised in the grain, which
will be the under side when the skirt is finished.

Stitch on the hogskin cover, making fine
stitches with yellow hemp, silk, or white linen
thread, and beeswax near the edge. Run a row
of stitches along the top ¾ in. from the edge from
end to end, and then rub, polish, and finish well.
When the piece to be nailed to the tree is dry,
stitch it with fine cord beeswax thread through the
holes previously made. Next prepare the flaps.

Knee-pads must be put in the front part of each
flap along the side ; then add the serge cover for
stuffing, which must reach from the point of the
skirt to the bottom, and be of the same shape
as the flap on the outside and straight on the
inside to within 3 in. of the top, and thence turned
round to the front. Spot the serge in from underneath, marking the straight line with a rule

and creasing the outer line far enough inside to allow of stitching over again between it and the edge.

Slip two or three stitches just at the turning from the straight line at the top, bringing the thread over the serge so that there will be a hollow to stuff through before making another stitch. Then take the flap or shafteau block, and through the flap put a nail into the board in each end of the pad; stuff it full and evenly through the opening left for the purpose, moving the flock to its place with the seat awl. Give the pad a good shape, full in front and sloping towards the inside.

Fig. 3.—Saddle Skirt.

A small flat padding must also be placed on the opposite side of the flap at the top corner just below the swelling of the skirts from the narrow part over the flap. Spot a piece of serge slack there exactly the same shape as this corner of the skirt, and straight towards the bottom edge of the flap. A small opening like that in the knee-pad must be left for stuffing; fill it level. The flaps must be cut in pairs, and, like the skirts, should be made with the grain side underneath outside.

When the pads are on the flap, paste a piece of hogskin over them; then let them dry on the shafteau block to its shape. The hogskin must always be damped before the paste is applied, then pulled tightly over, and the nails must be placed so that their marks can be cut off. A band of leather will also be needed along the straight side of the knee-pad to keep the hogskin close to the flap. Along the front run a smooth piece of string (nailing it at each end) to pull the hogskin into the hollow along the edge between the flap and the pad; let them thus dry. On removal from the block, cut the hogskin close to the edge of the flap and stitch the hogskin on firmly all round, and finish neatly, levelling the edges with sandpaper before polishing.

When the seat is dry the skirts must be stitched to it, the hogskin cover of the skirt being $\frac{1}{8}$ in. larger than the skirt along the top for stitching to the seat. Shave the edge of the hogskin to be stitched slightly, and, without removing the seat, place the skirt on the side of the saddle exactly in the position it should occupy when finished. It is better to arrange both skirts at the same time, employing tacks to keep them in place. Mark a line along the seat on the edge of the skirt, and also mark the various positions of the several parts of the skirt on the seat, so that if the former happens to stretch a little when being stitched, it can be pulled to place during work. Dots may be made with pen and ink in such a manner as not to be visible when the seat and skirt are stitched.

Before removing the seat from the tree, run a sharp knife along the mark from end to end of the skirt. Take enough dogskin welt to reach from end to end of the upper edge of the skirt and about 1 in. beyond; whip it to the edge of the skirt from end to end, employing single linen thread for the purpose, and making the stitches quite regular, so that when the seat is put in, the stitches can be run through the same holes. The welt must only just show when the leathers on either side are joined.

Having damped the edges a little, back-stitch

the seat to the skirt, .using a pointed needle and thimble, and employing the holes by which the welt was whipped; take care that the marks on the seat and skirt are exactly opposite. The pieces used in nailing the skirt and seat to the tree must be separate by 4 in. from the narrow part, and when these parts are being stitched together along this distance a piece of the hogskin seat should be stitched on with the skirt and seat; bring it back from the point of the skirt to catch the stitches in such a manner that the point will run out between two leathers, the seat being on one side and this piece brought back on the other.

Fig. 4.—Saddle Flap.

Two pleats must be cut behind the cantle and stitched with a pointed needle from underneath, the stitches being run half through the leather on both sides so as not to be visible on the outside. The points of the tree projecting beyond the saddle bars must be covered with thin basil or hogskin; damp and paste it down from the front round the sides of the point to within 1 in. of the bottom and a little above the saddle bar.

Now adjust the seat and skirts, previously damping the seat all over; be careful that it does not get stained whilst damp by contact with iron. Nail the front over the gullet underneath the tree,

making the skirts perfectly level like the seat;
nail it behind close by the edge of the iron plate
under the tree, and slit it to go through the
crupper staple. Small pincers may be employed
to pull it.

The sides can now be fastened, a nail being
driven alternately into each so that the seat will
be quite square and straight. Cut a slit in the
leather just nailed down, opposite the pieces of
straining web left hanging, preserving the same
width of leather as that of the web. Pull the
leather tight with pincers and drive a row of nails
through both into the tree. Trim off the surplus
web and the waste round the seat close to the
nails.

To adjust the flaps (Fig. 4), cut a nick upwards
in front of each, a little wider than the point at
this particular place, so as to run above it. The
other portion passes under the tree behind the
saddle bar, the next cut being above the hanging
web. The end of this should be cut half-round,
the farther portion being put round under the
tree and nailed close to the skirt. Thus when the
pad is fixed it will fit neatly to the corner of the
skirt. Then run two or three stitches through the
web piece and the piece above.

Now drive a tough silver nail through the top
of the knee-pad at the point and clinch it underneath; drive another in the fore part of the other
flap, and one behind on each side, just below the
centre of the seat pad; drive the nail slanting
through the tree and clinch it.

The next part needed is a gullet piece to run
all round the front of the gullet and from the
point of one flap to the point of the other. To
make it, cut a piece of brown leather of the required length by 1 in. wide, and a piece of hogskin
slightly wider. Stitch the hogskin on the other
piece along the edge at the same distance from

the edges as the stitches on the flaps, and finish neatly. Then damp the hogskin and push in a piece of cord, pasting the hogskin down afterwards; put the cord close to the stitches from end to end and press the hogskin flat on the bottom leather inside the cord.

After punching a hole about 1¼ in. below where the seat and skirt join, slit the hole on the inner side and nail it down along the gullet underneath, sufficiently close to the tree for the cord to come tightly against the edge of the tree. Be careful that the slit is at equal distances from the centre on both sides; then raise the other parts below the slits on both sides above the tree to meet the ends of the flaps, making them meet the latter closely. Drive two or three nails into the flap, and make sure that the entire front of the piece runs in a level line with the edges on both sides of the flaps; then join the gullet piece and flap by a stitch below out of sight.

Another method of joining them is to stitch the gullet piece to the end of the flaps by means of a hogskin reaching beyond each end of the gullet piece; then stitch these together before adjusting the flaps.

Take two silver saddle staples and put one leg through the point of the flap and the other through the gullet piece and the tree; knock them down to their necks and clinch them below. When there is no metal name plate, cut a piece of hogskin oval, and, having thinned its edges, paste it close to the staple over the nails in the gullet piece and its joint with the flaps. The breast plate is fastened to these staples and in some cases to coat straps.

Having cut six stout girth straps 1 in. by 1 ft. 3 in., shave one end and slant the other into a fine point; then edge and rub them. Crease them double on the flesh side and turn up the end of the web and leather hanging over the side until it is 3 in. long from the tree. Next stitch two straps on each side and nail the other straps, one on each side close to the first two; then make holes all along them. Then, in front of the skirt on each side at the point of the row of stitching, along the top, drive one tough nail and clinch it under the tree.

Two pear-shaped underskirts must next be cut and placed on each side under the straps; they should reach from the tree to a little more than halfway down the straps. Crease the underskirt with the hot creaser, and nail them under the tree, right under the girth straps. After cutting a piece of thin hogskin about $\frac{1}{4}$ in. wide, drive a nail in it close to the crupper loop and wrap it round the last from end to end; then fasten it on the other side with a nail. The flaps, close to their ends, are fastened to the tree by a leather chape put through and secured with fine tacks.

Some harness makers put silver dees under the saddle, nailing them with a chape just to show between the saddle tree and panel.

CHAPTER II.

PANEL FOR GENTLEMAN'S SADDLE.

THE saddle as made in the previous chapter is now complete with the exception of a panel (Fig. 5), and that is made as follows: Cut a good basil to the shape of the saddle underneath, and make it in two parts, joined along the middle. Drive a nail exactly in its centre at the front and back, and place the side of the saddle with the basil under it on the work bench in front. Now with the seat awl mark the basil all round the edges of the saddle, making it flush with the front and reaching at the back to the crupper loop, so as to cover the nails in the seat; it must also be flush with the side of the skirt as far as the flap; cut it to the same shape, but about 2½ in. shorter in the bottom only.

Cut a straight line from centre to centre at the front and back, and cut along the marks all round. About 2 in. from the centre, make a straight cut downwards for 1½ in. exactly, and from the end of this draw another straight line to the back, ending about 1 in. from the extreme point. Cut along that line and make one or two stitches at both ends to join the two sides of the panel. There will then be a hollow in the centre of the panel with each end attached.

Next line the panel along the top and front with basil or linen and allow it to dry, after which tack it on again, and see that it has not stretched in damping with the paste. If it has done so, mark the place, cut it off, and put a tack in the point, marking round the point for about 2 in. upwards

and around the bottom. Then cut two pieces of hogskin of the same shape as the point but slightly
larger. Stitch them on where the points on the
panel were marked, but sufficiently outside the
mark to allow the points to enter easily, because
they are pockets into which the points are placed
when the panel is completed.

The hogskin facing can now be cut for the
panel; it runs along the front on both sides and
in the turning under the flaps, also round the back
over the flap part of the panel on each side about
1 in. below the turning. Narrow it down gradually
to nothing in the points at both front and back,
and exactly opposite the gullet and opposite the
crupper loop narrow it to about one-half its width.
Back-stitch it to the panel with white linen thread
and a pointed needle, taking care to make the
facing ends level with each other at the points
both at the back and front. Damp the edges and
rub them down level with the rubber after they
have been stitched.

Next lay the white serge for the lining flat on
the bench, and place the panel on it with the
wrong side out; then with a single thread of hemp
coarsely tack the panel to the serge all round
inside the facing.

Cut the lining about 2½ in. larger than the back
of the panel, and narrow it to about 1 in. at the
extremity of the bottom. At the back also it
must be cut about 2 in. larger, and gradually
narrowed from the corners on each side of the flap
to the same width as the other side at the bottom,
namely, about 1 in. A little must be cut out of
the front of the lining opposite the gullet, removing about half the width of what is over the back
and likewise opposite the crupper loop.

After turning a little in all round the lining
with a needle and thread, run a coarse tack in it
close to the edge, and then whip it to the facing

and that part of the panel without a facing. Turn it inside out and make the lining equal on both sides; then put a little cord or a rounded piece of basil (damped and rounded) in the gullet just to meet the stuffing in both sides.

The panel being laid flat on the bench lengthwise, draw the lining smooth between the edges of the opening at the top and put a tack in the board at the back, with one on each side of the opening in front. Through the back and lining along the edge of the opening, from end to end on both sides, raise stitches about 1 in. apart at

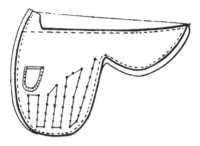

Fig. 5.—Saddle Panel.

the back, and a good 3 in. in front; the panel is now in two equal compartments with a hollow between them. Having cut a cross in the centre of its back near the lines, put one side of the panel on the bench, allowing the other to hang down by the side, after which, through the cross holes, each side should be stuffed pretty full with ready machined flock. Prepare the special quilting thread or a long three-cord beeswax thread to quilt the facing.

Holding the seat awl in the right hand, work down the flock to the facing, thus making a hard roll all round the panel to give it a permanent

form. With each stitch work the flock down, thus
keeping it in its place with the thumb and fore-
fingers of the left hand. Run the stitches from
below close to the joining of the facing and back
inside it in the panel; make very small stitches
in the lining, and pull them very tight. The roll
should be rather thick all round the back and
along the front, but gradually smaller towards
the front bottom. Turn the back upwards around
the part under the flap where there is no facing,
bringing the wool to the edge and tacking it there;
but do not make the roll so hard as in the facing.
Quilt along the gullet where the rounded basil
was placed, and draw the facing firmly and
smoothly over; begin and end at the back centre,
meanwhile keeping the panel lining on the work
bench in front.

The flock must be levelled by pushing it down
to the facing with the seat awl, more being added
to keep the panel full in all parts; be sure that
the flaps are quite smooth and well filled towards
the edges.

Five or six lines about $1\frac{1}{2}$ in. apart should next
be marked across the panel flaps, and two lines
at the top back part of it half-way across; again
mark them across with as many lines at equal distances from each other as will fill the space. Then
quilt the flap, making a stitch at each joining of
the lines, and on the two lines marked half across,
having three stitches in one and two in the other
at the back part of the panel. Add stuffing if
necessary along the top of the back, but do not
make it baggy.

The flock having been levelled with the seat
awl, the work should be placed in position as
follows:—After fixing in the pockets the points
of the tree, pull the pockets until the points are
right at the end; then tack the panel close to the
gullet piece around the front and put two tacks

through the panel between the points of the crupper loop behind.

On each of six medium-sized nails place a tuft of flock close to the head, then put one on each side of the panel near the facing, at about 8 in. from the crupper loop, and another on each side in the middle of the panel nearer the front of the tree ; finally, place one on each side in the front, about 2 in. from the top of the pockets, in the point outside the iron plate, and cut the flock close to the nail heads with a pair of scissors.

CHAPTER III.

CERTAIN important points must be attended to when ordering a tree for a side saddle. Such a tree is shown by Fig. 6. Sometimes this has a small off-head or point and sometimes a straight seat, or it may rise gradually towards the cantle, or, again, may have a long or short leaping head. Thus there is a great difference in the make of trees, and they are of plain hogskin, or with quilted, bolstered, or plain safe and skirts, or with doeskin in the seat or in the safe and heads. Others are quilted all over, seat, skirts, flaps, and safe.

The head or point is the part projecting on the side of the saddle in front, over which the rider's knee is placed; the other projection, head or horn, is now rarely of a size to which a name can be given.

The safe is the part in front which reaches beyond the saddle, covering the horse's shoulder to keep the rider's clothes from the horse; it either forms part of the flap or is joined to it straight down from the point.

To make a saddle with a small off-head and quilted or bolstered safe only, obtain a tree and strain the web thoroughly as for a gentleman's saddle. Adjust it in the same manner with the cross pieces and linen in a similar position to form a ground for the seat. Cover it also in a like fashion with white serge for stuffing, but make the sausage pad at the side where the rider sits twice as thick, or nearly so, as it is on the offside; if the seat runs down steep towards the riding

side there would be a danger of the rider falling
from the saddle. Nevertheless, gradually increase
the rounding, slanting it downwards as it ap-
proaches the front, for sharp corners here would
hurt the rider.

The point must be prepared and stuffed as
follows before the worker attempts to place the
cover on the seat: Cut two pieces of stiff leather
to the same shape as the head and to reach to the
bottom on the inside, and of sufficient size outside
the head all round to permit it to be stitched round
outside the horn. Place one piece on each side
and stitch each firmly to the horn ; then put two

Fig. 6.—Tree for Side Saddle.

or three tacks in the outer one at the bottom, and
thin the edges, giving them a good shape.

Shape a piece of white serge to the head, round
at the top and about 2½ in. wider along the sides
and as much longer at the top ; then run a tack
all round with white linen thread, turning in the
edges slightly under the stitches and puckering
round the top so that it will bulge when stuffed
in the same way. Put the serge in the inside of
the head and stitch it all round to the stitches
in the two leathers on the outside, catching the
edge of the serge and then running the needle
through the stitch in the leather so that the serge
will cover the edge of the horn. Be sure that it
bulges equally in every part at the top and sides.

Cut some clean carded flock small enough, and with it stuff from the bottom, pushing it to the top with the seat awl until the stuffing is firm and plump everywhere and smooth round the edges and top. Then from the back make a few stitches along the sides, backwards and forwards, to keep the flock in its place; do not pull the stitches very tight, for this would cause unevenness of surface. If the centre does not seem quite full enough when the edges are quilted, a little more flock may be put in place, and the surface afterwards made perfectly level all over with the seat awl.

The point being covered and stuffed, place a piece of serge on the outer side of the small head and nail it in the bottom and turn it in along the edge of the head; then fasten it down level. It need not be placed nearer the back of the saddle than where the seat cover is to be nailed. Adjust the serge, nailing it at the front, sides, and back, as for a gentleman's saddle; but cut it round the stuffed horn and turn the edges down underneath, nailing the ends in the front. Also, along the edge of the little horn, turn in the edges of the seat cover and whip this to the turned-in edge of the piece pasted underneath, along the extreme edge of the point. Cut the hole or slit in the centre of the seat and stuff in the same style as a gentleman's saddle, levelling down to all parts round the sides and round the top of the cantle.

To keep the flock in its place, quilt along the ridge to the root of the cantle from the point or horn on the near side, giving the seat the aspect of a flat, full square edge from the root of the cantle to the point; the other side is worked in a similar way.

In pushing the flock with the awl under the quilting, too much may have been pulled from the centre of the seat; if so, fill and level it again with the seat awl, taking care that the front point, and up to the tip of the small point on the opposite side, are well filled and smooth.

Now take a piece of hogskin large enough to cover the long point and nail it at the back, pulling it tight and tacking it close all round the top so as to obliterate every pleat; leave it on the point to dry. The hogskin seat having been damped, put it on the saddle and place a small piece of hogskin outside the small point to cover the serge put there for stitching the serge seat cover; both the hogskin and serge must run along the edge of the small horn.

The hogskin seat must be cut all round the long point, a hole being made of a size to suit the space required by the root of the points; draw the ends of the leather across each other in front at the outside, and tack them low down. When the seat and point cover have dried thus, cut a piece of firm leather to the same shape as the hollow at the back of the long point facing the operator, fitting it tightly between the stuffing at the top and along the sides. Then cut a piece of hogskin to cover this piece, and shave the edges of both; the hogskin should be about $\frac{1}{8}$ in. larger than the stiff piece all round.

After pasting the leathers together and allowing them to dry, adjust the skirts in the same way as with the gentleman's saddle, and cut along the line of mark likewise; then dot the position of various parts of the skirts and seat. Place the thin hogskin welt along the upper edge of the seat and stitch the skirt and welt together, but no farther than the root of the big point; run on the other side opposite under the short point.

From the point to which the seat is stitched, a wider welt doubled like the narrow one must be stitched to the skirt, running from this part to the end; a narrow welt must also be made

around the seat at the edge of the hole cut for the
point, and a broad welt stitched to that as in the
skirt. Likewise, at the other side, under the short
point, make a narrow welt and a broad one as in
the end of the skirt, and again make a narrow
welt along the edge of the hogskin piece placed
under the short point, and stitch the seat on it
from the place where the seat and skirt of the
saddle part.

The piece of hogskin, when put in place, will
go under the edge of the skirt to be nailed underneath. Be careful that the ends of the leather
which come round the long point meet and are
tacked neatly under the skirt on the near side
below the big point. Now remove the cover round
the long point and make a small welt around the
small back piece and cover it with hogskin. Stitch
the cover to it all round and take care that it does
not stretch or pleat round the top.

Having turned the cover inside out, damp it
and then slip it down over the point, cutting a few
nicks in the bottom so that it may go low down
with the bottom flat on the seat. As there is a
hollow between the two sides where the side padding bulges out at the back of the point, and as
the back piece does not run so close to the back
point as is required, put some paste between the
back piece and the point and press the former
hard down into the hollow, as though pasting it
to the point, until the sides stand out prominently
all round.

To keep it thus and make it stick to the point
by the paste, put over it two or three thicknesses
of soft leather, brown in colour, of the same shape
and size as the piece; then roll a soft rag round
the point and the leather so that it will press the
back piece close to the point; thus the paste,
when dry, will keep it in place. Nail the back
piece to the tree at the bottom with two or three

cut tacks out of sight, and cut the pleats in the seat behind the cantle and stitch them.

The points running to the pockets on the panel must be covered in the same way as those of the gentleman's saddle with thin hogskin or basil. After damping the seat, put it in place, nailing it in front and then at the back, and tightening it down well around the sides. Nail the piece of hogskin behind the short point, and pull the seam with the welt exactly along the edge in all parts. The points of the skirt must be drawn tightly towards the front and a tack put in the end, plac-

Fig. 7.—Lady's Near-side Flap and Safe.

ing the edge of the skirts at both sides under the points; cover the nails and ends of leathers fastened there, and cut the waste all round the back and sides close to the nails.

Some makers put a pocket on the centre of the off skirt to carry the rider's gloves or handkerchief; this pocket must be made before the under pieces are adjusted and before placing the skirt on the seat. The shape may be square, about 4½ in. long and 3½ in. deep. Stitch the leather along the bottom on the flesh side so that when the material is turned upwards the stitches will be hidden, and make a small gusset on each side, 1 in. wide at the top and tapering down to nothing at the bottom. Turn in the gusset at the centre, and stitch one side of it to the pocket and the other to the skirt. Cut a loop, and put both ends of it in the front, cutting holes for them; then stitch them across.

An overlap, of the same length as the pocket and like a pocket-book overlap, must be cut and stitched to the pocket in the same manner as the bottom on the flesh side, and turned down towards the front to cover the stitches. Hogskin is the material employed, and the overlap may be lined and stitched all round or neatly creased with a hot iron.

The near-side flap (Fig. 7) and safe are generally in two pieces, joined in the centre in a straight line with the point side in front. The back part is like a saddle flap, but is a little fuller in the round at the bottom; the back part reaches no farther than level with the end of the saddle-bar front side, but the fore part or safe in front runs a little beyond the centre at the top. The safe part and back part or flap are cut singly, and then joined together at the straight line by a closing stitch with strong black wax thread, crossing this from side to side every six or seven stitches.

For a bolstered safe, cut a piece of hogskin the same size as the safe part, allowing 1 in. all round for the bolstering, and covering in the centre the joint of the safe and flap part. Next quilt the hogskin and mark it all over with a regular pattern by a small single crease; press it hard with a pattern of flowers, leaves, or any other fancy design. A piece of calico large enough to line it should now be cut and stitched along all the marks with white or yellow silk or linen thread, either single or double. The outer lines must be stitched first and puckers avoided, leather and calico being perfectly flat; and a hole should be pricked every space in the pattern.

Now stuff all the spaces with very fine flock

cut small with scissors. A small edge tool can be employed for stuffing, the seat awl distributing the flock over the spaces; stuff just sufficient to show the pattern well on the outside and to give a pleasant feeling of softness to the touch. Then place the cover on the safe part, edge to edge, and cut it level with the safe, crease round the edge of the cover, and prick it very fine.

The underneath of the opposite straight edge must also be pricked, but not the top as for the outer side; the pricking must be much coarser than the top side. Stitch it, wrong side out, outside the joint of the flaps and safe; then turn it over towards the front to cover the stitches and bring the cover edge to edge with the safe. Next stitch it round the edge, double-handed, and finish neatly.

When the flap and safe are covered with hogskin and the safe is treated as described, the hogskin has only to be pasted on the flap part and stitched round. If, however, a covered safe is made without bolstering, paste a piece of serge over the safe; then place the hogskin as above described without pasting. In some cases the safe is not covered at all, the flap and safe being made in one piece and stamped, with the edges rounded and polished only; there is then no creasing on the saddle. Whenever flaps or skirts are lined with serge, do not let the serge come up to the edge or under the stitches; it should come only just to them.

The flap on the off side is, of course, a small one, exactly as for a gentleman's saddle, but fuller in the rounds below. If covered, make it like the other flaps, with or without serge. When putting the off-side flap in place, make a gullet piece from the end of the front of the flap running to a little over the centre in the top, so as to be covered by the point of the safe. Put the off-side flap in its place, nailing it underneath from the point backwards and above the point in front.

When placing the safe and flap on the near side, nail them likewise underneath; then on this and on the off side, where the web hangs down for the straps, cut a punch hole in the front of the safe close by the tree and near the end of the flap, and turn that part of the flap to the point underneath the tree, nailing it along the gullet.

When a leaping head is employed, a hole must be cut through the safe to screw the head in place.

Fig. 8.—Lady's Saddle with Quilted Skirt and Leaping Head.

Cover and stuff it exactly like the other long point, but use a piece of leather for the bottom. A hole must be made in it through which the screw peg passes, and it must be cut to the same size and shape as the point at the bottom. Finally stitch the point cover and this leather together all round. The straps for the girths are adjusted on the web.

The thin brown leather girth, a part which does not belong to a gentleman's saddle, can now be put on, its length being 3½ ft. and width 2 in. An inch buckle with a roller is needed at one end, and the chape should be cut slanting from both sides to its width. Make a loop for it, and another about 6 in. lower on the girth for the overlap of the strap, if there is any.

Cut another piece 1 ft. long and 2 in. wide, and a strap 1 ft. 6 in. by 1 in. stitched to one end. Having stitched them neatly, edge and rub the borders and make a narrow hot crease very near the edge ; the stitching may be made inside. On the girth have two rows of cross-stitching on the near side, and two rows on the off side ; the girth will buckle the reverse to the usual way, and can be adjusted whilst the rider is in the saddle.

Two cross straps for fastening the girth strap are employed by some makers, one being fastened through a hole in the flap at the top of the panel point, and the other under the panel behind, outside the flap ; these straps meet and are stitched to a ring on the centre of the flap, the strap being again fastened to the ring and hanging down. The tough nails are placed similarly to those in a gentleman's saddle, namely, one at each point of the skirts in front, one through the flaps on each side at the point, and one on each side at the narrow end of the skirts behind.

The panel is made as described in Chapter II., but slightly wider, to go under the safe in front, and the near side is filled rather more. Fig. 8 shows the finished lady's saddle with leaping head and quilted skirt.

CHAPTER IV.

CHILDREN'S SADDLES OR PILCHES.

A PILCH is the form of saddle used by a boy or girl, and is made as described in this chapter.

First the top is cut somewhat like a saddle panel, but smaller, and in a straight line along the back. At the joint a welt is placed, and stitched double-handed on the under side. This top can be made of plain, stiff single leather, or covered plain with basil or hogskin, or covered and quilted like a lady's saddle safe.

If it is covered, the cover must be tacked coarsely along the edge, and then bound with leather. A roll, if placed behind, should reach round the back and come to a fine point at each end. Cut some linen to the required shape and size, and double and stitch the edges together; then, after stuffing the roll hard with flock, quilt it firmly, and put a stitch here and there along the bottom through the linen and the saddle top.

Having drawn it tight all round the back of the seat, bringing the points down level to each other at each corner of the flap part of the top, cut a piece of hogskin or basil large enough to cover the roll. Raise a stitch along the bottom on both sides of the roll in the cover, and run the stitches up and down through the saddle top or cover, thus drawing the latter down tightly over the roll.

Next quilt the roll, making stitches from side to side, placing a little tuft of flock under each stitch, and drawing them tight; finally fasten the thread securely in the end.

If the saddle is a reversible one (for boy or girl), it must have heads, to be put on or taken off as required. Sometimes the heads are joined together at the top, with two long points running down, one on each side, at the shoulder. If such a head is employed, two long loops must be put on the side of the saddle for the points to enter and to keep the head in place ; make a hole at each end of the points, and rivet a strap at the near side and a girth on the other side to go under the belly and fasten the head when in use.

Another method is to have the heads loose and separate, in which case a piece of iron of suitable shape, with two tapped holes in it, is needed ; it must be in a proper position for screwing in the heads and there must be a screw on each head to enter the holes from above. The iron must be fixed on the panel by a piece of leather placed over it on the panel, and then stitched all round. Cut a hole in the leather of the saddle top for screwing in the points.

For stuffing the heads, cover with leather as in a lady's saddle ; two or three thicknesses of felt, however, can be employed instead of stuffing. With a common pilch it is not necessary to go to so much trouble ; a herring-bone stitch will do to join the cover together. When the heads are screwed in, cover their bottom with leather, stitching it to the· cover all round. When the heads go to the loops at the side, cover the points going down to the loop with thin leather, and herring-bone stitch it underneath.

To fasten the straps for the girths a piece of webbing will be needed about 1 ft. 3 in. long ; to its ends 2-in. straps, 10 in. long, must be stitched, the end of the web being turned in under the stitch. ˌThen take a piece of web about 1 ft. long, and whip it to the edge of the other piece at equal distances from both ends, and adjust two

chapes and a 1-in. buckle with the tongue taken
off for fastening the stirrup straps. Stitch this
to the lower part of the top cover right in the
centre, and before fixing the basil or hogskin cover
bring the buckles for the stirrup straps forward,
and cut a hole for them to come through on the
outside without making the web visible.

When the top cover is in position, stitch round
the hole, which should be close to the loops, where
the points holding the head run down in front,
or where they would be with loose heads ; see that
the holes are at the same distance on each side
from the centre. Stitch the web firmly through
the top from end to end ; add the cover and bind
it, and then put on the roll behind. If considered
necessary, a piece of web may be added at the
middle, and joined to the other web, together with
a chape and a 1-in. tongueless buckle, to come
out behind at the centre for fastening the crupper.

A safe will be needed when the pilch is for
a girl. Cut it to fit the front of the saddle neatly,
and cover or bolster it, or leave it plain. With
loose horns it can be shaped in cutting so that
it will fasten under the point, the screw of the
head being put through a hole in it to the iron
below, and fastened at the bottom with a buckle
and strap.

If the head is removable with points, it must
be fastened with straps and buckles at both ends,
and, if necessary, a strap placed in the middle.

The panel is made exactly like a saddle panel,
but is fastened by putting stitches through the
top here and there along the front and round the
back near the edge. A small tuft of flock should
be placed under the stitch on the panel, and every
stitch should be knotted over the flock as the
work proceeds. Cut the thread, and do not fasten
the panel quite at the bottom of the flaps, but
about 5 in. from it.

Make a pair of 1-in. stirrup straps, 1 ft. 8 in. long, and obtain a pair of boy's irons, which can be bought tinned for sixpence a pair; then a ready-made slipper for a girl, with a strap for it of the same length as the others, and a pair of girths, 1 ft. 6 in. and 1 ft. 8 in. long, will complete the pilch.

It has been shown that pilches are boys' and girls' saddles made without trees, but, according to some authorities, they do not properly come under the denomination of saddles. They are, at all events, an improvement on the old horse cover which in the beginning did duty for the saddle. Pilches are, or were, used also by rough riders and circus riders, probably because of the fact that pilches accommodate themselves to almost any horse, though they lose their shape under a heavy weight.

CHAPTER V.

THIS chapter will describe the making of saddle cruppers, breastplates, martingales, saddle girths, stirrup leathers, and saddle cloths.

Full-sized saddle cruppers (Fig. 9), which are used to prevent the saddle from advancing too much, are made about 1 in. wide, and sometimes a little more, the body being about 1 ft. 6 in. long, with a slit of about 5 in. in one end, the other being turned in for a $\frac{7}{8}$-in. buckle ; shave the points of the slits and the end of the chape.

Having cut a billet of the same width as the buckle, and 2 ft. 4 in. long, trim one end for the buckle and shave the other. Edge them and polish the edges, creasing them with a hot checker. Adjust the buckle and stitch the billet, making the first stitch by the buckle over the edge and the chape and billet together, and the next stitch through the loop. Now run four or five stitches towards the point on each side, and return to the buckle on the other side, making the last stitch over the side the same as the opposite side.

Put a loop on the flat lower down the body of the crupper, say about 6 in. from the buckle, stitching it across in each end, and then make a dock much smaller in circumference than the gig crupper dock, the leather being cut about 1 ft. 1 in. long.

Take a piece of string about 1 ft. long, and roll wet brown paper round it until it is of the required thickness in the middle ; thin the ends by cutting the paper before damping it. Stitch the leather over it as it is, without cutting a groove, drawing it very tightly over the paper. See that the leather is soft and pliable, and damp it before stitching. Having dried the dock, finish it in shape, and then stitch the dock to the slits, giving it about a 1¼-in. splice. Put about a dozen holes in the billets, and vary their lengths according to the size of horse for which they are intended.

Breastplates (Fig. 10) are made for hunting

Fig. 9.—Saddle Crupper.

saddles to prevent them falling backwards, just as the crupper keeps them from advancing too far. To make them, the following parts are needed:—One 1½-in. covered ring, two 1-in. covered rings, two ⅝-in. covered buckles, and one 1-in. covered buckle.

Cut two side straps ⅞ in. wide, and 2 ft. in length when turned over the rings in each end; round the top, place on the groove board, and stuff with strands of soft cord. Stitch them along both sides, very finely, with silk cotton or linen thread, placing a 1-in. ring at one end of each, and the two ends in a 1½-in. ring; polish the edges well after stitching. Then cut a 1⅜-in. strap to be 10 in. long when bent over the rings at each end; shave the ends and prick the sides finely like the shoulder piece.

Another piece must now be cut 9¼ in. long when bent for the rings, ⅞ in. wide at both ends,

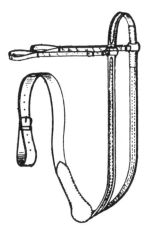

Fig. 10.—Saddle Breastplate.

but running gradually to a central width of 1¾ in. Put the chapes in the 1-in. rings, and stitch both pieces together. Two ⅝-in. straps, 2 ft. long, must be made, one end being prepared for the buckle, the other narrowed; then edge, rub, and crease them with a hot checker. Place one in each of the 1-in. rings to within 3 in. of the buckle. Double the 3-in. length with the buckle on the top, and make two loops between the two leathers. Stitch from the ring along both sides to the buckle, the loops, of course, being fastened at the same time, and, having finished the edges of the stitched part, make seven or eight holes in the points of the strap.

The long side straps must run down from the shoulder to the chest, and the short cross strap should pass over the neck at the top. The two small straps have buckles to fasten to the staples that are placed in front of the saddle. A strap is needed to go from the big ring to the girth

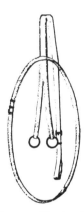

Fig. 11.—Martingale.

under the belly between the forelegs; cut it 1¼ in. wide and 3 ft. long. Narrow it down to 1 in. at 1 ft. from the bend at the ring, and turn it down for the buckle at the 1-in. end; edge, rub, and crease it, then put the buckle in the reverse way.

Now cut eight or nine punch holes, beginning about 8 in. from the buckle, and buckle the strap backwards, making a loop for the bellyband to go through. Place the other end in the ring, and cut a safe to go under it and run above under the ring round the top part, then passing down for about 3½ in. below the bend, and gradually growing narrower towards the end almost to the width of the strap.

Crease the safe, and place it in position under the chape and ring; then, having stitched it down

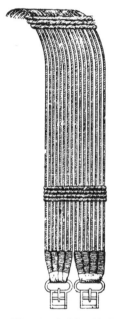

Fig. 12.—Saddle Girth.

neatly on both sides with a fancy stitch in the centre, line the safe with a piece of chamois or very thin buff, stitching it in all round the safe. Stuff a little flock through the opening in the bottom, and then close the opening with fancy stitching, such as an arrow point. It can be made of single leather without any lining, the bends only being stitched.

A combined martingale and breastplate can be made by cutting a strap 1½ in. wide and 15 in. long; the strap must then be slit for about 11 in.: the points of the slits are bent for a chape to suit a 1¼-in. brass, ivory, or leather-covered ring. A buckle and billet are put in the other end for

Fig. 13.---Saddle Girth.

fastening to the 1½-in. ring on the breastplate. The slits may be made round or flat, and the chapes must be narrowed a little at the rings and to ¾ in. at the buckle end, a billet made of this width.

Martingales (Fig. 11) are made with straps round the neck, either flat or round, and with or without a buckle; the total length is about 4 ft. 6 in., and the flat strap is ¾ in. wide.

When a buckle is used, a piece of leather is placed about 1 ft. 3 in. from the buckle for the breast strap, and is stitched at both ends. A piece is put in to make an opening, the rest of the neck strap being rounded, with about 1 ft. left flat for a ¾-in. buckle. If no buckle is employed, an opening can be made by simply over-

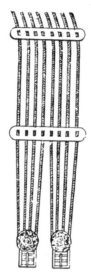

Fig. 14.—Saddle Girth.

lapping the ends and leaving space enough between the two splices for the breast strap.

The breast strap is cut 1¼ in. wide and 4 ft. long, is slit for 1 ft. 1 in., and may be flat or round; in the latter case, it must be wider to begin with, say 1⅝ in., and then slit in half. When flat, narrow it at the unslit end to 1 ft. 6 in. from the end, and, having fixed a 1-in. buckle there in the reverse way, buckle it to form a loop; this buckle must be adjusted before the rings. Then run the buckle end through the opening in the neck strap, and the martingale is complete.

Saddle girths (Figs. 12, 13, and 14) are made of linen, worsted, or union (that is part linen and

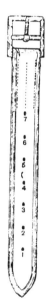

Fig. 15.—Stirrup Leather.

part wool); they are also made of raw hide, whipcord, and plaited brown leather. It is, however, more common to employ the first-named material.

Girth buckles must be obtained with safety bars across them, and the chapes should be cut pointed at the ends, swelling out at the sides to grow narrow to the width of the buckle at the

top, where they bend. Always stitch them round,
and put a straight line in the centre to keep down
the point of the turn-down; only about twelve or
fifteen stitches are put in the centre.

When this has been cut and prepared for the
buckle, stain the edges and turn in both corners
of the web to meet in the centre; then run a
stitch through them to keep them down, and cut
a little off the extreme point and tack the chapes
and buckles before stitching. The length varies
from 3 ft. to 3 ft. 6 in.

A Fitzwilliam girth is made of web 5 in. wide,
the ends being bound with leather and a chape

Fig. 16.—Saddle Cloth.

and buckle placed on each side—that is, in each
corner, two at each end of the girth. A 1-in. loop
is then put across the girth, 5 in. from the end,
on each side, and the loops are stitched across
twice at each end, an opening being left in the
middle for an ordinary girth to pass.

A single ordinary girth must then be made,
one end placed through each of the loops, and
the Fitzwilliam girth is complete. It is a very safe
girth, and keeps the saddle steady in place. If
so desired, chape punches can be obtained which
cut out the chapes at one stroke, or for cutting
partly round or cornered patterns the head knife
may be used.

Stirrup leathers may now be described. It may

be said that their purpose is to connect the stirrup
irons to gentlemen's saddles, and hold the irons in
place. For ladies' use, only one stirrup leather is
customary, and sometimes this is made in the same
style as a gentleman's; more often, however, a
single strap is employed to connect the stirrup,
this strap passing through a hole in the saddle
and joining the balance girth underneath the flap.

Stirrup leathers (Fig. 15) must be made from
stirrup middlings, and with stirrup leather buckles; the width may be 1½ in. to 1½ in., but 1¼ in.
is most common, whilst the length varies from
4 ft. to 4 ft. 6 in. There is no need to cut holes

Fig. 17.—Saddle Cloth.

for the buckle tongues, as these do not go through
the leather.

Having bent the strong end for about 2 in.,
stitch it firmly to the bottom of the buckle, narrow
a little on the buckling end, and nip a little from
each corner. Stain the edges, and polish them
well, and crease double and heavily with a hot
screw crease on the flesh side, instead of the grain
side as with other straps; finally turn the chape at
the buckle the reverse way, and make about eight
holes in them.

As a rule, saddle-cloths (Figs. 16 and 17) are
made of felt in the same shape as the saddle, but
a little larger. Each is cut in two pieces, with
a small curve at the back, rising a little at each

end, and stitched together with a whip stitch. A piece of binding is stitched along the joint, and the edges are then bound with red, yellow, or blue cloth. The felt can also be obtained in various colours—blue, brown, fawn, etc.

With regard to the use of the saddle cloth, it is shaped so as to go easily under the saddle, where it protects the horse's back and the panel of the saddle by absorbing the perspiration; the effect of the continued perspiration on the leather of the saddle panel is to render it hard.

The saddle cloth can be used also when the stuffing of the saddle is unequal; this is a good remedy, and one that has been used almost universally in the cavalry. In the army, saddle cloths known as numnahs, and are made of felt. This is certainly the best material to use for the purpose, but kersey, cloth, and holland have been commonly employed.

Kersey, it may be said, is a kind of coarse woollen cloth and usually is ribbed. Devon kerseys were famous as far back as the fourteenth century.

CHAPTER VI.

RIDING BRIDLES.

A SNAFFLE bridle is a single head and rein bridle, the cheeks being about $\frac{7}{8}$ in. wide and 9 in. long. The cheeks must have a buckle at each end, one with a chape turned down, and the other on the flat end of the strap, without turning, and with the billet underneath. For riding bridles (Fig. 18) the buckles are made square, round, or fancy shape, and are of brass, tinned or plated. Leave space for a loop before the buckle and the point of the cheek, the billet being placed far enough behind the buckle for two loops; a runner loop is needed on the cheek, and another stitched with the chape at the buckle, the billet being cut 9 in. long. They should be stitched-in single-handed, and back-stitched with linen thread or silk, according to the style of article to be made.

All the stitching must be done from behind, so that the best face of the stitches will be next the horse when the bridle is on. Make one hole in each billet, leaving enough material to pass through the two loops and cover the stitches.

The cheeks being finished, cut the head strap $1\frac{1}{8}$ in. by 1 ft. 10 in., and slit it for 5 in. on each side. The width of this strap varies with that of the cheeks and throat lash. A $\frac{3}{4}$-in. cheek should be slit $\frac{3}{4}$ in. on one side and $\frac{3}{8}$ in. for a $\frac{3}{8}$-in. throat lash, taking care that the wide slits are both on the same side in each end. After punching four holes in the wide slit, and six closer together in the narrow ones, make the front $\frac{3}{4}$ in. by 1 ft. $2\frac{1}{4}$ in. from the end of one bend to the other, after

bending. Turn it over the head strap, and mark
a line across close to the head strap, thus having
1 ft. 1 in. between the cross lines. Stitch the ends
down, with a row along each side, and make the
throat lash ⅜ in. by 1 ft. 7 in., after turning down
for the buckles. Put two runner loops on the
throat lash in addition to the loops at the buckles
of each end.

Now cut the reins, which measure 1 in. or ⅞ in.
by 4 ft. Prepare them for the buckles like the
bottom of the cheeks in the flat, place a ¾-in.
covered buckle at the other end, narrowing the

Fig. 18.—Riding Bridle.

chape down to the width of the buckle and the
end of the other rein also for buckling. Put in
the billets, with one loop before the buckle and
two behind, and always put the strong end of the
rein in the billet end; the length of the billets
is 10 in.

Sometimes the bridle is made without any
billets, the cheeks and the reins being stitched
fast to the bit; but the advantage of the other
method in making it possible to remove the bit
is evident.

The Pelham bridle (Fig. 19) is made like the
above as regards the head, but with a noseband,

which is made singly or lined along the front part
and stuffed; it is cut either straight or swelled
in the front, the length being 2 ft. 4 in. after adjusting the buckle. Any ornamental pattern in
the stitching on the centre must be put through
single leather, then lined, and the outer lines
stitched.

With a noseband the billets must be made a
little longer, so that a space can be left between
the two loops above the buckle unstitched for the
noseband to run through both cheeks.

The Pelham bridle also has two reins, one about

Fig. 19.—Pelham Bridle.

1 in. wide, and the other ¾ in., the length being
the same as that of the snaffle reins. They have
billets at the ends, and the wide rein has a buckle
at the top also, but the narrow rein is spliced
together in the centre without a buckle. The bit
has a curb and long cheek, with two rings for
buckling the reins, the narrow rein being at the
bottom ring and the wide one in the ring by the
mouth.

The Weymouth bridle (Fig. 20) has two heads
and two bits, a hackney and a bradoon. The head
fastening to the hackney bit is made as for the
Pelham bridle, with a noseband, but the head

fastened to the bradoon is made with one cheek only, about 1½ in. longer than the cheek of the other head, and from the other side is one strap with a billet and buckle at the bit; it passes over the head, under the other headpiece, and underneath through the forehead band loop below the other headpiece, and buckles in the cheek on the off side. This second head is ¾ in. wide, and the long side is about 2 ft. 9 in. long. The two reins must be exactly like the Pelham reins.

Bridles are made in different styles, and with fancy patterns; for example, rounded cheeks and part length rounded reins, leather rosettes, plaited throat lash with tassels, plaited fringe on noseband, etc.

Ladies' bridles are made like gentlemen's, but lighter and more ornamental. Sometimes they have plaited cheeks, hand parts for reins, rounded, plaited, or fancy covered fronts, and fancy leather rosettes, whilst tassels may hang from the throat lash.

Various styles of bits are specially made for a strong-headed or runaway horse; one style of gag bit is something like a snaffle, but has two holes in the ring opposite each other. The rein runs through these holes, being rounded for about 12 in. at this part, and a buckle and loop are put on the end of the rounded part after it is through the holes in the ring, whilst the buckles from the bit act instead of a cheek when the head strap is buckled, so as to form both rein and cheek. The total length is about 10 ft. Thus, the more the rider pulls the rein, the tighter the bit rises in the mouth, the pressure bringing the bit and headpiece together. To obviate the necessity of always keeping this tight, to hold the bit in the mouth, another rein is made as usual, and fastened to the bit, so that when quiet the horse can be driven with this rein.

A material that looks well in bridles is plaited cord, with billets and buckles like leather bridles.

Exercising bridles are made like snaffles, but, of course, with stronger leather and a slight difference in the bit, to which the rein is fastened at one end by a small bar of the same material as the bit, and at the other by being stitched to the bit ring. As the bar is too long to pass through the bit ring, pulling the rein at the centre during riding will not bring it through the ring ; but when the rider wishes to lead the horse, he takes the bar in his hand, and pulls the rein through

Fig. 20.—Weymouth Bridle.

the ring. Thus it will answer the purpose of a leading rein and a curb, giving greater power over a vicious horse. Exercising bridles are also made with winkers of light brown leather, blocked and stitched to the cheek quite close to the buckle, everything else being the same as for the snaffle bridle.

Stallion bridles are made on the same principle, but are much heavier and more ornamental. The cheek is of a wavy, swelled pattern, 9 in. long, and is ornamented as follows :—Mark a small diamond in the centre of each swell, then cut it out and keep the piece by. Next, out of thin, soft, coloured leather or American cloth, cut a piece twice or three times the size of the diamond removed, and place its centre over the hole from the under side; press it down into the hole, and put the diamond first made over it, exactly opposite the place from which it was taken. Beat it down into the hollow, with the coloured leather above, and there will then be a coloured diamond on the surface of the cheek; both cheeks can be made alike. Now place a piece of thin leather under the cheek, and stitch round the diamond pattern and along the edges of the cheek; then rub, and give the edges a neat finish.

For a stallion bridle, the front should be cut the same length as an ordinary bridle, or a little longer, and should be covered with fancy leather and ornamented with a pair of rosettes and streamers, which can be either made or purchased. The noseband also may be ornamented in the same way as the cheek, the front being scalloped and each swell ornamented.

Let the throat lash be cut $\frac{3}{4}$ in. wide, and have a buckle for the billets and top of the cheeks; for this, the headpiece must be wide enough to cut a 1-in. and $\frac{3}{4}$-in. strap, the latter for the throat lash and the former for the cheek. Consequently, the width of the headpiece must be $1\frac{3}{4}$ in., but as this size might cause the animal pain at the base of the ear, cut out a slanting piece on the front and back from the end of the slits opposite the ears.

There must also be a chape and buckle in the centre of the headpiece, and a drop with an ornament hanging down on the forehead. Line the drop, and make a loop for it under the forehead band.

As a rule, there is a riding rein like that for a snaffle, which can be fastened to the roller if not used for riding. Or, again, the rein can be made with a short piece on both sides, and a buckle and loop with runner, 1 ft. 3 in. long altogether, and with a centre piece to fasten in each buckle on the short pieces. There should be a dozen holes on each side of the centre part, so that it can be shortened on each side when fastened to the roller.

A leading rein must be made, with a safety bar and a check chain in one end and a buckle and long billet in the other; the leather must be 1⅜ in. wide and 7 in. long. The bridle buckles should be either fancy whole buckles or Scotch brass.

A breastplate may also be made for a stallion; a wavy pattern is selected, so that there will be two or three swells in the sidepieces, which are ornamented with patent coloured leather like the cheeks. Small straps also are placed at the top to fasten to the roller, but must be about 6 in. longer.

In place of a ring on the chest, cut the points of the two sidepieces slanting on the inside, so that they will meet together in a V-shape on the chest. The strap which runs between the legs to the girth can then be stitched on the joint, a fancy pattern being cut on the end, with a metal ornament in its centre to match the buckles. With worsted webbing make the roller long enough to fit the horse, the width being 6 in., and there must also be a 1-in. dee behind to the buckle crupper.

The chape which fastens the crupper dee must run on towards the front, with a 1-in. roller buckle in the centre and a loop; the other part will form a billet to hold the rein by the aid of the central buckle. There must also be two dees, one at each side, fastened with a chape to secure the breastplate straps. It is also advisable to place another dee on the near side under the pad for buckling the billet of the leading rein; and two straps, about 2 ft. long, should be fastened, one on each side. Thus, when the attendant carries a coat or feeding bag, he can strap it on the horse's back.

Under the strap place a small extra one about 6 in. long, with holes in it ; this rolls up inside the big strap, being buckled over it at the end. The crupper must be made with a body 2 ft. long. Having slit 6 in., and made a dock, put chapes and buckles on each end, and cut holes in the slits to fasten the dock to them by the buckles.

The billet is made 1 in. wide, forming one piece with the lay on the body of the crupper ; thus, it must be longer than an ordinary billet, say about 4 ft. Place the buckle at a distance of 4 in. from the point of the body, with one loop in front and three loops behind ; let it be stitched from underneath like a gig crupper, but without leaving an opening. Finally, make a runner loop on the billet.

CHAPTER VII.

BREAKING-DOWN TACKLE.

BREAKING-DOWN tackle is made in the same style
as the stallion outfit described in the previous
chapter, but it has side reins to fasten the horse's
head on each side of the roller ; this part may be
dispensed with for a stallion, but is indispensable
for horse-breaking, as the horse's head has to be
kept steady and under firm control. The nose-
band must also be made stronger, with a dee
fastened in the centre at the front for hooking
the leading rein, the dimensions of the last being
9 ft. by 1⅛ in.

Just as the chief feature in a stallion outfit is
ornament and show, strength is the characteristic
of breaking tackle. Girth and crupper are made
in the same way, but proper breaking tackle
(Fig. 21) has a cavison iron and dumb jockey.

The cavison iron (Fig. 22) can be purchased
ready-made ; it acts as a noseband, being strong
to hold the horse's head steady. In the centre
is a ring, which turns like a swivel, and another
ring is placed on each side ; there is also an opening at the sides of the iron to fasten the cheeks,
and one at each end for the straps running below
the jaw.

Begin by covering the cavison iron with thin
brown leather, and herringbone-stitch it underneath out of sight ; then make holes in the leather
opposite the openings in the iron. Adjust two
cheeks 7 in. by 1 in., then a runner and buckle
with a loop at the top.

In the centre of the cavison iron a 1-in. strap,

20 in. long, when passed round, ascends the face
and buckles in the centre of the headpiece. It
must be turned in sufficiently at one end to go
round the iron, and leave enough for stitching it
together at the upper end.

When placing it round the cavison iron, slit it
in half far enough to go over the ring in the
centre; then put it round, with half the slit on
each side of the ring, and stitch it above the
iron, with a hoop under the forehead to allow it
to pass.

In the next place, adjust a strap 9 in. long in
the off side opening at the end of the cavison, and
another 5 in. long, with a buckle, loop, and runner,
on the near side. Then make a pad as for a
cart winker cheek, but longer; this pad must run
all along the inside of the cavison iron, and reach
about 1 in. beyond at each end, being slightly
wider when stuffed and flattened. Do not make
it clumsy and thick with stuffing.

Four $\frac{1}{2}$-in. straps will be needed, long enough
to pass round the cavison iron, with a few holes
punched in them; stitch one at each end across
the pad, and one on each side of the central ring
which fastens the pad.

The head straps, made of good leather, are
like those for stallions, with a chape and buckle
in the centre to fasten the strap from the cavison
iron to the face. Make the strap 2 ft. 4 in. long,
so that it will fit a horse of any size, and slit it
8 in. or 9 in. on each side, so that, when cut, it
is $1\frac{3}{4}$ in. wide; it can be narrowed in the centre
between the slits.

The foreband is made like that for a stallion.
Having made the throat lash 1 ft. 8 in. long, when
turned in, and $\frac{3}{4}$ in. wide, put a buckle, a loop,
and a runner at each end. If required for extra
safety, a $\frac{5}{8}$-in. strap may be placed on each side
of the cheek, 6 in. long, and stitched in with

the chape at the top. Slant each strap slightly downwards, and make an extra throat lash, ⅜ in. by 1 ft. 4 in., to buckle to the straps. With two throat lashes the bridle will be firm and safe on the horse's head. No bit is employed with the cavison iron, but if straps are added to the cavison iron the bit can be attached to them.

A Corbett martingale, with cavison iron to hold the horse's head down, can be employed; fasten it to a strap to pass under the belly, and fasten

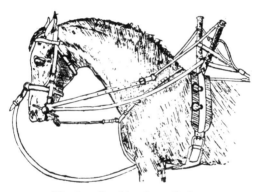

Fig. 21.—Breaking-down Tackle.

round the girth, or to a dee with a shorter strap, the dee being placed at the joining of the two sides of the breastplate on the chest. The fork on the end fastened by the horse's head consists of two short chains, which can be secured by two spring hooks attached to them in the side rings of the cavison iron, one on each side.

The style of rein depends on the make of the dumb jockey, which must be bought ready-made. As a rule, however, the reins must be strong, and at least 1 in. wide.

For preparing a double-horned jockey, rings

E

will be needed at one end of each rein to pass
over the horns, and a ring about 1 ft. 6 in. lower
down is stitched to both parts. On the end of the
fore part of the rein there must be a billet and
buckle to fasten to the side rings of the cavison
iron, and a buckle on the other end with two
runner loops, this end being fastened to the ring
in the other part of the rein, and then put through
runners and buckled. Thus, it can be shortened to
suit the size of horse, and is fastened exactly
like a bearing rein, but downwards instead of
upwards.

Two other similar straps must be made, with a
ring in each to put on the horns of the jockey,

Fig. 22.—Cavison Iron.

both the straps being joined in one ring at the
other end; these fasten the crupper, which is
2 ft. 6 in. in length in the body, and is slit 8 in.
along one end. Beginning at a distance of 2 in.
from the slit, narrow it down to 1 in., and then
put a buckle with two runners that end after the
fashion of a bearing rein, to secure it to the ring
in which the two straps are joined.

Make a thick, soft linseed dock, and stitch one
end of it to the off side slit, and lengthen the
other slit slightly by adding a 3-in. piece, in which
a few holes are punched. Place a buckle and two
loops on the near side of the dock, and, having
bought the dumb jockey, make a panel for it, and
also adjust a girth.

The panel must be made on the same principle

as the cavison pad, the centre being stitched somewhat better, and the length extending beyond the point, while the width is a little greater than the jockey seat. Quilt it in a straight line on both sides, placing a tuft of flock under the stitch on the panel face.

If the jockey is not prepared for fastening it, make some straps like those for the cavison iron to go round the jockey. Adjust two straps, 1⅛ in. by 1 ft. 8 in., one on each side of the jockey, for buckling the girth, this being 2 ft. by 2 in. Then fix a chape and two loops with a 1¼-in. roller buckle in each end on the flat of the girth, without turning the girth itself down for chapes.

Let the breastplate be made like that for a stallion, but, instead of joining the sidepieces on the chest, a ring may be adjusted, as previously explained, for fastening the Corbett martingale, instead of using a dee as when the sidepieces are joined.

CHAPTER VIII.

HEAD COLLARS.

HEAD collars, also called headstalls and stable collars, are made in various ways, and one of the most useful styles will be described in this chapter.

For a Newmarket head collar (Fig. 23) three head collar stop squares, a 1¼-in. tinned roller buckle, and a ¾-in. buckle will be required. Make two short straps 1 ft. by 1¼ in., and turn them in to 5 in. long, thus having 1 in. or a little more for overlap. Having shaved the ends, prick them eight to the inch, and put one square in the centre between them, and one in each end, with the stops on the same side.

Cut a strip of leather and lay it along the centre of each to raise the stay in the middle. Stitch them with beeswax thread, three-cord hemp, and make a strong cross-stitch at the end of each line, finishing carefully. Now cut the noseband 1 ft. 3 in. long when turned down, and, after preparing it, put one end forming a chape in each of the end squares in the shortstays. Stitch two rows along the edges of the turn-down, and trim the ends neatly.

Then cut a pair of cheeks 1¼ in. by 8 in. when bent in both ends, and prepare one end in each for a buckle, shaving the points of the other turn-down. After placing a runner on each cheek and a loop and buckle on one end, stitch the opposite ends to the two outer squares. Then cut the short upward stay ; this is stitched behind in the centre square, and the throat lash runs through at the other end, the length when doubled being about 4½ in. An opening is left in the top for the throat lash.

The forehead band may next be cut and made in the same way as the snaffle bridle forehead band. The top strap must be cut 2 ft long by 1¼ in. ; when finished, punch about four holes on both sides. The throat lash is 3 ft. 6 in. by ¾ in.

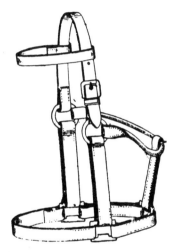

Fig. 23.—Newmarket Head Collar.

with a roller buckle of the same width, and a loop and runner, and with about nine holes in it.

Put the forehead band on the head strap, buckle it on both sides in the cheeks, and run the throat lash from the near side through the opening in the upward stay and under the head strap, then through the opening in the forehead band on each side, bringing the point down to the buckle on the near side. When the head collar is made with only one cheek on the near side, the strap situated on the other side should be 2 ft. 9 in. long.

The Albert head collar (Fig. 24) is made as above described, but always has two cheeks, which must be turned down to 6 in. long; it is either lined through or the chapes are stitched at each end, these being placed in the side square at the bottom, with a 1½-in. ring in the other end of each.

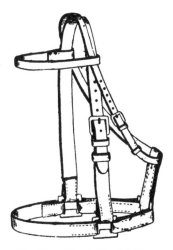

Fig. 24.—Albert Head Collar.

The throat lash may then be run from one ring to the other, and rounded by placing a piece of cord inside; it must be passed through the opening at the top of the short stay, and its length, after turning down the chapes in the rings, must be 1 ft. 6 in.

After cutting a piece of leather 1¼ in. by 5 in. turn it down double, and let it overlap 1 in., and put one end of it in the ring on the near side, and a buckle in the other end with a loop below, stitching it firmly from the under side.

The head strap must be cut the same width and then prepared; let it be 2 ft. long when turned in at one end, and stitch this end to the ring on the off-side, perforating it with six holes. The forehead band must be 1 in. wide. Run the

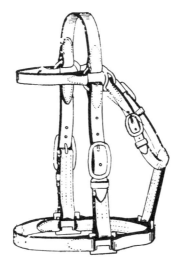

Fig. 25.—Queen's Pattern Head Collar.

head strap through both openings in the forehead band, and finally buckle it in the near side.

Head collars are made with brass or tinned fittings, the brass being either plain or whole fancy pattern, and the cheeks lined or single.

The Queen's pattern head collar (Fig. 25) is made with whole buckles placed on the cheek and not in the ring, with a chape, as in the Albert head collar. There must be a strap on each side, 6 in.

long, to buckle to them, and a centre piece across
the top of the head, about 1 ft. long, turned down
from ring to ring. On the ring there is a collar
to stitch to the throat lash straps; it is 7 in. by
¾ in. wide when turned down, the throat lash, with
buckles on each end, coming through the back stay
1 ft. 6 in. long, and being the same width as the
straps.

The forehead band, 1 ft. by 1 in., is turned down
and stitched opposite the straps at the front of the
ring; for a good head collar it should be made of
buff leather. A length of 6 in. will be sufficient
for the cheeks; the rest of the work has been
already described.

The head collar reins, 5 ft. by 1¼ in., are made
of strong single straps, with a buckle loop and
billet at one end, or part strap and part chain;
the latter is attached to the head collar either with
billet and buckle, or with a spring hook and a
3-ft. strap stitched to the other end. The ends of
the straps are narrowed in both styles to run
through the manger block, and a knot is made
on the other side.

Some head collar reins are also made of ropes
with a buckle chape and billet at one end for
fastening to the head collar; others are all rope
with an eye for the passage of the end of the rope
after it has been run through the head collar
square; then it is knotted below the block in the
other end.

Pillar reins are made in two styles; the first
has a buckle and billet at one end and a pillar
rein spring hook in the other; the second is white
cord with a buckle and billet and hook at the
other end, the leather being 2 ft. 6 in. by 1 in.
The reins are employed to fasten the horse in the
stall with its head outwards, when harnessed to go
out; and they prevent the horse from eating and
keep it from the dirt. The billet end is fastened

to the stall post on each side, and the hooks in the bit on each side of the horse's head.

Not much need be said with respect to the use of the head collar, its alternative names, "head-stalls" and "stable collars" sufficiently indicating its purpose. It serves merely to fasten up the horse in the stable. Several styles—the New-market, Albert, and Queen's pattern—have been described in this chapter, and each has its own advantages in certain circumstances. It has been said that the best kind of head collar is that with a round throat-lash, from which it is next to impossible for the horse to free himself; at each side there should be a ring for the reins to fasten into, and to the end of the reins a wooden log or ball should be attached.

CHAPTER IX.

HORSE CLOTHING.

Horse clothing is made of many different materials. Kersey, fawn rugging, princess check, and fancy checked and coloured linen stuff answer for day use, and for dust covers in the stable ; the shapes and patterns also vary.

The quarter sheet (Fig. 26) is made with only a slight cut backwards towards the shoulder, and a piece of the same material is placed from the off side at the front, with a strap 1 ft. 9 in. by about 2 in. on its point to buckle in the near side where there is a chape and a buckle. The sheet itself falls down straight from the shoulder on each side, there being a belt across the chest to hold down both sides.

The breast cloth (Fig. 27) is made to cover the front of the chest and to run up the side of the neck on each side in a point; there is a buckle and chape to fasten to two 1 ft. 3 in. by 1 in. straps coming down from the shoulder of the sheet to meet the buckles. The breast cloth must be in a line with the edge of the sheet at the bottom.

The padcloth (Fig. 28) goes under the body roller, and is about 1 ft. 3 in. by 1 ft. Use the same material as for the sheet, and after rounding the corners neatly stitch on the inside, straight with the edges, a piece of hogskin, of a wavy pattern and about 2 in. wide. Put one piece at each end in the centre, 7 in. long, and one on each side of the centre.

A hood is needed to complete the suit. A suit-

able shape is shown by Fig. 29. The hood must
be cut to the shape of the horse's neck and head,
from a point about 5¼ in. below the eye on the
nose, then along the ridge of the head and neck

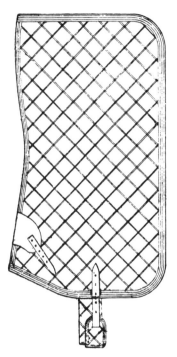

Fig. 26.—Quarter Sheet.

to the shoulder, where it should cover the front
of the sheet well. Cut the holes for the ears, and
make covers for them, the front part being about
1 in. larger than the face of the ear all around, and
the back part large enough to pass round the back

of the ear, and allow it to enter easily. Stitch the
edges, whipping them together; stitch also at the
bottom round the hole, all the stitches being on the
outside. Take care to put the front cut of the
cloth opposite the front of the ear.

Having made two holes, right opposite the
eyes, cut the hood under the neck all round the
throat and down under the head, so that the two
sides meet exactly in the centre. To join and bind
them, whip-stitch the two parts of the sheet to-

Fig. 27.—Breast Cloth.

gether along the back, and then put a piece across
underneath the shoulder to come down on each
side about 1 ft. ; let it be pointed at the ends, the
width in the middle being about 9 in., and all in
one piece to strengthen the point at the shoulder.

The padcloth (Fig. 28) is cut in one piece, but
the pieces of hogskin must be stitched in neatly,
having been previously pasted on and dried. The
breast cloth is cut in one piece, but the hood is
in two pieces, and sometimes in four, as pieces are

put on the side flaps to increase the size at the sides.

Whip the edges together level along the top of the neck and over the head, down the front of the face. If a piece is placed anywhere else, let it be joined in the same manner, and always bind the joint, stitching it on both sides; cloth, patent, or Newmarket binding can be employed for binding. To bind the breastcloth, padcloth, and hood along the edges, cut the cloth 1¼ in. wide, and turn it round the edges just sufficiently to catch the first row of stitching about ¼ in. from the edge. Draw it down as flat as possible, and stitch another row along the inner edge of all parts of the

Fig. 28.—Pad Cloth.

binding. When it puckers too much at a sharp turn, as at the throat of the hood, the puckers may be cut out and then stitched edge to edge.

A strip of cloth about 1 in. wide must be put across the centre of the padcloth, the ends passing under the hogskin piece and binding. Then add another strip along the centre of the sheet where it joins, and another along the joint on the top of the neck of the hood, the ends being always placed under the binding. Now place flat strips, ½ in. wide, along the joints at the side and the points of the ear-pieces, then round the bottom to cover the ends and the joint. This work can be done by machine.

The only difference in a Newmarket sheet is that

it is cut on a curve from the shoulder to the front
at the centre of the chest where both sides meet;
there is no breastcloth, the two sides being united
by a strap and buckle. The last mentioned must
be on the near side, and the shape like that for a
saddle girth. Line the shoulder and the corners
of the chest where the straps are stitched with a
piece of rugging underneath.

The hood is fastened under the jaw with a

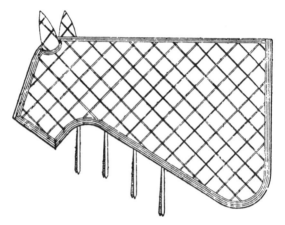

Fig. 29.—Hood.

small strap and buckle; cadez strings are run from
this point to about half-way down the neck on each
side to tie together.

The sheets can be bound in two colours, if preferred, or with patent bindings, one colour along
the edge and the other by its side. If red cloth
is employed for binding, bind it in all along and
then put blue cloth, about $\frac{7}{8}$ in. wide, just to cover
the edge of the red binding. Catch them both
under the stitch with the first row of stitching,

and finish the upper edge of the binding in the same style.

Princess check of various colours is fine worsted material, very light in weight, and of very showy appearance. It can be bound with fine worsted binding of one or more colours. When cutting the sheet for either of the above, the back must not be made quite straight, but should be scooped out

Fig. 30.—Horse Covered.

a little behind the shoulder towards the loin ; leave it full at the rump and slanting a little at the end. Fig. 30 illustrates the horse covered.

Body rollers (Figs. 31 and 32) are made of worsted, linen, union, webbing, or leather, with one, two, or three straps, a full-sized roller being 6 ft. 2 in. long. The pad is placed about 10 in. from one point, and the shortest end of the roller near the pad must be bound with leather and stitched with single thread ; let it be 1 in. wide

on each side, and bind the other end, the binding
being 1 in. wide on the front as at the short end,
but line the girth for about 6 in. below, and stitch
it along the edge of the roller. Then raise a stitch
over the edge of the leather in the girth without
running through, and with a lead-pencil mark a line

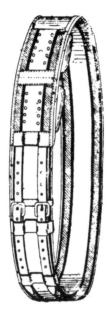

Fig. 31.—Body Roller.

across 10 in. from the end without lining, then
a second line 1 ft. away, and two more 5¼ in. from
each line in the space ; thus there will be a 1½-in.
space between the two last cross lines.

Cut out a piece of stiff cardboard to the same
width as the roller, and 1 in. below each of the
extreme cross lines thin the edges. Next cut a

piece of white serge (when the girth is leather use basil or hogskin) to reach 2 in. below the two end lines, and ½ in. wider on each side of the girth. Narrow the centre of a piece of hogskin, 1 ft. 4 in. by 1¼ in., to a little less than half opposite the space between the two inner lines.

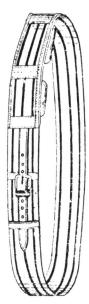

Fig. 32.—Body Roller.

Having rounded the four corners, cut slanting from the extreme rounded part towards the ends until the hogskin is about ½ in. wide at the point. Two of these pieces will be needed to face the panel on each side. Then turn down the serge along the edges lengthwise just ¼ in., and back and whip it to the facing along the shaped edge

F

—not the straight edge—placing them centre to centre ; the full and narrow parts of the facings must correspond on each side.

Two pieces of leather must be cut, 2¼ in. deep and of the same width as the roller ; crease them along the two longer sides with a hot iron, and then cut two similar pieces of basil and two strong 1¼-in. brown leather straps, 1 ft. 6 in. long. After pointing one end and shaving the other, crease them double with a hot iron and make eight holes in each. Place one of the pieces of basil underneath, level with the edges of the roller, the top part reaching a little above the line near the shorter end from the pad.

The two straps are placed within ¼ in. of the line, pointing towards the short end of the roller, and are then stitched down firmly through the roller and the under piece of basil. Next the first two pieces of hogskin of the same width as the roller are placed one on each end of the part to be occupied by the pad, their upper edges reaching about ⅛ in. above the two end lines. The other piece of basil is placed under the end where there are no straps.

After tacking down the basil, cut a piece big enough to pass across the roller from side to side and 1¾ in. wide ; crease it lengthwise and tack it in the centre to cover the two central lines. Now place the piece of cardboard underneath equidistant at both ends from the centre, and tack it down.

The other piece of hogskin goes at the other end of the pad to correspond with the similar piece on the opposite side, and cover the stitched ends of the straps.

The two pieces at each end can now be stitched through the roller and cardboard along the upper cross line of each ; also stitch the ends of the centre piece of the edge of the roller and cardboard, leaving the two cross lines unstitched. Take the serge lining and facing and put them centre to centre at each side of the roller; then whip the facing to the roller along both edges through the web and cardboard. Take care that the ends of the serge and facing reach equal distances just below the cross line stitched in the two end pieces.

A thin strip of hogskin should be cut for binding, about ½ in. wide. Both edges must be bound from the extreme end of the pieces of leather at each end of the pad to the end of the other piece at the opposite extremity of the pad. Distribute the lining equally on both sides of the centre, and stitch the two cross lines in the middle piece of hogskin from one side to the other, thus making two separate compartments.

Two rows of stitching must now be made through the leather at the strap end of the pad downwards between the straps and close to them; then make two corresponding rows in the leather at the other end of the panel. This can now be stuffed with flock through the opening at the bottom; both sides must be stuffed firm and level to the same size, and the edge of the serge turned in at the bottom. Raise a stitch to fasten the leather lining on the roller opposite the serge.

Then cut twenty small round or scalloped pieces of leather, a little smaller than a threepenny bit, of coloured roan or hogskin; quilt the panel with five stitches at each side on every part, making twenty in all. They must be in a perfectly straight line, and 1 in. from the edge, the needle being driven from below, then through the small circle of leather, and down through it again and the roller.

Having then firmly knotted it. to the panel below with a small tuft of coloured wool under each knot, cut two chapes for two 1¼-in. buckles,

and two loops. Stitch the chapes with the outside
of the buckles flush with the end of the roller,
and straight to the straps.

Another loop must be cut sufficiently long to
reach across the girth; finish it neatly and stitch
it across at both ends. Make also two cross rows
in the centre, with sufficient space on each side
of them to allow the two straps to enter. This
last loop must be about 6 in. lower down than
the chapes. Having blocked, creased, and finished the loops properly, place a fancy stamp in
the centre of each.

The above instructions apply also to the making
of a stallion roller, but this must have dees, which
are set in before the panel is adjusted; then the
binding can be placed round or under the chapes.
Wider web may be employed, and three straps
instead of two; also, there may be whole brass or
silver buckles to fasten them, instead of plain
buckles, and two long loops below the chapes
instead of a buckle.

The leather girths are sometimes made in the
same way, except that there need not be any
lining under the buckles when they are firm and
good.

Surcingles are made for the same purpose as
rollers, but have no panels.

CHAPTER X.

KNEE-CAPS AND MISCELLANEOUS ARTICLES.

KNEE-CAPS (Figs. 33 to 35) are of felt, fawn rugging, kersey cloth, union, buff leather, black rubber, etc.

It is better to buy the pads, but they can be made if so desired as follows: When there is no press available, damp some half-curried leather, and beat it as a shoemaker beats boot soles until it acquires the hollow cup shape. After it has had time to dry, cut it to a wide oval shape, about 5 in. by 4 in., and make the cloth, kersey, or leather about 8 in. at the top and 9 in. deep.

Round the bottom part, and bind all except the straight top with cadez patent binding or cloth; the buff need not be bound. Then, on the centre, place the leather block, with a piece of shaped cardboard underneath, pasting the two together, and pressing down the cloth to the hollow. Stitch the blocked leather to the cloth, about $1\frac{1}{4}$ in. from the top and $1\frac{1}{2}$ in. from the bottom, and cut a piece of leather $1\frac{1}{8}$ in. wide and 1 in. longer at each end than the cloth at the top. Make a hole at each end 1 in. from the point for a $\frac{5}{8}$-in. strap, placing a chape, buckle, and loop in the hole at one end, and a strap of similar width, 9 in. long, in the other hole, and stitching them both firmly.

If preferred, a small square may be placed in the strap side, with a chape to fasten in the hole, a second square being used for fastening the strap, with an indiarubber ring $\frac{5}{8}$ in. wide between the two squares.

A piece of chamois leather will be needed to make a roll at the top of the same length and

Fig. 33.—Knee-cap.

width as the strap, the chamois leather being stitched all along through the top leather and the cloth. The chamois must hang down in front

Fig. 34.—Knee-cap.

of the knee-cap while this is being done, the three edges being placed together; thus, they can be stitched, the top leather reaching to the same distance over each end.

Turn the chamois leather over the top towards the bottom, and stitch it along the bottom side

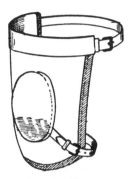

Fig. 35.—Knee-cap.

of the top strap through cloth and strap, leaving it rather slack. Then make two rows of stitches across in the centre, leaving an opening of about

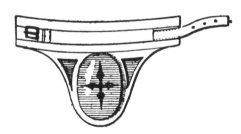

Fig. 36.—Fetlock Boot.

1½ in. exactly in the centre between the two cross lines.

After stuffing the two parts of the roll from each end with flock, close the ends by stitching

the chamois and top leather together. Next put
a ⅝-in. chape buckle and loop at the bottom of the
block pad, making them slant downwards slightly,
with a strap 10 in. long at the opposite side for

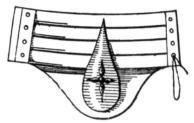

Fig. 37.—Fetlock Boot.

fastening. The buckles must be reversed when
making a pair, each buckle being on the outside.
Sometimes the best knee-caps have the knee

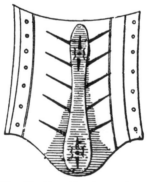

Fig. 38.—Lace Speedy-cut Boot.

block cut with a piece to come from the top to
catch the top strap, and to be stitched under it;
this is a great improvement, even when there is
a separate piece of leather.

Fetlock boots (Fig. 36) are made of leather, indiarubber, cloth and leather, or, as in Curtis's patent, of zinc and leather, according to the part on which the horse catches itself. It is scarcely worth while to make them, as they can be bought in all varieties and patterns ready-made, like perforated lace leggings, lace fetlock boot (Fig. 37), roll-cutting boot, top-roll fetlock boot, back sinew boot, lace or buckle speedy-cut boot (Figs. 38 and 39), over-reach boot of indiarubber to slip on over

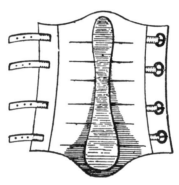

Fig. 39.—Buckle Speedy-cut Boot.

the hoof, and indiarubber ring boot (Fig. 40), either solid or hollow.

Fetlock boots made by the saddler should have a cup just like the knee-cap to cover the fetlock. A side leg boot, made for a horse that catches above the fetlock, must be cut to reach almost from joint to joint; it is stiffened along the centre inside, and has three straps and buckles on the outside.

Hoofswabs are made of felt or leather, the sole being cut the same shape as the hoof; leather is placed round to cover the top of the hoof, fitting

tightly and slanting upwards, and is fastened
behind with a buckle and loop.

Poultice boots are made in the same way, but
have a piece of strong canvas above to keep the
poultice round the top of the hoof; each is fastened behind with strings at the top, and a strap
with a buckle at the bottom.

False collars (Fig. 41) are very valuable when
all other means of easing a collar have failed.
They are made to fit inside a collar, but should
not be so thick as to interfere with its size, even
when quilted. Some are made of single leather,

Fig. 40.—Ring Boot.

others of one thickness of felt, and some are
quilted. All are alike in pattern, but the quilted
ones need a little allowance for the stuffing and
quilting, say 1½ in. in the width; the shape is
similar to that of a collar lining.

A brown paper pattern should be cut out first
to fit the collar, and then be manipulated so that
the creases come out in the trimmings. Run a
single thickness forward quite to the front to cover
the wide part of the body of the collar well, and
come out beyond the body all round about 1½ in.

The single leather and felt collar must be cut
to pattern, and seamed both ends together, with

a strap and buckle at both sides and at the bottom to keep them in place. Crease the leather double with a hot iron along the edges, and when felt is employed it is advisable to place a piece of thin leather over all the joints and stitch it on each side of them, having previously joined the felt end to end.

The felt must always be cut lengthwise, not crosswise, as it will only stretch across.

Fig. 41.—False Collar.

To make a quilted collar, cut the leather 1½ in. wider, but do not let it reach beyond the forewale outside. When cutting it, allow about 1½ in. more in width than the finished size. Four pieces of basil will be needed, two for each side reversed; each pair must be stitched together, whipped over the edges with the flesh outside and the ends stitched together, so as to form a bag from end to end. Having cut a hole so that it will be out of sight when finished on the side next the collar, turn the collar inside out, and cut a similar, though smaller, hole in the other side.

Both sides should be stuffed separately through these holes. A piece of strong, fine cane will be required, long enough to run all round the hollow between the body and forewale of the collar inside, meeting in the point at the top. Put it through one of the holes in front of the false collar, and spot it in, drawing the leather tightly over it all round. Thus, when the collar is finished, the cane will fit into this hollow with a spring, keeping it in place close to the body.

After that, stuff the collar with fine flock, putting more stuffing at the draught if necessary, and then quilt it and stitch up the holes in the sides. Run a row of quilting along the outside near the edge first, and then two rows inside towards the cane, a very small tuft of wool being also placed inside under every stitch.

The thread must not be cut and knotted at each stitch, but should be just pulled home, and the thread run from one stitch to the other; it must not be baggy, but smooth and even all over. Finally, place it in position, and catch it as firmly as possible with the spring cane in the hollow under the forewale.

CHAPTER XI.

REPAIRING HARNESS AND SADDLERY.

THE renovation and repair of harness and saddlery will be treated in this chapter. It is hardly necessary to point out that it is economical to repair harness and to keep it in good condition, rather than to let it be worn out straightaway and then to replace with new again. It always pays to attend at once to defective or broken parts, such a system saving time as well as money, and lessening the risk of accident that is ever-present where safety of life and limb depends on the strength of straps and buckles.

For the benefit of the uninitiated, the trade names of the many parts of a complete set of harness are given below, the letter references being to Fig. 42. A shows the blinker; B, cheek; C, front; D, headpiece; E, nosepiece; F, throatlatch; G, bearing-rein rounding; H, bearing-rein middle; I, collar; J, hame-tug; K, trace; L, backband; M, bellyband; N, saddle; O, flap; P, skirt; Q, swell; R, shaft-tug; S, saddle seat; T, terret; U, bearing-rein hook; V, breeching-strap; W, breeching-seat; X, breeching-tugs; Y, split hip-strap; Z, crupper; A', crupper dock; B', driving-reins.

When repairing trap or carriage harness of all kinds, such as reins, breeching straps, crupper billets, etc., shave the under side of the splice on the top and the top part underneath, making them as nearly as possible of the same thickness as a single strap.

A splice must never be stitched across in a single strap, but always forward along the strap. When, however, only two rows are made in a splice,

always put two or three stitches in the centre of
the top lay of the splice at the point.

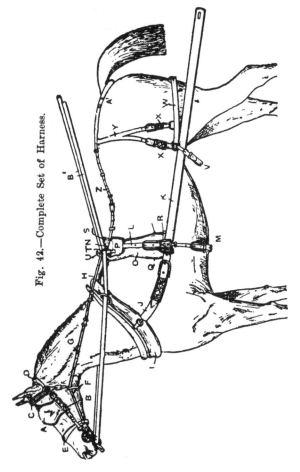

Fig. 42.—Complete Set of Harness.

To make a splice in a pair of reins, or where

the leather is of one thickness, only pare the ends and lap them as in Fig. 43.

The straps of the bridle have to be patched and replaced sometimes. When furnishing winkers with new chapes, make them like the old ones, and when treating a strap, shave the patch or splice as near as possible to the single thickness.

The bearing-rein rounding G (Fig. 42), when broken, is perhaps one of the most unsatisfactory parts to repair, because, its shape being round, sufficient cannot be pared from the old leather to give place to the new. The broken ends may be reduced a little, and the parts drawn together by stitches from one piece to the other and thin leather lapped round, extending 1 in. or so on each side, and stitched closely along the edge.

Fig. 43.—Spliced Leather Rein.

Chapes are put on head collar squares in the following manner:—Open the parts where the chapes are to be, and run them between the leathers, thinning the ends a little first, and making a strong cross stitch near the ends.

For lining shaft tugs, a somewhat frequent job, use, if possible, sole leather for the outer piece of lining. The stitches being made coarser than for a new tug, cut a groove in the outer lining all along on both sides, and sink the stitches. Never cut the old lining straight across without thinning its end and that of the new piece for splicing. It must overlap the old one, not merely meet it end to end.

In lining shaft tugs, try to make them level. Sometimes three or four thicknesses of leather will be needed, but the length must be regulated and

the ends of every piece shaved, so that, when placed
together, they will run down to the thickness of the
old parts. Always make the chapes long enough
for such things as bearers and breeching straps,
etc., shaving the ends to be joined to the chape,
and finishing neatly.

The inside of shaft-tug R (Fig 42), is specially
liable to damage owing to constant friction with
the shaft. In some cases only that part of the
lining under the loop is worn away. To repair this
part, take a piece of stout leather long enough to
reach beyond each end of the loop, and stitch it on
each side only where the loop is, with four rows at
each end. Use the screw-race for making a groove
in the leather, so that the stitches may lie well
below the surface to prevent unnecessary wear. If
the lining has to be continued all round, take out
the old one and cut a strip about 12 in. long ; bend
it down, grain inside, 1 in. from one end ; scoop out
a piece in the middle of the bend for the heel of the
buckle tongue to lie in, and pare both ends for a lap
splice. When put into the tug, it will appear to be
too long, but the thin end of the strip must be bent
and fastened in its place by a nail on each side of it,
and the lining then worked into place by rubbing
the fingers round inside until it assumes its proper
shape.

Forcing in the lining by this means makes the
tug solid and strong. A strip of sole leather
soaked in water and sewn in wet makes a better
lining than harness leather where a tug is subjected to very rough wear. Use the tug clamp for
any of this work. These special clamps are illustrated by Figs. 52 to 55, pp. 24, 25, of "Harness
Making."

In the hame-tug J (Fig. 42) there is a clip (Fig.
44) with which to connect the tug to the draft of the
hame. This clip sometimes snaps at one of the
rivet holes and causes the leather to break. The

broken leather must be pared away from each side of the break laid on as described on p. 96 in repairing the middle of backband. Owing to the iron clip inside, this can only be sewn along each edge.

If the clip has become very much worn, it is best to put in a new clip at once, and so avoid further trouble. Rip the stitches holding the top and bottom pieces to the middle, knock out the two rivets which fasten the clip to the tug, and fix in a new one, forcing the prongs of clip together in a vice and riveting them firmly. New leather may now be put from the end of tug to the loop instead of splicing in a piece ; and if this new piece is to go

Fig. 44.—Hame Tug Clip.

on the top of the tug, stitch the two inside rows first on the new leather before fixing it in its place.

Always trim and finish the work off neatly, and where the edges, as in this case, cannot be polished with a cloth, a finished appearance may be imparted by the free use of a smooth bone (the handle of a worn-out tooth-brush, for instance). The bone rubber is illustrated on p. 28 of "Harness Making."

Some parts of a set of harness being subjected to rougher wear or more intense strain, naturally get damaged much sooner than other parts. Say the end of a trace (K, Fig. 42) breaks at one of the holes. This may be repaired either by splicing the broken parts together, or by putting on a new point. The first method is not always satisfactory, because

G

when finished this trace will be shorter than its fellow.

In splicing the end of a trace, cut the broken ends off square, and open the one on the short piece by running a knife between the two layers of leather for about 3½ in. and separating them. Bend them well apart, lay over the edge of the bench, and with the round knife pare away until there is a gradual taper on each. Now take the long piece and pare the end away, top and bottom, until it resembles a wedge. This is fitted into the other part, and two or three nails are driven through to hold it whilst being sewn. The next hole towards the point should be level with the hole in wear on the other trace.

Lay both traces on the bench to see that all holes are even, or an unequal strain may sooner or

Fig. 45.—Spliced Trace.

later cause the shorter one to break, and probably give the horse a sore shoulder in the meantime. Full instructions for making threads are given in Chapter II. of "Harness Making." Judgment must be used in making a thread of suitable size. This will depend principally on the number of stitches per inch. Sew in the old holes, drive the awl straight through, and pull the stitches well in. Shave the edges evenly with the spokeshave, put on some dye, and rub up with a cloth to give it a polish. Fig. 45 shows this kind of joint.

To put a new point to a broken trace, cut off at the last hole, and measure it. A new point should never be put on between the holes, as the splice would be stiff, and difficult to get through the buckle and loop.

Cut a strip of good leather with the cutting gauge, and from the thickest end measure off two pieces the length required. Cut the end of one piece to a point, mark it with the compasses, and prick it with an iron the same number of teeth per inch as the old stitching, using the small mallet for this purpose; pare the ends for the splice as just described, and tack the pieces together with a few nails. The bottom piece should be $\frac{1}{4}$ in. shorter than the top piece at the splice; this makes a more even joint.

After it is all sewn, lay it top side downwards on the bench, and with a stout round stick (a hammer handle will do) rub the stitches well down. Cut off the surplus leather at the point (bottom strip), run an edge-tool along all the edges, and with the spokeshave finish the edges to a crescent shape. Dye these, and, before rubbing them with a cloth, draw a piece of tallow along. This will give a nice smooth finish. Lay the trace on the bench and place the other above it; mark through the holes of this on to the new leather, and punch on the lead-piece.

In repairing thick backbands and traces, splicing should if possible be avoided. Shave both ends of the break, and just tack the ends together, then put pieces of leather at both sides until the required thickness is obtained, the pieces being shorter and thinner-shaved at the ends nearer the centre. As a rule, stitch four rows along the patch, and one or two stitches in the centre of the points. If the entire part, such as the holed part in a trace, is not worth patching, put in a new piece, keeping the old one to mark the new; the joint at the splice must be very neat, not thick and clumsy. In the same way, if the other end is gone, add a new piece, making it thicker than at the other parts.

When the centre of the backband is not worth patching, make a new centre, but generally the strap end and bellyband part can be used. Having measured the part, cut off and allow enough extra to make a splice in each end; put the strap in one end and the bellyband in the other.

A backband, L (Fig. 42) generally breaks at one of the tug buckle holes, or at some part near the middle where it passes under the saddle-skirts, P, or seat, S. This part of the backband is sometimes made up of three thicknesses of leather, and it may be that only the top or bottom strip is broken. Take off both tugs, lay the backband, broken side up, across the bench, and with the round knife skive out a piece about 2½ in. each side of the break. Cut a piece of new leather to fit, and if it is for the top of the backband, mark the number of lines and prick them. See that the part under repair is of equal substance with the rest, then sew it and finish off.

Before putting the backband into the saddle, the off-side tug must be put on. The point of the backband is passed through the loop first, from the bottom, then over the tongue and through the buckle, when it is easily got into position. Then pass the point of the backband under the off-side skirt on the opposite side of P, and through to the near side. Buckle the other tug in its place.

If any difficulty is experienced in getting the backband through, bend the point down at the start, and if not successful then, put a piece of strong string through the first hole and pass the two ends of the string through; by this means it can be readily pulled into place.

The bridgeband is frequently torn across in some part or other of the body; to repair it, shave the ends thin, and join the break with a few stitches. New pieces must be put on both sides, and, when necessary, another in the centre. Let the top lay be 1 in. longer at each end than the lower lay, and shave it thin at both ends. Next make four or five rows of strong stitches from end to end, but never stitch the patches across; also make a few stitches at the centre in the points, keeping to a uniform thickness as much as possible.

The above remark applies to the backband, bellyband, or crupper of the leading gear when they are torn. In case of chapes like those for bridgeband tugs, use strong leather, shave the ends, and let the upper side be a little longer than the lower; also thin the part put in a little.

Broken loops in harness frequently occur. To repair them, cut a piece of leather the same width as the broken loop. Its length should be reckoned at about three times the width of the strap it is going into. Take off the edges with a small edge-tool and rub them up; push one end half-way through the opening made by taking out the old pieces; sew in this side; then, turning in the other end, sew that also, running the awl in a slanting direction towards the edge as the middle is approached. Block it up on a loopstick, which must be the same width as the strap, warm the creasing tool, and mark the loop along its edge.

Surcingles and saddle girths often break in the centre; stitch the ends together, and make a basil cover tight enough to pass round them, stitching each side, and then put it over the end of the girth, making four or more rows of stitching along it.

In the skirt of the saddle, s (Fig. 42) a large stud or bolt is shown. Many saddles are made without this, and it often happens that the stitching at this part breaks away, and if not repaired at once is likely to lead to the whole of the saddle-top being pulled off.

To do such a repair, knock out the nail under the iron crupper loop and loosen the panel from the flaps o about half-way down one side. The skirt can then be sewn down to the flap again. If the panel was fixed in with copper wire, a close examination of the old wire will give the size and method to be employed in replacing it in its position.

Very often the panel, especially when the saddle is old, is merely stitched to the flaps at intervals, four or five stitches being made at each place, and this is an easier plan. Fasten it under the iron crupper loop with a small clout nail padded with serge, and trim this off to a small tuft.

Re-lining collars and saddles is dealt with in detail in the next chapter, but a note or two on the subject may here be given. A saddle panel may need a new lining and stuffing. Begin work by removing it, and, if the back and facing are good enough, cut off the old lining close to the stitches running by the side of the facing, but let part of the lining and stitches be there to keep the facing in place. Cut the new lining as for a new panel, and tack it with hemp, turning in the edges and spot-stitching it down by the facing along both sides. On the outside, the stitch must be small and neat. Stitch the lining in at the top along the old marks, and whip it in at the bottom.

The panel is stuffed like a new panel, and for a good saddle is quilted and adjusted with wire, or spotted and stitched all along; for a common saddle, five or six stitches together here and there will suffice. When the back is good and the facing bad, stitch on a new facing with new cord, and stitch the lining like a new one.

Sometimes a saddle panel has to be stuffed and raised without lining; to do this, cut a hole across at the centre, and fill each end, levelling the stuff with the seat awl.

In repairing riding saddles, the same principles are followed as for making new ones; as a rule, the back of the panel can remain with a new panel affixed, and also the hogskin facing. Remove all else, put in a new lining, and stuff like new.

When a riding saddle tree is broken, a blacksmith will often repair it, especially when the plate is broken, but it must be stripped and everything put back as before.

When a saddle needs a new tree, begin by taking off the old top, doing as little damage to the flaps and skirts as possible. The skirts can often be utilised again like the flaps, so that only a tree seat and cantle cover will be needed. Make it up like a new one, and damp the skirts and flaps to make them easier to handle; also remove the old nails from the leather before employing new ones. If the skirts are gone, new ones must be cut out to the same pattern.

When the cover of a collar forewale is worn in any way, put on a piece, and shave both ends well and thinly; then stitch it along the bottom of the forewale between the forewale and the body. If the lining is worn in some places, line it without taking off the old straw, and put in new flock; place the lining along the forewale, and stitch it with a lace-collar needle and handiron, turning it down to cover the stitches, and drawing it in along the old stitches in the sidepiece if necessary. A little fresh straw can be placed under the draught, a wisp or two being placed in with the stick, and hammered with the mallet to fill it and tighten.

The best plan, however, is to take the sidepiece off entirely, and make a new body as for a new collar, the sidepieces being damped and put back just like new ones. When the leather to which the lining is stitched at the forewale is worn too much, the stitches can be run through and out at the same side, as with false lining.

Collars also are half-lined, and a strip of new lining is sometimes placed under the draught; the straw and flock required are then put through the

opening. The last two methods do not interfere
with the sidepiece; the lining is merely drawn to
it and stitched on. The subject is dealt with more
fully in the next chapter.

A collar can be reduced in the following way.
Open the top, remove the top piece, and then, with
pincers, pull some wisps from the straw in the forewale until both sides meet easily. Now stitch the
ends together to the required size, turn down the
sidepiece and lining, cut the straw in the body to
size, fasten both ends of the body together, and put
the sidepiece on as before.

To put a piece in a collar to make it larger,
shave the ends of the forewale thin, and again remove a few wisps. Cut a piece of leather of the
same width as the leather in the forewale, and
stitch it, joining it well with the old leather and
shaving the joint thin. Put in some fresh wisps
and a short collar iron, one after the other, until
the forewale is hard enough, taking care to join
the straw well, so that there will be no hinge.

The iron must be beaten in with the straw on it
by a mallet, as it cannot very well be knocked on
the block. When long enough, close the top, and
unless it is much enlarged, flock in the body will
suffice to lengthen it. Stitch a piece of lining or
basil to the new piece on the forewale, and fasten
it in the shape of the body by stitching the other
side; then stuff it tightly with flock. Join the top
and put a cap on the forewale and a patch in the
sidepiece of sufficient length to cover the new part.

Wtih regard to cleaning and renovating, it is
obvious that harness and saddlery, to be maintained in good order, should be kept thoroughly
cleansed from all dirt, whether splashings from the
road or exudations from the horse.

For cleansing harness use warm water (not hot),
a stiff brush, and a little soft soap. After well
washing it, wipe with an old cloth, and before it is

quite dry apply a dressing of pure neatsfoot oil, and hang up for a few hours in the shade. It will then be found quite pliable, and if there is any objection to the dull appearance of the leather, it may be brushed over with a thin coat of harness composition and polished with another brush. A soft cloth will give it quite a lustre, and a set of harness treated in this way will always be found to look neat, and to last twice as long as it would if never cleaned.

The collar and saddle linings should be kept free from scurf and other dirt, either by applying a stiff brush or by scraping with a blunt knife, and should always be hung up and thoroughly dried before being used again. This careful treatment not only preserves the collar and saddle, but is also very beneficial to the horse, preventing sore shoulders and back, and tending to greater comfort altogether.

An occasional loosening of the padding by beating the lining all over with a thin stick will keep it soft and prevent irritation. All buckles should be unfastened, and the under part of each one thoroughly cleaned and polished. If only the parts in sight are cleaned, an accumulation of verdigris will ultimately destroy the leather where the buckle rests on it, causing it to crack across at the hole, with the possible result of a serious accident.

Where harness is required for daily use it is advisable to have an alternate set. Of course, this implies double outlay at first, but the advantages of possessing an extra collar and saddle will afford ample compensation.

Shifting the buckle to another hole occasionally is another means—small, but not to be despised—of extending the life of a set of harness; but in altering traces, breeching-straps, and such like, it is necessary to proceed equally on both sides in order to avoid unequal strain.

Where there is room for it, and where its cost does not preclude its use, a saddle-cleaning horse as seen in harness-rooms attached to stables might with advantage be employed. Such a horse may be a high table with substantial legs, these supporting, besides the table top, one or two shelves for holding miscellaneous articles. The saddle rest fits on the table top, and in section is shaped thus: $\wedge$. It is desirable to add two side leaves so that the horse can be conveniently used for many purposes other than saddle cleaning.

CHAPTER XII.

RE-LINING COLLARS AND SADDLES.

BEFORE undertaking the re-lining of collars and saddles, all sores and abrasions on the horse, to which the collar or saddle belongs, must be noted and the collar or saddle marked, so that any cavity to be formed for the relief of these may be in the right place.

In the case of a collar, the best place for a guide-mark is on the afterwale c (Fig. 46).

A cart saddle usually hurts in the gullet under the bearing-rein hook or beneath one of the terrets, the discomfort being generally due to lack of sufficient padding. If it hurts in the gullet, it may be altered by padding the sides well; but if the injury is on one or both sides, then the stuffing must be removed, and the lining drawn firmly down to the back of the pannel.

The various parts constituting a collar are indicated in Fig. 46, in which A denotes the cap which covers the stitches made in joining the ends of the forewale B; the afterwale C is the outer covering of the body side. That part of the collar marked E is called the throat, and through the line F is the draught. The substance of the collar at F is greater than at any other part, the increased substance being necessary, not only on account of most of the wear falling here, but also in order that the tugs and traces may be kept clear of the horse.

When collars are very much worn down at the draught, it is sometimes necessary to place a pad under the point of the hame, so that the tugs may be kept clear of the shoulders. This pad may be sewn to the collar or kept in place by small straps buckled round the hame point.

When repairing collars, it is preferable to
remedy any defect to the afterwale before the new
lining is put in.

The materials employed in lining collars and
saddles are (1) collar cloth, (2) serge, (3) leather.
For cart collars and saddles the first is used, and
for cab and gig work either serge or leather.

In re-lining a cart collar the lining is not carried
completely round the inside; it seldom reaches
beyond the points indicated by x x (Fig. 46). Each
end of the lining is gathered to fulness, and, when
stuffed, keeps the collar clear of the horse at the
throat and on the withers.

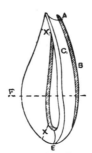

Fig. 46.—Cab Collar.

Cab and gig collars are not re-lined in this
manner, but the new lining is made to cover all the
inside. Fig. 47 represents the method of cutting
the lining for one side of the collar. When leather
is used, it is necessary, of course, to reverse the
pattern in cutting the other half. The lining is
made to lap at the throat, as shown at E (Fig. 46),
and is fitted in quite close at the top.

With regard to the tools used in re-lining collars,
etc., the hand-iron is used for pushing the needles
through the collar. It is made with either a
straight or bent stem, the latter being preferred by

many on account of its being less liable to slip
through the hand. Half-moon needles are made in
sizes ranging from 3 in. to 7 in. in length, the
thickness increasing proportionately. One each,
4 in. and 5 in. long, will answer all the requirements
for ordinary work. Straight collar needles, 4 in.,
5 in., and 6 in. being the most useful sizes, are also
necessary. Seat-awls will be required for shifting
and finally adjusting the stuffing, or " levelling " as
it is called.

Collar cloth, 40 in. wide, costs 1s. 4d. to 1s. 9d.

Fig. 47.—Lining of Cab Collar.

per yard ; serges, 2s. to 3s. ; and collar basils, 2s. to
2s. 6d. per lb. The basils are unstrained, this condition rendering them more pliable to work and
softer in wear than those which have been strained.
Suitable basils may be bought at any large leather
warehouse, but serges and collar cloths can be
obtained only of saddlers' ironmongers. Flock for
stuffing will also be necessary ; it costs from 16s. 6d.
to 24s. per cwt. ; some houses supply 14 lb. of good
drum flock at 2½d. per lb. Collar twine, 9d. per
½-lb. ball, and fine tarred twine, 1s. 2d. per hank,
are used for sewing in the linings, but these are not

absolutely necessary; a ball of brown hemp, some shoemakers' wax, and beeswax will answer the same purpose.

For a saddler's black wax melt in a pan over a slow fire till thoroughly amalgamated ½ lb. of pitch and ⅓ lb. of resin, stirring slowly the while, then add about half a pennyworth of boiled linseed oil, and pour a small quantity of the mixture into a bucket of cold water. Allow to stand for half a minute, then pull the mixture hand over hand; if it sticks well together without cracking or breaking, it is right as to softness, but if it cracks and breaks, put in more oil; if too soft, add more resin or pitch. If the mixture is of the desired consistency, pour it all into the cold water, and pull it hand over hand till it floats on the water; cut a small piece and throw it in to try. Add more or less oil (or tallow will do), according to the weather.

Having procured the necessary tools and material, and made careful observation of any sores and tender places on the horse, the work of re-lining may be proceeded with, a cab collar (Fig. 46) being dealt with first.

The lining, whether of serge or leather, is cut the same shape, the only difference being that the serge is reversible, whereas the leather is not. Begin sewing in at the top; use a straight collar needle, passing it through from the outside below the forewale and into the crease where the old lining is joined to it. The edge of the new lining is turned inwards, and the needle passed through it and brought out again so that the stitch lies hidden in the folded edge. Push through to the outside again, then return, and repeat until the throat is reached, when the other half must be lapped about ½ in., and the sewing continued until the top is reached again. The splice at the throat should be exactly in the middle, as shown at E.

When the stitching has been completed, the

collar will be ready for stuffing. Loosen the flock
well, and lay it evenly all over the body side, using
very little at the throat and the top, so that the
depth may not suffer. Remove the stuffing from
the parts to be eased, and stitch the lining down
firmly to the body side; then pad well round the
edges of the cavity.

Begin to sew the remaining edge to the collar,
using the half-moon needle for the purpose. It will
be noticed, by turning up the edge of the afterwale, that it is stitched to the body side about
$\frac{1}{4}$ in. from the edge, and that all the stitches are

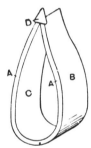

Fig. 48.—Collar.

hidden from the top. The new lining must be sewn
in the same manner, if neatness is aimed at. Press
the edge under the afterwale, and alternately pass
the needle through, pulling each stitch well home
when made.

If the collar has been lined with serge, the stuffing may be worked as desired by using the seat-
awl, and any unevenness disposed of. Pass the awl
through the serge into the lump to be removed and
gently work it in the required direction. Passing
one hand along the lining will show when evenness
has been obtained.

A collar should fit the horse perfectly, or it will

probably produce either galling or choking. One that is too wide, or deeper than it should be, will produce galling; whereas if the collar is too small, choking will result.

When lining a gig collar, it is better to take off the lining and make it like new. But when it is a question of healing sore shoulders, though many put pads near the sores to keep the collar away, the most commendable system is to chamber the collar opposite the sore, which can be done as described in the next two paragraphs.

In the lining opposite the sore part make two cross slits, their lengths varying according to the

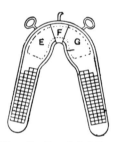

Fig. 49.—Panel Saddle.

extent of the sore. Then damp the leather well, and turn up the four points. With a knife scoop a big hole in the straw underneath, taking it out to a good depth, and making the hollow slant towards the sides; but cut in farther than the leather can be turned up, so that there will be no sharp edge to the hollow to cause another sore.

A small collar needle and a long thread with a little twist will be needed for stitching. Make some stitches from the outside of the collar to draw the leather lining down deep into the hollow; stitch round the edges, and also put several stitches in the centre. Some makers put flock under the stitches inside the hollow. The collar can also be patched up again when the sores are healed.

Another method of providing for sores, etc., is as follows:—The stitches which connect the lining C (Fig. 48) to the afterwale B are cut, and the wool or other material with which it is padded at the place touching the injured part is taken out. The lining is drawn down to the form of a hollow by putting a stitch or two right through the body of the collar with a needle. Additional wool may be put in above and below the cavity by the use of the stuffing-rod. See that the wool does not form into lumps, but lies evenly all round the cavity. In

Fig. 50.—"Swelled" Flap Cab Saddle.

sewing the lining to the afterwale, use a needle and collar twine. A shows the forewale and D the cap.

The dotted lines in Fig. 49 show the parts which are likely to cause any injury found on the back or withers of the horse. To remedy this, knock out the nails round the gullet at F, and loosen the panel on the side causing the injury. An opening will be found in the back of the panel; take out the padding from where the lining is stained, and pad round the cavity as in easing the collar, according to the instructions given in the last paragraph. If the injury is caused by the part at F chafing, then

H

both sides, marked E and G, must be padded more fully.

Re-lining a saddle is a somewhat more difficult job than re-lining a collar. That shown by Fig. 50 is known as a "swelled" flap cab saddle. The panel (Fig. 51) must first of all be removed. It will doubtless be found to be fixed to the flaps with copper wire, which must be cut, the best tool for the purpose being an old hand-knife made into a rough saw by jagging the edge with a chisel. It will pass freely between the flap and panel roll and sever the wires. Remove all pieces of old wire, then cut the quilting stitches on the back of the

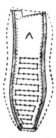

Fig. 51.—Panel of "Swelled" Cab Saddle.

panel. The dotted lines (Fig. 51) show how to cut out the new lining. Fold the serge and lay the panel on it, then cut as indicated.

There are two methods of stitching in the new lining of a saddle:—(1) By entirely removing all the old one, and stitching the new to the facing, as in the case of a new panel ; or (2) by cutting the old lining near the stitches made in quilting in the roll, folding the edge of the new lining, and hiding the stitches within the folded edge, as in the case of lining a collar.

The first of the above plans is always adopted in the case of best gig saddles. When the lining has been stitched in, quilt it all round near the facing, to keep the roll in its place. This done, lay it, lining side down, on the bench and begin to put in the stuffing, using a long flat rule for the purpose; fill it firmly on each side as far as the quilting reaches. The quilting must next be proceeded with, long stitches being formed on the back of the

Fig. 52.—Straight Awl.

panel, as shown in Fig. 51, and the lining just caught, as shown in Fig. 50. Needles for this work should be 4 in. long.

The proper method is to lay the panel, lining down, on the bench, and quilt it from the back. If the needle is driven straight through, the stitches on the lining will appear uniform. When both sides are quilted, the panel must be sewn across at the top, as in Fig. 51, and the rest of the stuffing pushed in through the **V**-cut. Fill this part well, and work it out towards the front and back by using the seat-awl; it will then be ready for fixing in again.

No. 22 copper wire will be the best to use. Cut sufficient pieces, 4 in. long, then take a straight, sharp awl (see Fig. 52), re-open the places in the flaps where the old wires were, and put in the new. This done, put the panel in the saddle, fix it by two nails under the crupper loop, and nail it round the gullet with ¾-in. cut tacks; then pass the points of the wires through the panel close to the roll, cross them, and twist up tight. Lastly, cut off the ends, but leave ½ in. of twisted wire to be bent down into the channel.

CHAPTER XIII.

WHIPS, HUNTING CROPS, ETC.

A GOOD whip, properly used and cared for, will last for years ; and in this chapter it is proposed first to give the chief points to be observed in maintaining whips in a suitable condition for the work expected of them.

The varieties of driving whips may be summed up under three heads—the bow-top (Fig. 53), drop-thong (Fig. 54), and gig (Fig. 55).

When whips are not in use, they should not be carelessly thrown into a corner or left in the trap, but they should be carefully hung up on a hook, so that the stock and thong may retain a perfect shape, which is not otherwise possible.

The mounts should never be cleaned without first rolling a piece of stiffish paper round the stock to prevent it becoming soiled by the material used in cleaning. Good whiting, free from grit, is un-equalled as a polish ; but if the mounts have become much tarnished, Monkey Brand soap or one of the many metal polishes should be applied with a piece of flannel, the polishing being done with a piece of soft chamois leather.

The handle should be sponged occasionally with a damp sponge, and, should the varnish have be-come dull, give it a very thin coat of either white or brown hard spirit varnish, which will revive the lustre. Stick stocks, such as holly, yew, malacca, thorn, lance, and other woods may be dried with a soft cloth after sponging.

It is a good plan, when hanging up a whip, to make a noose of string or other material, which should be first slipped round the stock and then passed over the hook or nail. In the case of a whip with a quilled or bow top, see that the noose escapes the part which naturally bends over; it should be placed on a gig whip where the thong is bound on to the stock. This will keep the stiffened part more erect, and prevent the whalebone inside becoming broken or otherwise getting out of shape.

Solid brass, nickel, or silver mounts will, of course, wear all through alike, and those mounts which are hard plated will stand a lot of polishing before the foundation metal shows through; but mounts which are lightly electro-plated on very common metal quickly lose all signs of the silver. These should be gently rubbed with a soft chamois, and not allowed to tarnish, which always means either more violent rubbing or the application of some substance to remove it.

The thongs and keepers should receive an occasional dressing of tallow, which not only preserves them but keeps them pliable. This must be well rubbed into the parts with the hands to ensure it penetrating into the leather.

The commonest injuries which happen to whips are: A broken keeper either on the thong or the stock in the case of the dealer or drop-thong class (Fig. 54); the stock broken, in or near the bow, in the class shown in Fig. 53; a broken point to the thong, the quills broken where the thong joins the handle, or the handle itself broken, in the case of gig whips (Fig. 55).

To repair a broken chape or keeper, first of all remove the old one, if it is the keeper on the stock which is broken; if it is that on the thong, cut the broken pieces off nearly level with the plaited part. Take a piece of white horse-hide, of good quality and pliable, and skive this down at each end, leaving the full substance slightly beyond where the binding thread will reach when it is folded end to end and placed in position.

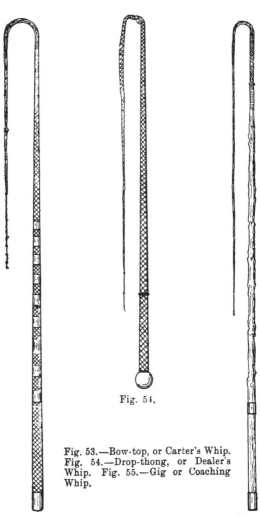

Fig. 54.

Fig. 53.—Bow-top, or Carter's Whip.
Fig. 54.—Drop-thong, or Dealer's
Whip. Fig. 55.—Gig or Coaching
Whip.

Fig. 53.

Fig. 55.

This skived part must be well waxed by laying it on a board or bench, and rubbing a ball of shoemakers' wax down it several times so that a thin coat of wax covers it. Treat the end, to which it is to be fixed, in a similar manner, and, to ensure perfect adhesion between the parts, warm them gently, place the keeper in position, and press them well together with the fingers.

If there should be any surplus of leather where the edges of the keeper meet, trim it off with a sharp knife, and see whether there are any uneven places; if so, put them right before proceeding to bind it on. There should be a uniformly even, but very slight, taper from the top of the binding to the bottom. The full thickness of the leather at the top of the stock over the reduced part lower down will naturally produce this.

If the stock should be a brown one, either gut or thread, use a beeswaxed thread made of white hemp; if black, then use fine brown hemp and black wax. Make a long thread by passing the strand of hemp, held in the left hand, over a hook, bringing it down to the same hand again, repeating the operation until there are three strands on each side of the hook. See that the three strands on one side are quite separate from the others; hold these firmly between the thumb and forefinger of the left hand, about eight or nine inches from the end, and with the right hand rub this part down the thigh of the right leg, releasing the grip of the left hand during each stroke. When this part is well twisted, repeat with the other half of the thread; draw the wax sharply down the twisted strands and along the part round the hook. When sufficiently waxed, tie a slip loop at one end and pass this over the hook.

Begin binding on the keeper by laying about an inch of the other end on it lengthwise, so that the first few turns will secure it. By standing away from the hook the full length of the thread, and holding the stock in a horizontal position, the thread can be wound tightly and evenly on.

The method of binding on a keeper for splicing a stock is fully explained by Figs. 56, 57, and 58. The method of starting the binding is shown in Fig. 56, and Fig. 57 shows how to finish it off securely.

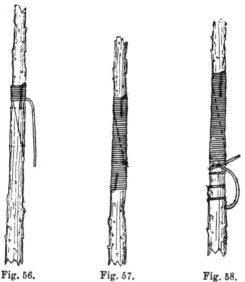

Fig. 56.   Fig. 57.   Fig. 58.

Figs. 56 to 58.—Methods of Splicing Broken Stock of Whip Stock.

Of course, the start and finish of the thread should lie perfectly hidden beneath the coils, but in order to illustrate the method clearly they are shown in the diagrams. Let each coil lie perfectly close to the preceding one, and in finishing off, as in Fig. 57, drop down sufficient slack, and wind the end of the thread back towards that already wound, passing it under the last turn. Then, by continuing the original, the other unwinds, and a portion of the thread lies under the last few coils. Pull the slack well home and cut it off.

Lay the bound part on a hard, level board, and with another piece of hard wood roll it backwards and forwards, using plenty of pressure ; this will give it a nice smooth finish. For better appearance still, a little spirit varnish may be put on.

Now proceed to put thong and stock together. The method of doing this is fully explained by Fig. 59. Pass the loop at the end of the thong over the keeper on the stock, then take the point of the former and pass it through the latter and draw it well home ; the two parts will then be as shown in Fig. 54.

A fresh piece of whipcord is generally put on a thong in a very bungling fashion, and not always securely. The proper way to do this is shown in Figs. 60 and 61. Unbraid the end of the thong and separate it as in Fig. 60. Lay the cord between the four ends—two on each side of it—with sufficient left for making the loop. Fold over the ends of the thong, and pass the end of the cord round them and under the cord as in Fig. 61. Draw down tightly by the knotted end of lash, and trim off the surplus not too closely ; this will be found not only a neat but a secure way.

The knots in the points of lashes prevent the lash ravelling away quickly, and the neatest method of forming them is to separate one strand of the cord from the other two, and tie this over at intervals, twisting it into its place again in the spaces between the knots.

Whips of the class shown in Fig. 53 generally suffer at the part forming the bow, and to repair these place a piece of thin whalebone about $1\frac{1}{2}$ in. long on each side of the whip, and bind these to it. Twisted points, made of raw hide dressed in oil, are always put on this class of whip, and the whip-

cord point fixed to these.   Fig. 62 shows the way to
put them on.

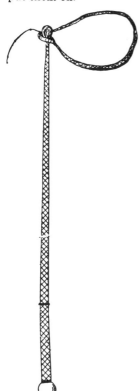

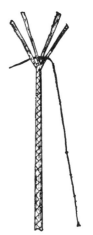

Fig. 59.—Method of Joining
Thong and Stock of Drop-
thong Whip.

Fig. 60.— Method
of Fixing Silk or
Cord Lash to End
of Whip Thong.

In the case of a gig whip (Fig. 55) having a
broken thong requiring a new point, it may be said
that such points are made in various lengths, and

differ in thickness, so that it will be necessary to choose one of suitable substance and length to match the old thong. The number of strands constituting the plait carries from four to eight; and the strength is generally in proportion to the number of strands, but the process of putting on is the same with all.

If the old thong is not already unplaited, proceed first to do this for about 1½ in., and see that

Fig. 61.—Method of Fixing Silk or Cord Lash to End of Whip Thong.

Fig. 62.—Method of Fixing Twisted Gut or Hide Point to Carter's Whip.

the new point is opened about the same length. Figs. 63, 64, and 65, which show a four-plait in each case, give the method of fixing them together. The separated ends are put between each other, as in Fig. 63, and the ends are brought down and held close to the part they should lie on. Take the strand first which is farthest open, and pass it over the other three, as in Fig. 64. With a pair of flat-mouthed pliers pull this as tight as possible. Take

one of the others which comes best into position,
and, when all have been turned through and pulled
well home, treat those on the other part in the
same manner.

The joint will now appear as in Fig. 65, and it
will be impossible to pull it asunder, because the
greater the tension the tighter will be the grip on

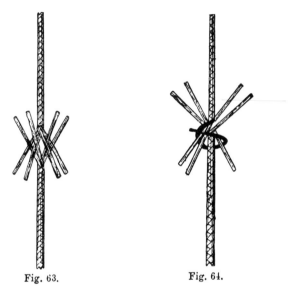

Fig. 63.   Fig. 64.

Figs. 63 and 64.—Method of Joining New Plaited Point to
Old Whip Thong.

the strands, separately and collectively. The projecting ends must be trimmed off, but not quite
close to the thong now formed ; lay the joint on a
level board and roll it as described previously for
putting a keeper on a drop-thong whip.

Carelessness in leaving the whip in the socket,
whilst running the trap into the coach-house, is

generally the cause of broken quills. For repairing, get a few good goose-quills and slit them with
a knife into halves. Take off the thread round the
old thong, and pass one or two half quills down
inside the old ones. Some people use steel pens
instead of quills, but generally they are too short
to make a satisfactory job. Having fixed the new
support, bind up again, following the plan adopted

Fig. 65.—Method of Joining New Plaited Point to Old
Whip Thong.

when the thong was new, and which is easily found
out by carefully noting the way in which the old
thread comes off. Use good black sewing thread
for these repairs, and apply a little spirit varnish
as a dressing to protect and brighten it.

Another injury to this class of whips is a broken
stock, which usually occurs towards the top and
at one of the knots. First trim off with a knife any
knots in close proximity to the breakage, and before
paring down for the splice place the broken parts

together and endeavour to ascertain the natural fall of the whip, or the way when it is spliced which will give to it the best appearance.

Reduce the wood so that it can be joined as shown in Fig. 56, using for this purpose, besides the knife, a moderately fine wood rasp, which should also be used on the part to be covered by the thread. Use good glue in uniting the parts together, and when firmly set bind with a thread of suitable size and colour. The method of binding has already been explained in the instructions for fixing on a new keeper to a drop-thong whip.

The joint may be given greater strength by putting a pin through each end of it, as indicated by the dotted lines in Fig. 56; this prevents the parts drawing asunder. Make the holes with an Archimedean or other small drill.

The mounts at the bottom of a whip handle sometimes get loose or come off. These can be refixed by scraping all the old resin out of the mount and cleaning off that clinging to the wood, and then partly filling the mount with crushed fresh resin, gently warming it until it becomes liquid, pressing it on to the handle again, and allowing it to cool.

Whip lashes are generally plaited with four tapering leather ends, round a tapering "heart." The plaiting can be done with any even number of ends, and is termed "cross-pointing." If, however, four ends only are worked, and no "heart," the result is the same as a sennit made with four ends, explained in the next paragraph. This method is the quickest where two can work together, but for single-handed work another method will be found easier.

For plaiting square sennit having four ends, take four ends of gaskin, and tie them to a hook in a post. Take two ends, and cross them beneath the hook. Hold these two ends out, then cross the

two others beneath them. Thus proceed to cross
the two ends alternately, as indicated in Fig. 66,
where A and B are shown in the act of being crossed
between C and D. Pull each tight, and hammer
square when complete.

Eight-stranded square sennit is shown partly
completed in Fig. 67, which explains the position
of the 8 ends during the work. Begin by crossing
the 2 centre strands—say right over left—then take
the outside right strand, pass it round at the back
of the rest and up between the strands on the left.

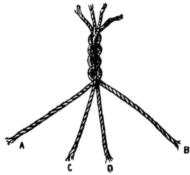

Fig. 66.—Plaiting Four-stranded Square Sennit.

bringing it over in front to its own side again; then
take the outer strand on the left side, and bring
it up between those on the right, and back to its
own side again. In the figure, strand 4 was
taken from above 1 and passed up between
6 and 7, and brought back over 5 to its
own side as shown. Strand 8 will be next taken
and passed up between 2 and 3, then brought back
over 4 to x. This done, each opposite face of the
sennit will appear the same. In working, remember to keep the same face always uppermost;
the end A must, of course, be secured to something
at a convenient height.

The following methods of cross-pointing are recommended for making whip lashes. The methods
of plaiting square sennit, shown by Figs. 66 and 67,
may be useful on occasion, but the whip maker is
more concerned with plaits that have cores or
hearts. However, Fig. 68 shows a coreless plait
popular in the trade.

In Fig. 68, the end c was taken from o, passed

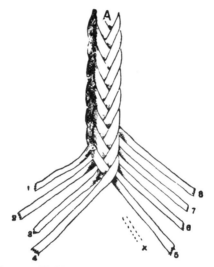

Fig. 67.—Plaiting Eight-stranded Square Sennit.

back to the left, then forward between A and B, and
crossed over to its present position, c, on the right.
The end A will next be passed back to the right,
forward between c and D, and crossed over to the
left, as shown by the dotted line, x.

In Fig. 69 the plait is precisely the same as in
Fig. 68, only round a heart. The end c was taken
from o, passed round to the left at the back of the
heart, and brought forward between A and B, then

I

crossed over in front of the heart to its present
position. A next goes round the back of the heart,
and forward between C and D, and across in front
of the heart, to X. When the tapered end of the
heart is reached the process will be as explained
before (Fig. 68).

When about 2 in. from the end of the lash insert
a piece of whip-cord, as W P (Fig. 68), pull through
one-third of its length, then taper the leather ends,
A and D, off to about 1 in. in length; proceed as
before, but whenever A or D are worked, carry its

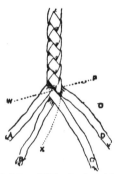

Fig. 63.—Plaiting Whip Lash without Heart.

accompanying whip-cord end with it till A and D run
out, then taper B and C off in the same way, and
work with four ends as before, two being leather
and two whip-cord; when B and C run out "lay up"
the whip-cord tight, and splice the shorter end into
the longer.

There are few things more difficult to find out
for one's self, perhaps, than how to work buttons,
collars, and ferrules on whips, hunting crops, and
walking-sticks. Undoing the work is of little avail
except to those who have some knowledge of it;
this plan may then be profitably employed in dis-

covering the method of working any new pattern which one may come across.

The material used for working buttons and ferrules on whips is generally gut, similar to violin strings but not of such good quality. For ferrules on walking-sticks silver wire is used. This varies in price according to the gauge. Any size up to No. 22 B.W.G. is 3s. 1d. per oz.; from No. 23 to 25 the price is 3s. 3d.; and from No. 26 to 30, 3s. 6d.

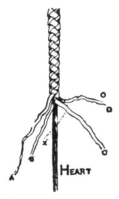

Fig. 69.—Plaiting Whip Lash with Heart.

per oz. As a guide, it may be mentioned that about 27 ft. of No. 22 B.W.G. weighs 1 oz.

As the groundwork is the same, whatever the pattern may be, it will be seen that when the manner of doing this is once mastered any pattern, however elaborate, can be worked by carefully observing the course of each strand and making a complete record of the manner in which the strand, in course of manipulation, passes through its counterpart in forming the ferrule. By adopting this method a complete guide for future reference will be obtained which, if closely followed, will furnish the means for carrying out the work in a satisfactory manner.

In taking one of these ferrules to pieces, a commencement should be made at the finished end; therefore, in making a record of each course taken by the strand which has been interwoven to form a ferrule or collar, begin at the bottom of a sheet of paper and work upwards; there is then a straightforward guide in attempting to work a similar pattern. Be careful to mark down every change made when passing from one stage to another; the slightest error will cause endless trouble and prevent a satisfactory completion. If, being satisfied

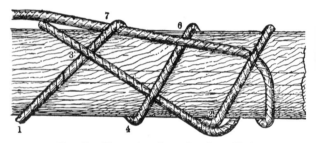

Fig. 70.—Beginning Groundwork or Mesh.

that the guide is correct, it is found that the pattern will not come right, it is certain that a mistake has been made in reworking it; at once try to find out where the mistake exists, and rectify it. The work must be undone to this point, the mistake remedied, and another attempt made.

There is no work in which the advice to "make haste slowly" could be more usefully given than to the tyro at this work. The greater his diligence, the sooner will his aim be accomplished; but haste and carelessness will inevitably lead to failure.

By referring to Fig. 70, the first portion of the groundwork or mesh will be seen. Begin at 1, and

bring the cord round at 2; it is then carried round
again, and brought under the thumb at 3. Pass it
round, and bring it midway at 4, then over the top
and up at 5. Here it is passed under the second

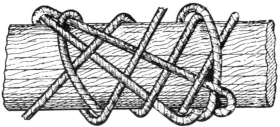

Fig. 71.—Second Course of Mesh.

turn which was made, carried over the fourth at 6,
under the first at 7, and over the third at 8. It is
then brought round and passed to the left of 4 and
over to the left of 6. Pass it under the next cross
strand, and bring it up outside of 5; carry it over

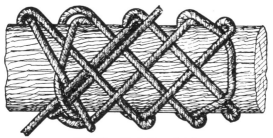

Fig. 72.—Mesh Completed.

the first strand back, then under one, over two,
under one, over one; now turn again when the
stage shown in Fig. 71 is reached.

The cord in its course is here seen to pass over
the first, then under one, over one. In continuing,

it passes over the next two, then over one, under one. Turn again, and pass it under one and over the next alternately, when the mesh will be completed. This is shown in Fig. 72.

Fig. 73.—Ferrule Complete.

The second course is then begun. There is no difficulty now in completing the ferrule, as the cord or wire is simply passed under and over to correspond with the mesh. Always keep to the right of the start—to pass beyond this throws out the pattern.

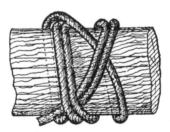

Fig. 74.—Mesh on Single Turk's Head.

The finished ferrule shown in Fig. 73 has three courses. There is no limit to the number which can be made, provided the mesh is slack enough to allow a greater number being passed through it.

If the ferrule is found to be too loose, an additional course will tighten it; but this might not always prove satisfactory, especially if a given number of strands in each direction is desired.

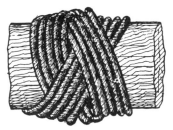

Fig. 75.—Single Turk's Head Completed.

The length of ferrule must also be considered at the commencement, and this is decided by the number of turns in each direction of the mesh. There is no limit whatever to its length.

Fig. 74 shows the groundwork of a very simple

Fig. 76.—Raised Turk's Head.

collar used on dog-whips and some hunting crops. This is commonly called a "Turk's head." It generally has several courses or strands. Fig. 75 shows five. Fig. 76 is a "raised Turk's head." This is formed by working a small one on the stick first, and then working another over it, carrying it beyond each end of the first button, so that the raised part is in the centre.

Fig. 77.—Small Button for Hunting Crop.

Small buttons for finishing the ends when binding on the keeps of hunting crops are shown in Figs. 77 and 78. The method of working these is given in Fig. 79. The cord is passed once round the stock, and in its next course threaded through it to form the twist. It is then kept to the right of

Fig. 78.—Four-strand Button
for Hunting Crop.

Fig. 79.—Beginning
Small Button.

the start and made to follow the direction of this as many times as desired. Fig. 77 shows a button formed with two courses and Fig. 78 one in which there are four courses.

CHAPTER XIV.

SET OF GIG HARNESS.

THE making of gig harness is not strictly the work of a saddler, though, of course, the country tradesman has often to do both harness and saddle making. The two branches of the trade must be distinguished between, however, and whilst this handbook is devoted chiefly to saddlery there is a companion volume dealing with nothing but harness making. Considerations of space forbade the inclusion in that volume of a chapter on mak-

Fig. 80.—Nose-band.

Fig. 81.—Drop, or Breast plate Ornament.

ing gig harness, and as the work is of a superior kind, and is likely to fall to the lot of the majority of saddle makers in country shops, there need be no apology for inserting such a chapter here.

The bridle of gig harness is made as for a van harness (see the companion volume), but the work is finer and the material better; the nose-band is often cut in some fancy wavy pattern, and the work is much finer.

Sometimes the nose-band (Fig. 80) is rounded by placing a piece of leather or card underneath; when it is stuffed only the outer row is, as a rule, stitched through both top and lining, the first ornamental rows or patterns being stitched through one thickness only at the top part. The winkers are also made smaller and stitched finer with two inner rows close together.

A drop (Fig. 81) is often made with some fancy ornament to run down the face from the buckle or head-piece; it must be 1 ft. 1 in. long, with a fancy pattern cut at the hanging end where the ornament is fastened. The drop may be made of patent leather, lined and stitched all round with two fine rows of black linen thread. Finish it neatly and make a hole in the point for fastening the buckle on the head under the winker strap. If preferred, a loop for it can be put on the forehead band, or a runner may be used to keep it and the winker strap together at the top below the buckle. The drop and winker strap can also be made in one by leaving an opening in the drop 5 in. from the point for the winker strap to pass; the last is made round like a bearing rein with a small cord inside.

The winker strap also is sometimes lined and stitched fine with two rows, or it may be ornamented with stitching without lining, or again with rounded slits. In making the best harness, a piece is put along the centre of the head-piece to form a loop for the winker strap point, and runs down on each side as far as the slit, being raised in the centre as much as possible, and stitched very fine; all this is for the sake of strength and ornament.

With bradoon fittings, however, this piece is turned outwards at each end, and a chape is made to go over and fasten the eyelet for the hook of the bradoon swivel chain (Fig. 82); or a small brass dee is used to fasten the small straps by which the swivels hang, because with bradoon fittings no swivels are put to the throatlash. These fittings are made by stitching two straps, about 6 in. long, underneath the head-piece right at the top of the slit; make very fine stitches on the head-piece, and let the straps hang down inside the cheek. Run the bearing rein through the swivels and down through the bit rings to buckle in these straps at

each side. Thus a bearing rein with bradoon does
not need billets, but at the round part must be
made about 1 ft. 1 in. longer than an ordinary
bearing rein.

The winkers are frequently made with ornaments; for adjusting them, holes must be cut
through the winker plate and the leather with a
fine hard steel punch. The legs of the ornament
must be put into these holes and then cut short
as close to the leather as possible underneath;
then flatten the points well down. These directions and what is said in "Harness Making" on
van harness will suffice for the making of the
bridle

The instructions regarding collar making will
apply, in general, to all, but gig collars must

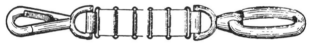

Fig. 82.—Bradoon Chain.

always be made of patent leather. The forewale
is always lined with calico to prevent the leather
cracking, and must be turned down for about $1\frac{3}{4}$
in., or altogether for $3\frac{1}{2}$ in. For stuffing, employ
a fine collar iron. It is also well to have somewhat shorter wisps than for cart or van collars;
see carefully that they join properly.

Cut the lining out of the best basil leather and
put it in place while stitching the forewale, making
the collar lighter and of better shape than the
heavy types. Let the lining and flock be made
quite smooth, free from lumps or wrinkles. The
patent leather side-piece is bound as described,
but a paper pattern can be cut in one piece all
round so that no housing will be needed; it is
joined at the bottom under the throat, and is
called "London top." If in two parts, join it at

top and bottom, like a van collar, the top piece and
housing being made likewise, but with finer
stitches. The width of the collar at the widest
part is 8 in. to 10 in., as required by the neck,
the length being fixed on the same principle.
Black basil may be employed for lining, or instead,
black the lining when finished with soda and iron
dye, afterwards rubbing it with a ball of tallow
and the palm of the hand to "kill" the dye.

For the gig saddle (Fig. 83) obtain a tree (Fig.
84) 4 in. to 4½ in. broad at the top (they are often
smaller), put on it a thin sheet-iron seat plate,
shaped like a saddle seat, nail it against the cantle
at the back with two or three tacks, and at the
front or gullet with a short piece of leather underneath to raise it a little. Then cut a piece of thin
basil a little larger than the plate. Shave all the
edges thin, damp and paste it over the seat, and
turn it down round the edges at the sides and over
the cantle as well as in front; this prevents the
leather above being rotted by the rust from the
iron seat.

Now cut a piece of thin pliable patent leather
slightly larger than the seat and sufficiently long
in front to be nailed underneath, and about ½ in.
above the cantle. Having damped it, tack it down
tight to the tree and leave it there to dry.

The skirts (Fig. 85) are now cut; these are the
other parts of a gig saddle which cover the portion
through which the backband passes. Make them
of stiff patent leather to reach about ⅜ in. over the
tree at each side and about 1 in. below the bottom
of the tree where the backband runs, but not covering the points. These three sides must be cut
straight, and the top level with the edge of the
seat plate in front and of the same shape as it is
in the narrow part, running downwards to ter-
minate in a rising point and rounding upwards just
by the root of the cantle. Cut both skirts exactly

alike, quite square with the tree when in place on the seat.

Run the race compass along the edges and bottom of the skirts, about ⅛ in. from the edge, and then make another groove ¼ in. inside that all round the four sides and at the top, but do not let the top groove run farther than the points of the side grooves; all will then meet at a terminal point. A piece of plain leather must now be cut to reach about half-way up the skirt from the

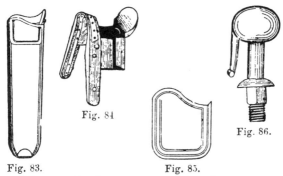

Fig. 84.

Fig. 86.

Fig. 83.   Fig. 85.

Fig. 83.—Gig Saddle.   Fig. 84.—Gig Saddle Tree.
Fig. 85.—Gig Saddle Skirt.   Fig. 86.—Stand Hook.

bottom, the upper part being shaved thin, with grooves pricked all round, and the inner groove stitched all along through the top and under-piece. Then stitch the bottom line across and over the corner at each end, twelve per inch, and trim and polish the edges. Then skive a little along the top edge and mark out the seat along the top edge of the skirt from end to end, having a piece of patent thin welt about 1 in. longer at each end than the skirt to run along the edge at the top. Run a stitch over the welt and skirt along the top, after doubling the welt by turning it down along the centre. Along the mark **cut** the seat,

and mark this at the place where the skirt is first
to be joined and at the other end; thus, after
stitching it will be in its proper position.

The seat and skirt may now be back-stitched
together, the welt being kept in the centre of the
joint; use a pointed needle and linen thread and
a thimble. Work both sides in the same way and
rub down the joint underneath. Cut a piece of
patent leather for the back of the cantle $\frac{1}{2}$ in.
longer all round, and make two punch holes and a
slit for it to pass over the crupper loop at the
bottom, one part of it running through the centre
of the loop inside. Nail that piece down under the
back of the tree and drive two nails into it at the
centre of the crupper loop. Cut it at the sides to
meet the seat at the edge of the cantle, and then,
after damping the seat and placing it in position,
tack the seat at the back-piece together all round
the cantle close to the wood, using a pointed needle
and thread.

Cut round the stitches with the edge tool,
leaving enough margin to bind the edges, and then
cut out a thin piece of patent leather binding sufficiently long to go round and with 1 in. extra at
each end. Lay it on tightly over the edge and
stitch fine with double thread black linen, beginning work right at the bottom at the root of the
cantle and finishing on the other side at the
bottom.

Nail the front part of the seat neatly with $\frac{3}{8}$-in.
tacks just under the edge of the tree and cut two
holes for terret sockets with the brace, one on
each side of the tree in front, just by the side of
the groove. Raise the skirt out of the way while
working, and make another hole opposite those
just made in the skirt. Having inserted the
sockets from below, nail them securely and then
cut a hole through the seat opposite the hole in
the tree through which the stand hook (Fig. 86)

is put. It is taken for granted that the skirt is made perfectly square, but the corners may be rounded; whatever the shape, the method of work is always the same.

The saddle flaps (Fig. 87) must now be made; they should be about 1 ft. 8 in. long in front, and 1 ft. 9½ in. at back, and for a 4-in. tree must be 4¾ in. wide at the top. Cut them straight down to the bottom, gradually narrowing until 2 in. from the base, where they taper in a rounded form to

Fig. 87.

Fig. 88.

Fig. 87.—Gig Flap Showing Cuts.   Fig. 88.—Hame Tug
         with Safe.

about 1¾ in. Cut a groove along the sides and bottom a little farther than ⅛ in. from the edge, and another ¼ in. inside it; do not cut the last quite to the bottom, however, but with the race make a half circle from corner to corner at the bottom and join the middle grooves to the edge of this. Now cut out the lining from uncurried brown belly, paste the lining on the flaps and let them dry. Prick them, double-stitch twelve per inch, all but the half circle and the cross line at the bottom.

The edges can now be finished and well polished; make them as level as possible, but do not

round them as much as the edge of a trace or
backband, merely edging the patent leather top.
From this trim them level inwards below so that
the flaps lie close to the panel facing. The longer
side point must reach close to the crupper loop
underneath the tree; mark this therefore. The
other side at the front must be above the tree, but
if it is too high the flap will be drawn too much
forwards, and if too low it will start backwards;
make sure that it is quite square with the tree.

A piece must be cut out at the top to fit the
flap and to keep it in position as regards the point
at each side. Opposite the groove in the tree
mark a line across the flap, and from the back end
of the line to within an inch of the outer top back
edge make a slanting cut. Now from the front
end of the mark run a slanting cut upwards to
within an inch of the front edge; the middle part
must be cut square to the same width as the
groove, and $1\frac{1}{2}$ in. long from the line. Shave the
end of the piece thin and also the inner sides of
the slanting cuts underneath.

The saddle flaps can now be put in their places,
hind point below and front point above the tree,
the middle cut entering the groove. Nail the point
behind close to the loop, then the front under the
skirt and the middle cut in the groove. Make sure
that the flap points are at equal distances from
the edge of the tree, and perfectly square to each
other and the tree.

There now remains a space, between the ends
of the flaps at the gullet in front, which must be
filled, and for this purpose a piece of patent leather
is cut to the required length. If necessary, line it
so as to obtain the same thickness as the flaps,
and stitch the outer line in the same way as the
flaps along the outside. Thin the inner side all
along and make a punch hole a little below the
junction point of the skirt and the seat on each

side. Put it in place, by measure central between the two holes which cut at about half the width of the leather. Shave it thin from that line inwards, letting it approach close enough to the tree in front to be in a straight line with the flaps. Make a slit running from the two punch holes towards the inside, and nail the centre part under the tree all round the gullet. Raise each side of the lower part above the tree—from the punch hole downwards—under the skirt to meet the points of the flaps. Bring them together quite tight and nail them to the tree ; if the inner side happens to cover the terret hole it must be cut.

A stitch is now made with copper wire from the point of the flap to the point of the gullet piece underneath, and is tightly twisted to draw the edges together. Tack the front of the skirts square down on the flaps and stitch the outer line left from top to bottom on each side through both skirts and flaps. The flap should project beyond the side of the skirt for about $\frac{3}{8}$ in. Now place a piece of thick leather under the edge of the skirt behind, to make it level with the rest of the face. As the flaps are nailed under the tree they fall below the surface during the operation of stitching. Add enough to raise them and stitch the skirts down again from behind the crupper loop to the lower corner of the skirt ; trim and black this piece afterwards by the edge of the skirt. (Fig. 88 shows the hame tug).

The flaps may be cut like the skirts of another pattern, swelling them at both sides and rounding them at the bottom ; in this case the skirts must be rounded to match. Nail a piece of thin leather on the side of the crupper loop, twist it round from end to end, and drive a nail in the other side, and then two tough nails through the tree at both the top front corners of the flaps, and one on each side through the point of the cantle, binding at the root of the cantle behind. Clinch the front nails under the tree and cut the hind ones slanting about half length before driving them into the tree.

To make the girth, work as explained in the companion handbook, but let the stitches be finer; the lay may have to be put all along the girth, this being narrowed from the last loop to the top, about half the width of the front part and the edges being shaved to bring the lay close to the body. The strap may also be shaved, lined, and edged, the top part being rounded; fill it along the middle and put on the wide piece at the top to fasten to the flap of patent leather. Then stitch it round the edges, narrowing it at the bottom to the same width as the strap, the under-part of this being placed under and the other above it for stitching; finish the girth, strap, and loops, neatly. After placing them between the flap and the lining, stitch along the half circle with strong thread.

The panel should be made exactly like the other, but with a paper facing; then stitch it finer with patent facing cover and quilt it closer and finer than for the van panel. To adjust it, nail it round the gullet and at the crupper loop and stitch it with wire.

The traces (Fig. 89) must be cut 5 ft. 9 in. to 6 ft. long by $1\frac{1}{2}$ in. wide, the top part at one end being rounded and the corners only at the other end. As ornament outside the stitches, with the hot screw crease make a row of creasing near the edge, then make another row of creasing inside that, and a third row a little more than $\frac{1}{8}$ in. inside. Cross the inner rows neatly about 5 in. from the square end and 1 ft. 4 in. from the other or holed end. Prick the two inner rows, eight to thirteen per inch, according to the quality of harness, but be sure to reverse the two outward pieces, placing the stronger against the weaker end. Line them level all along, adding an extra piece about 6 in. long, with the inner end shaved at the square end for fastening the trace to the trap; tack or paste them down and stitch along the four inner rows.

Now dip the trace in water just for a minute and level the stitches by rubbing them on the underside with the handle of the hammer; an old flat iron without a handle is very good for this work.

The trace is now placed in the clamp, which must be held between the knees, and the edges are trimmed round with the spokeshave down to the line outside the stitches and to the same depth on the other side. Some harness makers draw the spoke towards them, others push it outwards, but

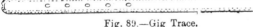

Fig. 89.—Gig Trace.

this is a mere matter of choice. Scrape and smooth with glasspaper, black, and polish well as directed. Cut two holes in the square end, one 1 in. from the end and the other $1\frac{1}{4}$ in. farther in; slit the piece between them by making two cuts, one on each side of the holes, round the edges a little, and black the opening inside and finish.

At the other end four holes must now be punched for the buckles, the first 4 in. from the point, and the others $2\frac{1}{4}$ in. from each other. Cut a little in front of each hole out of the leather underneath, either with punch or hand knife; if this were not done, the point of the tongue, which goes slanting into the hole, might tear the material. Holes should always be punched big enough, and are much better too large than too small. Both traces must of course be made alike.

The hame tug (Fig. 88) fastens the trace to the hames, and is to be made as follows:—For a 1½-in. buckle, the tug should be cut 1 ft. 4 in. by 1¾ in., with a piece for the centre 10½ in. long. Turn down the tug pieces in the centre, making both ends of the same length, and turn down the other piece level to form a chape for the buckle as far as it will reach at the short turning. Now make a punch hole about ¾ in. from the bend through both lining and cover to form a chape for the buckle. Open the punch-hole to the front by making a cut on each side, and shave a little inside the hole in the lining so that the buckle can go close to the bend.

Next slightly round the corners of the top part of the outer long piece, and as the tug is 8 in. long when doubled, the loop to be put on measuring 4 in., make a mark 4¾ in. from the bend at each side, the middle piece being in its place. Now through the three leathers run an awl down each side at the marks, so that there will be a mark on both sides above and below.

Open out the tug and cut ⅛ in. from both sides, mark to mark; when the tug is bent, see that the cuts on each side are square with each other and the opposite cuts. From the mark in the lining now cut ⅛ in. on each side as far as the point and shave this thin. The fore part of the tug will now be of the same width as the buckle, and the other part ¼ in. wider; thus the hind part will have a full neat appearance and the clip be covered when put in. Crease a line near the edge all round the wide part as was done for the traces, and a second line not far from it; then put a third line ¼ in. inside that round the ends as well, being careful to keep the shape in the second line of the turning in the corners.

Prick the two inner lines the same as the trace and shave a little on the edges of the wide parts

on each side both above and below. Stitch all
the inner line through the single leather and about
¾ in. in the outer line of stitching at the centre of
the point, so as to produce the appearance of
stitching all round when the leather is put above
the clips. Now make a groove exactly ¼ in. from
the edge on the lower side of the narrow part,
from the beginning of the cut to both sides of the
buckle, for stitching the loop. Let the last be
4 in. long, and wide enough for the trace to enter
and meet in the centre.

Use strong double-waxed thread for the loop,
blind-stitching it on the last side, and make two
strong cross stitches on each side of the buckle.
Make this part neat in appearance and crease the
loop, checking it to match the winker and shaft
tugs.

With the prongs fix the clip in the draft of the
hames and push it inside with one prong on each
side of the middle piece. Mark the last at the
place where the holes are to be cut for the rivets.
Remove it and punch the holes, then put it back
again until all the holes are opposite. Place the
clip in the vice as far as its neck, tighten it down
close to the leather, and rivet it; then cut the
rivets to length in the vice with a cold chisel.
Rivet them down well as smoothly as possible on
the top side.

The upper and lower part of the tug leather
must now be turned down over the clip, then
tacked at each side and neatly stitched. Join the
stitches on at each side, with the few cross stitches
made over the clip at the end. Then having neatly
finished the edges, run a single hot crease along
the outer line of the crease made outside the
stitches; repeat this operation with the outer line
on the traces, making both tugs the same.

A safe is often put under the hame tug, in
which case the top layer of the tug need not be

cut to go all along both sides, but may reach
about 3 in. over the buckle underneath, and exactly
the same on the upper side as if there were no
safe. The lining also must be the same, right
over the buckle and for attaching to the clip. The
inner row of the wide part must be stitched like
the other, with the cross stitches at the point;
the buckle can now be placed in position and the
chape turned down as though for stitching.

Place the buckle end of the tug on the leather
intended for the safe, allowing it to pass a little
more than ⅛ in. beyond the end of the buckle and
flush with the other end of the tug; thus, it serves
the purpose of the turn-down part in the other
method. Cut it all round the buckle, having first
marked it for a little more than ⅛ in., and then
taper it in a straight line on each side of the
buckle, beginning at the lower corner and bringing
it to the same width as the tug at the other end.
Make a round hole opposite the tongue of the
buckle for the trace; its diameter should equal
the width of the buckle.

Another piece, of identical form, is now cut,
made from light leather like the first. Having
slightly shaved the edges and the edge of the
round hole in each piece, make an outer row of
creasing near the edge around the hole and other
edges. Another row must now be made close by,
and one piece placed on the other, to act as a
lining; prick the inner row very fine, and stitch
the pieces together, giving the edges a neat finish.
The safe being placed in position, stitch the loop
as for the other style, but, instead of having sunk
stitches, the safe should be stitched coarse from
underneath; attach the hame clip at the other end
and stitch it and finish.

When placing the loop on, and also afterwards,
be careful to keep the safe in the centre. Some
makers place the prongs of the clip one on each

side of the inner part of the two leathers of the safe. Then the safe must be made in the same manner and stitched on both sides as far as the loop end farther from the buckle. After fastening and riveting the clip, stitch the other part on both sides and then the top lay through them both.

The backband must be 8 ft. 2 in. long, the strap end 1 ft. 6 in., and the centre 3 ft. 3 in., the remainder being for girth. Make four rows all along, crossing the lines at each end of the middle part and making a line outside the stitches as in traces. Stitch about twelve per inch, and add three loops, but instead of stitching them with backband, do so when the latter is finished. Run a hot crease over the outer line and finish the backband. Punch holes in the same manner, and cut their edges a little for the shaft tug on the lower side.

The shaft tugs are made on the same principle as the cab tugs (see the companion volume), but are a little smaller and finer to match the backband; this and the tugs are 1½ in. wide. Safes are sometimes placed under the shaft-tug buckles as well as on hame tugs, and a hole is cut for the backband as for the trace in the safe. This should be in one piece with the outer lay of the tug, overlapping just at the centre of the back, the safe running up from under the buckle. A paper pattern of the entire piece will save much waste.

The crupper is made in a similar style but lighter, the billet being 1 in. wide as a maximum, and the loop 1½ in. The billet and body, however, are often lined, the edges being shaved even and the billet stuffed and rounded on the groove board; make one row of creasing outside the stitches as on the traces. Line the body with something very light and finish the work as with other parts. For extra fine harness there may be four lines of stitching in the billet. Leave about $2\frac{1}{2}$ in. at the end of the slits unstitched for the dock, which must be lighter than for cab harness but of the same length and stuffed with linseed.

When the dock has buckles, loops, and chapes, the slits must be stitched to the extreme point and finished like other parts of the body. Adjust the lay in the same manner with two openings, but as the body is lined, stitch it a little coarser than usual from the underside, instead of sinking the stitches.

To make the hip strap for the breeching, cut the leather 4 ft. 4 in. by $1\frac{3}{4}$ in., and slit it at each end 1 ft. 5 in. by $\frac{3}{4}$ in. The extra width between the two slits must be cut off at the top with a punch, the point of the slits being rounded and a wavy pattern cut on each side in the centre between the slits. The edges being shaved and all parts rounded on the grooving board, an outer line of crease and another line for stitching can be made all round ; then make four rows between the central slits. A wave or other pattern is then pricked at each end of the middle rows unless the ends are covered by an ornament

Another of similar size and pattern is now to be cut for lining the hip strap. After shaving the edges, stitch it with fine thread and finish off well ; about eight holes must be made in each slit, beginning at 4 in. from the point. These parts, instead of being tacked, can be pasted together and allowed to dry before being stitched.

All lined straps for the best harness are stuffed in the centre, that is, shaves which are thicker on the outer side, owing to the way they are cut, are placed in the centre of the strap, the shaves having their thick sides abutting ; thus the surface will be rounded from edges to centre. Having pasted the pieces on the strap, lay over them the top part, rounded and pasted closely along the edge of the lining; an ornament at the junction of the slits will be required for the hip strap of good harness. Cut a pear-shaped piece of patent leather a little wider than the hip strap, and make two rows of fine stitching all round. Stitch the inner row, singly, through the leather, place a lining underneath, and stitch the outer row through both, leaving spaces at the sides of the bottom and top end unstitched.

Finish the edges and stitch the spaces through the hip strap for securing the patent piece. If this is adjusted singly, after stitching the inner row, stitch all round the outer one, raising the centre by stuffing it with leather. The metal or silver ornament can then be placed on the wide part, and then riveted, the legs being cut close below.

The breeching is only 1½ in. wide, and there may be four rows of stitching all along. Stitch it finer and finish it better, rounding it well by placing a piece inside. The bearers are finer checked and better finished. The breeching straps must be lined; give them and the loops a neat finish. These straps may be 2 ft. 6 in. by 1 in., and, if desired, two narrow loops can be put on the top with one wider and stronger underneath.

Some people prefer a kicking strap (Fig. 90) instead of a breeching strap, and in this case the breeching, shaft, and hip straps are not employed, the opening in the crupper being used for the kicking instead of the hip strap. For two-wheel traps the kicking strap must be 5 ft. 3 in., and for four-wheeled 6 ft. 6 in., long and 1 in. or 1⅛ in. wide; a lined strap should be made as directed for lining.

If the kicking strap is in three parts (Fig. 91) two brass or silver squares will be needed with a chape at each end of the centre-piece round the square and one at an end of each of the points;

when finished it must be of the same length as
the full-length strap.

A patent leather centre-piece, with swelling
middle, may also be placed between two squares
for supporting an ornament; now join the centre-
piece and points. There must be four rows of
stitching in the ornamental piece on the hip strap,
a metal ornament being placed in the centre. The
kicking strap may also have in all parts two or
four rows of stitching. After finishing, make half
a dozen holes at each end. The kicking tugs
should be 1 ft. long and of the same width as
the strap. Having obtained proper kicking-tug
buckles, put a loop below the buckle, line it like

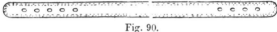

Fig. 90.

Fig. 91.

Fig. 90.—Kicking Strap. Fig. 91.—Kicking Strap in
Three Parts.

the strap, finish, and make a hole 1 in. from the
point.

Single leather driving reins are made as described for van harness (see the companion volume),
but often have a piece on the centre of the fore-
part, called "Melton reins" (Fig. 92). There is
a thin neat strip of leather about half the width
of the reins running all along the fore-part from
the buckle to a little beyond the splice of the
fore and hind part. The edges below are shaved
and the strap is rounded in a groove board. The
stitching is fine, with an outer fine line of creasing
just outside the stitches, the centre being raised
by placing a piece of thin string underneath the
stitches and bringing it down over the string on
both sides.

For this style of reins brown leather is employed for all parts of the reins and not merely
for the hand parts The stitching is done with
fine yellow or white hemp beeswaxed thread. The
hand parts (Figs. 93 to 96) are sometimes plaited,
laced, lined, etc., to give the driver a firm grip
when driving a strong-headed animal.

The lacing is made by punching holes about
¼ in. apart in the centre of the rein, for about
3 ft. along the part held by the driver, and then

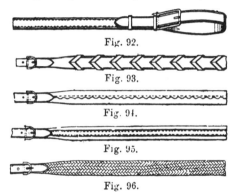

Fig. 92.

Fig. 93.

Fig. 94.

Fig. 95.

Fig. 96.

Fig. 92.—Melton Rein with Billet. Fig. 93.—Laced Rein
Hand Part. Fig. 94.—Stuffed Hand Part. Fig. 95.—
Lay on Hand Part. Fig. 96.—Plaited Hand Part.

running a lace through the holes. Place the
centre part of the lace under the rein below the
first lower hole ; bring it up on both sides of the
rein and run one point from each side down
through the hole, and so on till the last hole is
reached, where the points are stitched together on
the rein.

For plaiting, the hand parts must be cut in
three strips, none of them being cut right off ;
plait them firmly, and finally bring the end through
to fasten the plait. In working the end it has

often to be put through the strips, and it is rather
difficult to explain the operation. It will be found
that as one end is plaited the other must be undone, because, when fast, both ends get plaited.

The stuffed hand parts overlap with specially
dressed leather. Make a serge lay inside and
scallop the upper edge very finely ; stitch one row
from end to end at the foot of the scallop, and
place a chape and buckle with a strap stitched to
them at the end of the hand part.

For a martingale a pair of ivory or bone stops
(Figs. 97 and 98) will, in the first place, be required
for the reins to prevent the rings catching in the
bit ; two ivory or bone rings will also be wanted
to match them. Stops can be obtained either to

Fig. 97.   Fig. 98.

Figs. 97 and 98.—Rein Stops.

run along the reins or be stitched to them. Cut a
piece of leather, 1 ft. 3 in. by 2 in., to fasten to
the rings, and slit it for 1 ft., narrowing it down
at the other end to $\frac{3}{4}$ in. Turn it in 2 in. at the
end of the slit and narrow towards the bend to
$\frac{3}{4}$ in. ; shave the point thin. A groove in width
equal to half the thickness of the leather must
now be cut on both sides of the slit and very near
the edge. Round the slits and get pieces of cord
to put in both. Line the point below the slit from
the commencement of the rounding of the slits to
the end. Shave the ends of the lining thin and
stitch it fine.

The rings can now be stitched in the forepart
and afterwards the round part stitched, the cord
being kept deep down during the work. Get a
firm hold and join the end of the ring chapes and
the points of the lining at the bottom with the

round piece, making two good stitches through all at the beginning of the round end. Finish, close the grooves well, and rub, round, and polish the material bright.

The breast-plate part (Fig. 81, p. 133) can now be made as follows:—Cut a piece of patent leather, about 4½ in. long, to a fancy pattern, and swell it at the sides to match the drop-piece in the bridle and hip-strap piece; narrow it gradually for about 1½ in. towards the top to ¾ in. A buckle hole must now be made in the centre of the narrowed part, the point and edges being shaved. Then run two rows around with the race compass and prepare it for stitching. The inner row is stitched single leather, a piece of the same size and shape being cut to line it as far as the buckle hole and no farther.

Having obtained a ¾-in. ring to match the buckles, cut a chape for it, which, when bent, will be 2 in. long; shave the ends thin and narrow them a little. Now, quite in the centre, make a hole in the lining ⅜ in. from the bottom for the chape to pass so that the ring will hang down outside. Two rows of stitching must now be run upwards through the chape from the hole; then, having placed the lining under the patent leather piece, stitch the outer line through both.

Put the buckle on the top without turning down the chape, and make a billet 9 in. by ¾ in.; shave one end and round the other. After creasing it, prick the part to be joined to the buckle and stitch in the billet with a loop below the buckle, the end of this billet being below to join the lining previously stitched. The loop should be slack enough to admit two straps.

When the entire piece is finished and rubbed, make a runner loop to pass on the billet above the buckle, and then cut a strap 2 ft. 4 in. by ¾ in. wide. Adjust a buckle and loop to one end, in the

reverse way to the usual position, so that the strap
can be buckled back through it. Now make a loop
for the bellyband and punch six or eight holes in
it, beginning about 8 in. from the buckle and
continuing in the opposite direction to it. Buckle
so as to form a loop, turn the other end in for
about 1½ in. and shave the point, after which stitch
it to the ring right side out and finish.

Now stitch a ¾-in. double piece of leather to
another ring about 1½ in. long when doubled, leaving an opening in one end and the ring in the other.
The opening allows the hame strap at the bottom of
the collar to pass, the billet of the martingale
being fastened to the ring. Give this a neat finish.
Now punch a hole in the martingale billet and two
or three holes in the point of the ring part; adjust
the ring and small piece in the bottom of the
collar to the hame strap and fasten the martingale
billet to the ring.

Buckle the ring piece to the buckle of the
martingale over the billet and through the same
loop; this shows why the loop had to be made
large. The girth must be passed through the loop
part of the martingale. When driving, the reins
must be put through the rings from the hand-part
end because the stop prevents this being done
from the billet end.

There is another style of martingale made with
a single strap, a buckle being placed at one end.
The length should be 5 ft. Round the end opposite
the buckle end for a distance of 2 ft. 4 in., placing
a cord inside it to shape it and cutting a groove
for the stitches. Make an eye for the noseband
by turning the end backwards at the round end and
then, having placed the points between the edges
of the round, stitch them firmly; give every part
a neat finish. Now put a chape on a 1¼-in. ring,
leaving an opening at the other end for the hame
strap, as in the other martingale, this opening

being for the round part at the bottom of the collar running from below the chest to the noseband. Having unbuckled the noseband, put the buckle part through the eye of the martingale, which will make all complete.

A long breeching may also be made instead of the short one with straps to go round the shaft. The breeching should be 9 ft. 6 in. long by 1¼ in. wide; taper it to the end to about ⅞ in. for 3 ft. along each side, and then line it to within a distance of 1 ft. 6 in. from each point. Owing to its length the breeching must be joined in the centre, the best end of the leather being always placed

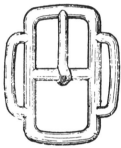

Fig. 99.—Breeching Loop Buckle.

towards the points. Stitch the centre all along, the 18-in. part being single, with two or four rows of fine stitches; leave two openings, one on each side, 1 ft. 6 in. from the centre for the bearers to pass and give it a neat finish. Make a chape at each end and prepare it for a buckle; then punch six or seven holes on each side, beginning about 6 in. from the end and moving towards the centre. Finally make four runner loops to pass round the points double.

The bearers should be made like ordinary breeching and the hip strap like the kicking strap, but 4 ft. 4 in. long. The hip strap may also be made to act as a kicking strap as well, when it will be fastened to a pair of breeching loop buckles (Fig. 99), whilst the breeching runs through the loops in the buckle which acts as a carrier. The hip strap must be 5 ft. 6 in. long, made as described; then make the kicking-strap tugs. Thus the breeching can be employed with the tugs to form a kicking strap as well or without them, and the kicking strap can be employed without the breeching.

Two dees will be needed in the shaft tugs to fasten a long breeching. When making it, take two 1-in. dees and fill the flat part of them for about half the width towards the round part with a piece of leather, then place them inside the side of the shaft tug in the centre on the part next the saddle, and stitch them as the shaft tug is made. When adjusting the breeching, after the loops, without bearers, have been placed on the body, put two of the runner loops in the points on each side with the buckles before them. Then run the points through the dees on the shaft tugs and through the loops, after which they can be buckled; now tighten the loops, one near the buckle and the other close to the dees.

As can be observed, the chape is made on the same principle as the bearing rein, and the buckle is never stitched down; the breeching can thus be lengthened at both sides. There is another style of make which is a combination of long and short breechings; for this, ordinary breeching rings, and straps round the shafts, also with bearers, are employed. Other straps may be stitched to the ring and fastened like the bearing rein to the shaft tugs. Thus both styles are combined and the breeching is made doubly secure.

INDEX.

L

CONTENTS.

LIST OF ILLUSTRATIONS.

HARNESS MAKING.

———•••———

CHAPTER I.

HARNESS making and repairing is a branch of
leather work that can often be undertaken profitably by many persons, and the information given in
the following pages has been adapted specially to
the amateur's requirements. Doubtless the readers
of a companion handbook on "Boot Making and
Mending" have wished to pursue further the subject of leather working, and will take up the making
and repairing of harness with pleasure. Aspirants
to more highly skilled work will find "Practical
Saddlery" of the greatest possible use to them,
whilst readers less ambitious may look to "Leather
Working" for instructions on making a number of
articles, such as bags, portmanteaus, and cases, for
which there is general employment and a consequently great demand. The two books just mentioned are issued uniform in style and price with
the present work.

In this handbook it is proposed to treat the subject of harness making so fully that anyone possessing tact and sense can make a set of harness from
the instructions given, or, at any rate, keep harness
in good repair. A start will be made by describing
the tools that will be necessary. In the list given
below, every essential tool is specified and its uses
explained. The tools are very numerous, but the
amateur may dispense with many of them; for
though all of them may have to be employed by a

tradesman in turning out finished work, an amateur
may be content with a much smaller outfit. The
tools are not bulky, however, and all that are necessary for making a double set of harness could be
carried in a small handbag, excepting, of course,
the mallet and collar-iron.

Fig. 1.—Paring Knife.

The tools are here classified as (*a*) cutting tools,
(*b*) punches and tools of percussion, (*c*) tools for setting out, marking, and ornamenting, (*d*) awls and
needles for perforating, (*e*) tools for gripping and
holding work, (*f*) tools used in stuffing collars
and saddles, and (*g*) miscellaneous. It may be re-
marked that saddlers' tools, as well as harness-
makers', are included in this chapter.

With regard to cutting tools, a paring knife (Fig.
1) and a hand knife (Fig. 2) are used for cutting
thread, paring down, and splicing, and are otherwise generally useful. The round knife (Fig. 3) is
used by saddlers instead of the hand knife for cutting, splicing, and thinning leather ; they can be had
in different sizes, suited to light and heavy work ;
their chief use is in thinning the edges of leather,

Fig. 2.—Hand Knife.

and for giving a rounded appearance to lined straps,
such as nosebands, traces, breeching straps, etc.
The head knife (Fig. 4) is used for cutting the holes
for buckle tongues and cutting any circular shapes
or holes in leather.

Fig. 5 is a cutting gauge made in iron or wood. A

knife passes through the ruled stem, and is held
firmly by a screw. It is adjusted by shifting the
block, which is also held by a screw.

A plough or plough gauge (Fig. 6) is very useful
when much strap or belt cutting has to be done. By

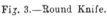

Fig. 3.—Round Knife.   Fig. 4.—Head Knife.

means of it, straps can be cut from $\frac{3}{4}$ in. to 4 in.
wide, by sliding the knife backwards or forwards
along the marked gauge. Straps can be cut much
more quickly by this machine than by hand, and it
quite dispenses with the use of the round knife and
compasses. A slightly different plough is illustrated by Figs. 7 and 8.

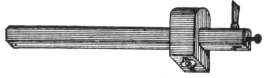

Fig. 5.—Cutting Gauge.

The slitting machine (Fig. 9) is useful for thinning
straps which are to be drawn down to half or one-
third their thickness. A saddler's spokeshave (Fig.
10) may be used for the same purpose as the slitting

machine. It is suitable for thinning light straps, and not only takes less time to adjust, but does the work more quickly than the slitter. The chief use

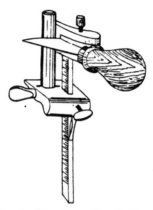

Fig. 6.—Plough, or Plough Gauge.

of the spokeshave, however, is to trim and finish traces, backbands, etc. After a trace or backband or other lined strap is stitched, the uneven edges require to be rounded and smoothed; this is done by clamping the strap between the knees, holding

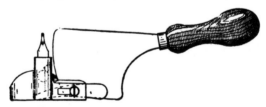

Fig. 7.—Side Elevation of Plough Gauge.

the clamp a little straighter than when stitching, and using the spokeshave.

Edge trimmers (Fig. 11) are for running along the

edges of straps of all kinds to take off the sharp edge
and sides before dyeing. It is made in sizes 1 to 8.

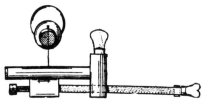

Fig. 8.—End Elevation of Plough Gauge.

Sharp and strong scissors are necessary for cutting
linings, basil, and other kinds of thin leather. The

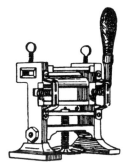

Fig. 9.—Slitting Machine.

washer cutter (Fig. 12) is used for cutting round
pieces of leather by rule; the knife can be set at
all sizes up to 6 in.

Fig. 10.—Spokeshave

Punches are indispensable, and half a dozen different sizes each of round (Fig. 13) and oval (Fig.

14) tools should be obtained. Round punches are made in sizes from No. 1, suitable only for very narrow straps, to No. 16, which make a hole $\frac{5}{8}$ in. in diameter. Oval punches are numbered, according

Fig. 11.—Edge Trimmer.

to size, from 17 to 32, and make a hole of similar dimensions to the round punches just mentioned. Punches of intermediate sizes, Nos. 3 to 13 or Nos. 19 to 29, will, however, answer for most repairing jobs. The ovals are preferable in most cases, as they make holes in the straps large enough for the purpose without impairing the strength so much as the round ones do. Buckle tongue punches, or

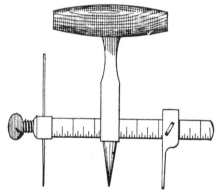

Fig. 12.—Washer Cutter.

crew punches (Fig. 15) are handy; these are made in three or four sizes, and they run from No. 33 to No. 43, and are used for making the holes that take the heel of the buckle tongue when the buckle is

placed in its chape. This hole may also be made
by punching two holes at a suitable distance from
each other, and cutting between them, thus ⟨○▭○⟩
The strap has to be bent and a hole cut through the

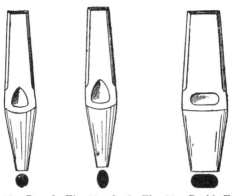

Fig. 13.—Round   Fig. 14.—Oval   Fig. 15.—Buckle Tongue
     Punch.   Punch.   or Crew, Punch.

bent end, the piece between the holes for the
tongue of the buckle being afterwards cut out.
The punches shown by Figs. 16 to 18 may be used to
cut saddle girth chapes, brace ends, etc.

A hand punch (Fig. 19) is useful for punching holes
in small straps, or for making holes in harness
whilst it is worn by a horse. Saddlers are some-

Fig. 16.—Girth Chape Punch.   Fig. 17.—Brace End Punch.

times called upon to do this, and without a hand
punch the work is awkward, necessitating the use
of mallet, punch, and lead. Fig. 20 shows a loose

nipple which can be obtained in various sizes to
screw in the handle.

Scalloping irons (Figs. 21 to 24), vandyke, round,

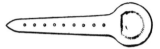

Fig. 18.—Forepart of Brace End Punch.

straight, and half-moon are used for cutting any
fancy or ornamental designs in American cloth
or fancy leather. Rosette punches (Figs. 25 and 26)

Fig. 19.—Hand Punch.

in sets of three or four, are useful for making
rosettes in patent fancy coloured leather or for cutting out round scalloped edge pieces.

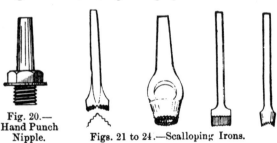

Fig. 20.—
Hand Punch
Nipple.

Figs. 21 to 24.—Scalloping Irons.

A lead piece (Fig. 27) for punching on should be
from 6 in. to 8 in. square, and about 1½ in. thick.
Lead is used because, being soft, it does not
damage the points of the punches; but if lead is not

handy, a block of wood 5 in. or 6 in. thick will do, if set up on end so that the punch does not cut across the grain.

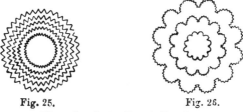

Fig. 25.   Fig. 26.

Figs. 25 and 26.—Rosette Punches.

A wooden mallet (Fig. 28) for punching is also required, and a lignum-vitæ round mallet to work the forewales and shape the stuffed bodies of

Fig. 27.—Lead Piece.   Fig. 28.—Wooden Mallet.

collars. Other useful mallets are shown by Figs. 29 and 30. Two hammers are necessary, one fairly light—the proper saddler's hammer (Fig. 31)—and the other a heavy one for heavy work.

Figs. 29 and 30.—Useful Wooden Mallets.

Tools for marking and ornamenting leather may now be mentioned. Fig. 32 shows a tool used in stamping the lines preparatory to stitching. These

M

tools vary in width from three teeth, which are used
only for round points and scalloped work, to twenty-
four teeth for straight lines. The teeth on each
iron are cut to mark a certain number of stitches

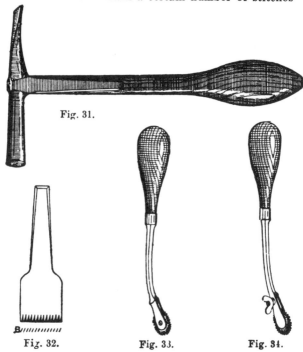

Fig. 31.

Fig. 32.

Fig. 33.

Fig. 34.

Fig. 31.—Saddlers' Hammer.   Fig. 32.—Pricking-iron.
        Figs. 33 and 34.—Wheel Prickers.

per inch, from six to sixteen, and these teeth are
not at right angles to the flat part of the iron, but
are cut on the slant as at B, thus making an impression on the leather which acts as a guide in
forming a stitch perfect in shape as well as in
length.

Wheel prickers (Figs. 33 and 34) are used in sizes from seven or eight to sixteen teeth to the inch. They are round pieces of steel, having serrated edges and a hole in the centre, and are provided with a handle in which they are adjusted with a pin and nut. A change of stitch, say from fine to coarse, necessitates a change of wheel. The wheel is run along the stitching line, and in the holes made by the pricks the stitches are run.

The screw-race (Fig. 35) is a tool for grooving

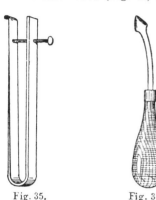

Fig. 35.   Fig. 36.   Fig. 37.

Fig. 35.—Screw-race.   Fig. 36.—Single Crease.   Fig. 37.—
                   Screw-crease.

lines in any part where it is desired to sink the stitches below the surface. It is easily adjustable.

Single creases (Fig. 36) are for marking in places where neither the screw-crease nor the compasses can go, as for instance, in the centre of a large piece of leather or wide strap. They are also used to mark thick and heavy loops, for which purpose they are heated before using.

Two screw-creases must be obtained, one light and the other heavy (Fig. 37); one is used for light lines and the other for heavy lines along the edge of

the leather, and for marking the lines for stitching. By means of the screw, the points are closed

Fig. 38.—Checker.

Fig. 39.—Beveller.

or opened, thus bringing the line nearer to the edge
of the work or taking it farther away.

Checkers (Fig. 38) are small double creases with

Fig. 40.—Compasses.

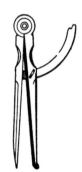

Fig. 41.—Race Compasses.

two parallel edges, one of which marks the small
ornamental checked lines on loops; one edge is run

along the last line done, which thus serves as a
guide for keeping the lines parallel. Sizes 1, 2, and
3 will be sufficient. A brass foot-rule, of course,
must be obtained.

Fig. 42.—Awl Blade.

Bevellers (Fig. 39) resemble the single creases,
but are much thicker and bevelled ; they are used
for the sole purpose of creasing or marking loops on
portions that require ornamenting. In use, they
are heated and then made to form a deep, wide
groove on the loop, such as the straight cross lines
on the front, and any fancy shapes worked on the
outside of the loop.

Compasses (Fig. 40) should have a screw and regu-
lator so that they may be set at different widths.
They are used for marking the widths of straps to
be cut and for marking distances, etc.

Race compasses (Fig. 41) are for the purpose of
cutting a slight groove or line along the edges ; they
just take off a narrow strip of the grain and leave a
faint line, which is blacked with the edges. It
answers the same purpose as the line cut with the
screw-crease, either ornamenting the straps or
marking the line for the stitches.

With regard to perforating tools, a few awl blades
(Figs. 42 and 43) and hafts may be obtained. Stitching blades vary in sizes from $1\frac{1}{4}$ in. to 3 in. long.

Fig. 43.—Awl Blade.

Hold the blade fast in the vice, and with a few sharp
blows of a light hammer drive the haft or handle on
the awl, which is then ready for use. Fig. 44 shows
a sewing awl. Strong thick awls will be required for

coarse work, to stitch, say, a thread of seven, eight, or even more cords of hemp in one thread, and the thickness of the awl should diminish until the fine awl for stitching fine silk and cotton threads is obtained. Bent awls (Fig. 45) in one or two sizes,

Fig. 44.—Sewing Awl.

such as shoemakers use, are employed for putting in wire in saddle flabs for fastening the panel ; they have other uses also.

Half a dozen packets of harness needles (Figs. 46 and 47), varying in size from No. 2 to No. 6, will be necessary ; the lowest number is the coarsest. These needles are for wax thread and all other stitching threads. Needles will also be required as follows :—2-in. or 3-in. needles for quilting saddle panels, etc. ; pointed needles for thimble work in stitching linings to saddle panels, etc. ; collar needles of different sizes, half-moon shape and straight with bent points ; these are from 3 in. to 6 in. long, the longest being for heavy cart collar work and the lightest for patent and light harness collars.

The seat-awl (two shapes are shown by Figs. 48

Fig. 45.—Bent Awl.

and 49) is for easing and levelling stuffing in collars, saddles, and other stuffed or padded articles. It is also useful for levelling thread ; this is turned once around the round awl, which is then drawn sharply

backwards and forwards, the lumps thus being
taken out of the thread.

The hand- or palm-iron (Figs. 50 and 51) is a kind
of thimble used on the palm of the hand when driv-

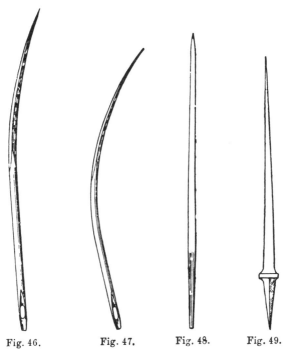

Fig. 46.　　　　Fig. 47.　　　　Fig. 48.　　　　Fig. 49.

Figs. 46 and 47.—Harness Needles.　Figs. 48 and 49.—
Seat Awls.

ing collar needles through leather. A shallow honey-
combed well is formed in the hand part, which prevents the needle from slipping, however great the
pressure may be ; and at the end or point a hole is
bored lengthwise, about ⅛ in. deep, to take the eye

end of the needle and force it closer to the leather
when the broad part of the iron is not available

Holding and gripping tools include the clamp,

Fig. 50.   Fig. 51.
Figs. 50 and 51.—Hand-irons or Palm-irons.

known also as the pair of clams.   Fig. 52 shows the
ordinary type, while Fig. 53 is the kind used in sewing shaft-tugs.   Held between the knees in a slightly
slanting position, the clamp keeps the work firmly
in position while the stitching is being done ; it lies
against the left knee, and by throwing the right leg
over it the work is held fast between the gripping
points.   Note that the saddler has the clamp between his legs in a slanting direction, and not as
the shoemaker, who has them straight up, almost

Fig. 52.—Clamp or Clams.

against his nose, when bending over the work.   One
reason for this is that the work done by the saddler
with the clamp requires more force to press the awl

through than the work done by the shoemaker; consequently the saddler must set his clamp against some firm object (his left knee) so that it will not yield under the pressure. Another reason is that

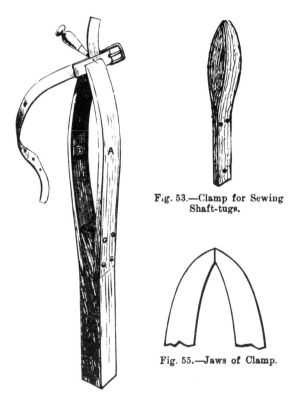

Fig. 53.—Clamp for Sewing Shaft-tugs.

Fig. 55.—Jaws of Clamp.

Fig. 54.—Home-made Clamp Holding Work.

the saddler stitches with needles, while the shoemaker uses bristles, and must see the hole made by the awl, as the bristles cannot force their way, as

the needles, to some slight extent, are able to do.
The saddler feels for the hole with his needle and
thus becomes accustomed to finding the hole without looking, and to getting his needle to follow the
awl as the latter is drawn back ; in fact, the needle
is inserted in the unseen lower side with more
accuracy than on the top side, which is in view.

A clamp can be made easily by the worker at
home. The parts A and B (Fig. 54) are made from
two oak cask or barrel staves. The lower portion
c may be a sound piece of white deal, 20 in. by 3 in.

Fig. 56.—Nail-claw.

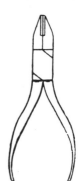

Fig. 57.—Cutting Pliers.

by 3 in., and the only other requisites will be eight
stout 2¼ in. screws. The staves should be cut 2 ft.
long by at least 3 in. wide, the points of greatest
convexity being in the centre ; the more bent the
staves are the more useful the clamp will be. Clean
up the outside with a spokeshave, leaving one end
the full thickness of the staves, or about 1 in., and
thinning off gradually to about ¾ in. towards the
upper ends, which are to form the jaws of the
clamp (Fig. 55). Round off the outer corners, and
clean up the inside surface flat, smoothing both
sides with glass-paper. The dovetail-shaped tenon

in the lower part c, should be at least 6 in. in
length, and will require careful cutting, the depth
of the shoulders and the width of the upper end
depending upon the amount of curve in the staves

Fig. 58.—Iron Collar Rod.

which are to be attached to it. It should be borne
in mind that the object is to embed the staves so
firmly that their upper ends, or the jaws of the tool,
press tightly together. With this object the tenon
should be cut, so that energetic screwing will be
required to bring the staves home into their final
position. The screws should be countersunk flush
with the surface of the staves.

A small wrench and a medium-sized vice will
often be found useful. A nail-claw (Fig. 56) is required for pulling out the nails used to keep the
work together. Pincers, nippers, and cutting
pliers (Fig. 57) will be found useful as occasion
demands.

An iron collar rod (Fig. 58) for stuffing the forewale must be obtained, as well as a hardwood stick,
about 2 ft. 6 in. long, and having a **V**-shaped point,
for filling the body of collars with straw; the stick

Fig. 59.—Steel Seat-iron.

is flat towards the **V**-shaped end, and round at the
other end, the corners being rounded off smooth.

A steel seat-iron (Fig. 59) is used in putting flock
into cart-saddle panels, but chiefly for stuffing the
peak of riding saddles, as the tool bends nicely with

the shape of the saddle without tearing the cover or stretching it immoderately.

Loop-sticks (Fig. 60) are made of hardwood in various sizes to suit the width and thickness of the straps. A set made of hard boxwood or iron, varying in width from ½ in. to 2 in., and in thickness from ⅛ in. to ½ in., should be obtained. Less room is wanted in shaping a loop for a single strap than when a strap of two or three thicknesses is required to go through a loop. (A loop is the piece of leather placed crosswise on straps having buckles, and it keeps the point of the strap in its proper position.) A loop stick must be obtained that is thick enough

Fig. 60.—Loop-stick.

Fig. 61.—Rubber.

and wide enough for a trace 1¾ in. wide and proportionately thick ; there must also be one sufficiently thin and narrow for a ½-in. strap ; loop sticks for intermediate sizes are also necessary, and it is as well to get two each of some of the sizes. For instance, those things that are done in pairs, such as bridle-cheeks, shaft-tugs, etc., will require the use of two loop sticks of the same size. Good loop sticks are essential to turning out good work.

A rubber (Fig. 61) made of a piece of hard, close-grained wood or of thick glass about 6 in. square and V-shaped on one edge is used to smooth down two edges whipped together, or for flattening and levelling any two thin substances, such as leather and linen pasted or stitched together ; it is also used to rub stitching on the underside of traces or any double straps, and for rubbing or stretching damped leather.

The straining fork (Fig. 62) is sometimes employed for stretching wet webbing or leather, one end of which is nailed down and the other end strained with the fork and secured until dry.

Fig. 62. —Straining Fork.

A coarse file or rasp may be necessary to file down wooden and cane driving whip-stocks, etc., when putting on thongs and in splicing whip-sticks to level the splice so that both of the parts may lie flat against each other. A small round file and a small square one, as well as two or three coarser ones, are sure to come in handy. Amongst their uses will be the filing down of the brass or ironwork of saddles, and the making of holes in saddle trees, etc.

CHAPTER II.

It is now proposed to give some particulars of the materials used in saddle and harness making.

The threads used in the trade are many, but the principal is waxed thread, made by the saddler himself, and used to stitch harness and straps together. By waxed thread is generally meant thread dressed with black or cobbler's wax, but the saddler also uses thread dressed with beeswax and sometimes with white wax. The linen thread used is in various colours, yellow, red, black, white, etc., and is on reels or in hanks. Silk threads of the same colours are used for best work, such as stitching best brown saddlery, riding bridles, martingales, etc. The white and black linen thread is used for whipping-in lining in panels of both gig and riding saddles, and for stitching saving pads in any thin material for light work, and also in stitching along with the red and yellow thread in making riding bridles, and all kinds of brown light work. The hemp for wax threads, of various strengths, is to be had in black, yellow, green, and white. The white hemp is considered the best and toughest, though the coloured perhaps is a little cheaper. Fine No. 15 and coarse No. 3 will probably meet all requirements.

Beeswax, as already hinted, is used to make threads for work that is light as regards both colour and substance. Single linen threads of all colours are, before using, rubbed with beeswax, which does not deaden the colour. White wax is sometimes made for brown harness by melting together white-lead and white wax; instead of the latter, the wax from best white wax candles may be used. If the wax when cold is too soft, add more white wax; if too hard, add a little more white-lead.

Black cobbler's wax is made by melting together ¼ lb. each of resin and pitch. When thoroughly mixed, remove the pan from the fire, and add one pennyworth of boiled linseed oil, or less, according to the weather. Thoroughly mix this with the other ingredients and then pour a little into cold water to test it. Let it remain for a minute and then remove it from the water, taking care to well wet the hands in doing so, or in the subsequent working it will stick to them. If it cracks when working it in the hands, it is too hard; if it pulls out properly and sticks well together, it is all right. Put it back into the water, and pour in the rest of the stuff after it. It is important that the piece tested be not put back into the pan containing the rest of the wax, as the water absorbed will evaporate and make the hot wax frothy and spongy. Gather the wax together in the water without loss of time, remove it with wet hands, and pull it fast hand over hand as quickly as possible till it attains a light golden colour. Pull off a small piece with the hands, or cut it off with wet scissors, and throw it into the water. If it floats on the surface it has been pulled enough; if it sinks, the wax requires more working. If not pulled enough, the wax is brittle, becoming tougher and better the more it is pulled. In making the wax it must be remembered that only half as much oil is required in summer as in winter. The colder the atmosphere the more oil will be required.

The quantities of ingredients mentioned will make about thirty handy lumps of wax, and as a rule a pennyworth of oil is enough in the coldest weather. If, after working it, the wax is too hard, melt it again and add more oil; if too soft, add more pitch and resin. Hard wax may be used in a way that avoids re-melting. The thread, previous to being dressed with the wax, is rubbed with tallow, over which the wax will run smooth. Cut the wax into lumps the size of a large pigeon's egg and keep it in water.

Directions will now be given for making wax threads. So that the hemp may be kept tidy and not mixed up with the tools on the bench, place the ball of hemp in a wooden or tin box having a small hole in the centre of its lid, through which the hemp can pass. Take hold of the end of the hemp with the left hand, twist it once around the fingers, and draw it through the right hand. When a sufficient quantity has been drawn out, break the thread by rubbing it on the knee to take out the twist, at the same time giving it a sharp pull; the strands thus loosen and break in a ragged end. Throw the hemp over a nail or hook in the bench, pull it until the sides are each about 2 ft. 9 in. long, keep the hemp tight with the end in the left hand, and with the right hand spin or rub it on the knee as before to untwist the strands; then pull it sharply to break it. The more ragged the broken end is the better will be the point on the finished thread. There is now one strand 2 ft. 9 in. long and pointed; with the right hand put the points together in the left hand, and draw the hemp again over the hook, spinning and cutting it as before, and repeating the operation till the required number of strands is obtained. The number varies with the required strength, from three to sixteen.

In putting the ends of the cut hemp together, do not leave them exactly the same length; by leaving some shorter than others a nice pointed thread is obtained at the finish, fine enough to go into the eye of a needle. When the required number of strands is obtained, take a ball of wax in the right hand, and hold both ends of the thread separately in the left; draw the wax over the points two or three times to keep the ends together, taking care to keep the ends on the left of the hook twisted round the left hand, and holding them tight with the third and fourth fingers, leaving the thumb and forefinger loose to manipulate the other end in the process of twisting ; the wax on the ends or points is a great help at this stage.   Having an end between the thumb and finger of the left hand, set it on the knee, and spin or twist it as when cutting the hemp.   The knee should be raised about 12 in. from the floor by placing the foot on a support.   Continue spinning with the palm of the right hand until the thread is twisted enough.   If twisted too much, it will work into knots when used in stitching.   Then put the twisted side round the left hand, kept firm by the third and fourth fingers as before ; and take the other side between the thumb and forefinger of the left hand, and spin it to the proper twist with the palm of the right hand as the other side was done. If the thread is required very smooth, twist both of the sides of the thread once round the seat-awl and draw the latter sharply backwards and forwards along the thread, all unevenness being thus smoothed away.   For coarse work and repairs this is not necessary, but for best and new work the thread should always be smoothed.

To wax the thread, hold the two ends of the thread firmly in the left hand, and with the ball of wax held in the palm of the right hand, rub all along the thread, pulling the thread from around the hook into the open to enable that portion to be waxed also.   Pull back the thread into its former position, and, with a piece of soft leather or the bare hand, rub the thread sharply from end to end to smooth the wax and make it even all along.   The thread is then ready for use.

Yellow or white hemp thread is made with either beeswax or white wax in exactly the same manner, but the point of the thread is not dressed with white wax, being left unwaxed until the rest of the thread is finished.   The end has to be pointed with black wax, which will not stick over beeswax or white wax.   Black wax is the only kind that will keep the thread fast to the needles.

N

Nails are extensively used both in putting materials together for working and as ornaments. The nails used in putting work together are generally cut tacks, ranging in length from $\frac{2}{3}$ in. to 1 in. Neat wire nails can now be had, however, much cheaper than the tacks, and are to be preferred, as they are of uniform size and leave a much smaller hole when withdrawn. Clumsy nails spoil good work, as the holes made by them are larger than the awl used in stitching. Very fine nails do not spoil the work, and can be obtained in sizes suitable for heavier and clumsier work; and they may be used over and over again if care is taken in pulling them out with the nail-claw. Cut tacks are used in putting gig saddles together, in nailing the leather to the tree, in adjusting panels in the gullet and behind, between the two prongs of the crupper staples, for nailing seats in riding saddles, etc. Cut tacks can be obtained as small as $\frac{2}{3}$ in. in length.

Saddlers' tacks of different sizes from $\frac{1}{2}$ in. to $\frac{3}{4}$ in. long are used in putting in cart-saddle and riding-saddle panels and flaps, and for many other purposes. Clout nails are used now and then in putting houses on cart saddles, and for nailing on straps and girths, etc. Clout nails and saddlers' tacks are made of wrought iron. Round-headed and japanned nails may be used for nailing cart-saddle housings, and have a neater appearance than common iron clouts. Tough nails are used in making all kinds of saddles; they sometimes have heads covered with black patent leather, and sometimes japanned heads only. Others have heads of silver, nickel, or brass. They are used partly as ornaments and partly to hold the work together, and are in two sizes, cab and gig. There are usually four in a gig or cab saddle, one in each corner of the skirt in front and one on each side behind, holding down the binding that comes over the cantle of the saddle. The front ones are driven through, bent, and beaten close to the tree backwards, whilst the hind ones are cut to taper for about half their lengths to a point; they are driven into the tree.

In a riding saddle there is one nail in the front, one in each of the sides, one in the corner of the skirts driven through and bent, and one on each side just at the thin end of the skirt, driven inwards so as to catch the tree and be flattened close to it. There is also one in each flap under the skirt in a line with the stirrup fastener, driven through the tree on the outside of the plate running along the points from the gullet; these are bent and flattened underneath. Sometimes brass nails are used as ornaments, but brass beading has done away with their use to a great extent. Formerly country cart saddles were ornamented by nailing the housing to the tree with brass nails; the covers of van saddles, as well as the opening over the boards, were also fastened down with these nails.

Such pieces as loop leather, the edges of black straps, etc., often have to be dyed. The dye or stain is made by boiling together for half an hour 1 lb. logwood chips, 4 oz. crushed nutgalls, $\frac{1}{2}$ lb. copperas, a little gum arabic, and 5 qt. of water. Keep a little in an old bottle hung in a handy position near the bench. The dye is applied by a stick having a piece of felt attached to its end. The ink can be thinned by the addition of water. In dyeing brown leather, it must first be coated with soda solution to kill the grease. The solution is made by dissolving a piece of washing soda the size of a pigeon's egg in a quart of hot water. The black dye may then be applied. If it does not strike well, rub over it a coarse brush and again coat with dye. Rub it well and dry with a rag, afterwards well rubbing in a little tallow with either a rag or the bare hand. The tallow gives a finish and counteracts any injury the dye might do the hand, there being in the copperas a tendency to burn.

Flocks, both white and coloured, are extensively used in the trade, and can be bought at from 20s. to 50s. per hundredweight; the material can also be had in small quantities—even as low as a pound. Best white flock should be free from cotton, and should be tested by putting a small quantity in a candle flame; if cotton is present, it burns fiercely and with a big flame, but fine wool burns slowly and smoulders. The best flock is used for stuffing riding-saddle panels, etc., and the best drummed flock is used for collars, being put near the horse's breast under the lining to make the collars easy for the shoulder.

The drummed flocks are in large sheets, and these are cut to the size and shape required, and, being of even thickness, will not be lumpy, an important consideration in making a collar. Coarser flock of a white, brown, or any dark colour will do for stuffing and restuffing gig-saddle panels. Curled horsehair is sometimes used for stuffing panels, and is found very cool for an animal with a tender back or shoulder; goat hair is very suitable for stuffing. Neither this nor horsehair is so liable to be clogged by sweating as sheep's wool, though the latter, when dry, containing but very little oil and being well carded, is used extensively in country places.

All these materials before use should be put through the flock machine once or twice to loosen the fibre, and care should be taken when stuffing with a rod that the flock or wool is not put in lumpy or uneven. After stuffing, the work should be levelled with the seat-awl until it is as smooth as a board. The drummed flock, of course, is already level and even; it is not stuffed in, but laid on the inside of the collar lining before stuffing the collar with straw.

Thick felt is a good substitute for pads to ease collars and saddles, and can be bought in various thicknesses by the pound. Large cuttings and waste pieces can also be bought very cheaply, and two thicknesses can be put together if necessary, a strap and a buckle being on one side with a strap on the other to fasten to a saddle or collar. Felt is useful to put under cruppers and to line breechings when chafing, or under any strappings that chafe the horse's skin. They can be fastened to the above by stitching them with a spot stitch, thus - - - - -, about ¾ in. apart, and slanting the awl underneath to make the stitch small there as well as on the top ; or nails may be used when the felt is sufficiently thick. False collars, pads to be used like saddle cloths under gig or cab saddles and under cart-saddle panels, riding-saddle cloths, and many other articles are made of felt.

The harness maker and saddler uses many different kinds of leather, and, unless the worker possesses some knowledge of the particular purpose of each variety, much waste is likely to result. Stuff too light or too heavy, too thick or too thin, spoils a job, and of course entails loss.

In Fig. 63, which is a diagram showing a cut hide, A A show the sides of a harness hide with belly on ; C C, backs of harness hide with belly off ; B B B B, bellies of hide ; D D, middlings ; E, shoulder ; and F, uncut middling.

Harness leather can be bought in hides (A A) cut only along the back, having the belly part attached, at the rate of from 1s. 2d. to 1s. 11d. per lb. The best part can be used for harness and cart gear ; the belly will come in well for repairs, linings, and fillings. Harness backs (C C) are half hides from which the belly (B B) has been cut off ; these have all pure firm leather suitable for making all kinds of harness. The price is from 1s. 9d. to 2s. 5d. per pound.

Trace backs (C C) resemble the above, but are picked and more carefully dressed, and are made of the finest and best grown hides. They cost from 1s. 10d. to 2s. 7d. per pound.

Rein hides have the bellies attached but are dressed and of picked quality and thickness and uniform strength ; they are suitable for making into driving reins. For the best part can also be made any good light single straps, where strength and durability are required. The best part of the belly can be cut up into small straps of any kind and into linings. These hides cost from 56s. to 72s. each. Rein backs resemble the above, but have the belly cut off ; the price is from 40s. to 70s. each.

Black strap butts (D D) are the best part of the hide from which the belly and shoulder have been cut. They are from 4 ft. 6 in. to 4 ft. 9 in. long, and are suitable for any kind of good single strap. The price is from 56s. to 72s. a pair.

Black spur shoulders (E) are light shoulders dressed and flattened ; from them are made spur and similar straps, garters, wrist straps, etc. The price is from 8s. 6d. to 10s. each. Japanned horse hides for patent harness collars cost from 40s. to 46s. each. Cow hides, japanned for the same purpose, cost from 38s. to 44s. each. Japanned cowbacks for collars, etc., cost from 30s. to 39s. per pair. Japanned flap hides for making gig, cab, or brougham harness saddle flaps are priced at from 2s. 3d. to 2s. 6d. per pound. The middlings cost from 2s. to 2s. 6d. per pound.

Winker hides, japanned for making bridle winkers, cost 54s. to 56s. each, and the middlings (F) for the same purpose cost from 32s. to 36s. per pair. Japanned welting seals for making welts for gig saddles, etc., are priced at from 7s. 6d. to 8s. 6d. each. Japanned and enamelled hides for making military belts, etc., cost from 54s. to 60s. each, and middlings for the same purpose from 40s. to 42s. per pair.

There is great variety in brown or stained leather. Bridle hides for all sorts of riding bridles cost from 50s. to 56s. each. Backs (C C) from the above cost

45s. to 50s. each, whilst the butts cost 32s. to 40s. ; these are in varying qualities and prices.

Brown shoulders (E) dressed for coat straps, garters, braces, or small straps in general can be bought at from 6s. 6d. to 10s. each, and driving-rein brown hides at from 56s. to 72s. each. The backs cost from 56s. to 66s. a pair, and the butts for hand-parts of reins 38s. to 42s. a pair.

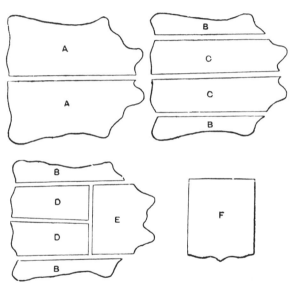

Fig. 63.—Cutting up Hide.

Double-rein hides—that is, brown leather speci-ally selected and dressed for making reins of double thickness stitched together, cost from 44s. to 50s. each. The backs cost from 40s. to 48s. per pair. Head-collar rein backs for making head-collars, stallion bridles, etc., can be bought at from 2s. 6d. to 2s. 11d. per pound.

Stirrup hides for making stirrup straps cost from 2s. 6d. to 2s. 9d. per pound ; there are also inferior qualities. Butts for stirrup straps cost from 3s. 6d. to 4s. per pound. Brown harness hides cost from 1s. 6d. to 1s. 11d. per pound. The backs cost from 1s. 8d. to 2s. 2d. per pound. Skirt hides for making ladies' and gents' saddle skirts and flaps are priced at from 1s. 10d. to 2s. 2d. per pound. Skirt backs are from 2s. to 2s. 4d. per pound, and shoulders, 1s. 5d. to 1s. 10d. per pound.

Hog-skins suitable for all purposes, but chiefly used for saddles, can be bought at from £9 to £12 per dozen ; they can be bought singly, and there are also inferior qualities.

Sheep-skins in imitation of hog-skins can be bought at from 30s. to 60s. per dozen, or copper plates for printing basils and a printing press for the purpose can be bought instead. Basils for gig-saddle panel pads and repairing collars, and cart-saddle cheek pads, etc., can be bought at from 10s. to 30s. per dozen. The common ones are good enough for repairs and cheap work.

Specially dressed hides for making braces or any light straps can be bought at from 36s. to 40s. each ; the shoulders (E) or bellies (B) dressed for the same purpose can be had apart from the hide. Purse and pocket-book hides are also specially dressed, and cost from 30s. to 40s. each. Calf-skins dressed for the same purpose cost from 9s. to 10s. 6d. each. The brace and pocket-book and purse leather can be obtained stained in various colours, red, brown, yellow, orange, etc. The brown harness leather also can be had natural or tallow colour or stained fawn, nut brown, yellow, or orange. Brown gear hides for cart work are from 1s. 3d. to 2s. per pound, the backs from 1s. 7d. to 2s. 3d. per pound, and bellies from 10d. to 1s. 4d. per pound.

Mill bands for making driving belts cost from 1s. 6d to 2s. 2d. per pound. Engine butts for makıng strong engine belts, either single or double, cost from 2s. to 2s. 6d. per pound.

Fancy coloured leather for bridle fronts and rosettes cost from 40s. to 42s. each middling. Striped patent frontings leather costs from 1s. 6d. to 2s. 9d. per square foot. White buff hides for hunting-crop keepers, razor strops, belts, etc., cost about 5s. per pound. White bleached buff middling is about 5s. per pound.

A country saddler is often called upon to work in coach-builders' leather; leathers for this purpose are not included in the above list, but, as a rule, they can be obtained at the same place as harness leather.

Enamelled cow, ox, and bull hides for carriage tops, etc., are sold whole, and not slit along the middle, at from 40s. to 70s. each. Coach hides and backs for dashes and wings cost from 26s. to 40s. each. Seal-skins for the same purpose cost from 7s. 6d. to 12s. each. Hides for window straps, enamelled and prepared, cost from 56s. to 60s. each. All coloured carriage cushion hides for making carriage cushions cost from 40s. to 60s. each. Dyed and enamelled leather for cushions is sold by the square foot.

It is scarcely necessary to state that all the above prices fluctuate with the market. A great quantity of harness leather, nowadays, is prepared by the quick tanning process, but it is inferior stuff. The best leather is that which has been through a pure oak tan. It is very hard, however, to tell when the inferior process has been used, but as a rule the colour, smell, and even taste of the leather decide the question; soft, mellow leather that has not a hard feeling to the touch is as a rule good leather, especially if it has a close grain and a light yellow colour when cut. The inferior quality feels and looks dry and hard: it has a dull grey colour and an uneven grain facing. A good test is to bend it.

poor and badly dressed leather cracking in the bend,
and the grain giving way ; these defects show that
either chemicals or excessive heats have been used
in the finishing and tanning. Well tanned and
dressed leather stands the bending test well.

A few rules on cutting up hides may now be given.
When cutting a strap from a hide, do not cut down
lower than the width of the strap required, so as
not to interfere with the next cut into the hide. All
possible care should be taken to prevent waste, and
pieces of particular shape should be cut from a pattern. It is sheer waste to cut off a piece of stuff
larger than is required and then to trim it down.
In cutting up a hide, lay it on the bench with the
back part against the worker ; use a straightedge
at least 8 ft. long, and mark with a blunt-pointed
awl or the seat-awl, using the straightedge as a
guide. Take care not to cut the grain of the leather
with the point of the awl, as in the case of the
straightedge being shifted an indelible mark may be
left.

If the strap is to be cut with the round knife, set
the compass to the right width, and put one point in
position to run along the edge of the leather, and
the other on the leather so that it marks the width
to be cut ; pull the compass towards the worker,
pressing it so that it leaves a plain line. With
the round knife begin cutting at the right-hand end,
keeping the leather steady in its place on the
cutting-board with the left hand. A cutting-
board ought always to be employed, as nails
on the top of the bench would interfere with the
work. Push the knife along the marked line stead-
ily, taking care that the knife does not slip ; if it
does, it may make a bad slit and spoil the work.
Straps are always cut along the hide and not across
it, the hide being much stronger lengthways.

The first cutting from the hide is suitable for reins,
and then in order come traces, back-bands, bridg-

ing-straps, hip-straps, and hip-strap tugs; then crupper billet, shaft tugs, name tugs, bellyband, bridle head-strap, cheeks, etc.; and from the belly part or third quality in side of hide may be cut linings and layers for folds. In making cart harness, cut bridge-band, crupper, and bridge-band carrier or hip-straps and bearers, and then cart-saddle bellybands and bridle; the best part of the belly, with the top well lined, will do for side pieces of collar, unless this can be cut from a specially dressed piece.

Specially curried leather must be obtained for cart-saddle housings and winkers, as the harness leather is not firm enough and contains too much oil. The special leather also must be got for the saddle flaps, the pieces lying against the ribs of the horse under the ridgworth.

A leather that is cheapest in first cost is not always the cheapest to use. That leather is the best from which the greatest weight of firm straps can be made, and which will continue firm for the greatest length down towards the belly part.

The compass and round knife only were mentioned in the description of cutting straps, but the plough is very useful for cutting straps varying from $\frac{1}{2}$ in. to $5\frac{1}{2}$ in. in width. The plough does away with the use of both compass and round knife, and cuts much more evenly and straight than it is possible to do by hand. Its use effects a great saving of time, the knife merely requiring to be adjusted on the gauge and made fast by the thumb-screw. Hold the leather firm and flat on the board with the left hand, and press it forward to the plough, keeping the guard close and tight to the edge all along. The uses of the head knife in cutting will be fully explained later.

Brown harness work, as small straps, traces, backband, and breechings, may be finished with a thin solution of gum and water, and should be well

rubbed with a smooth bone until polished. Machines
for trimming the edges are made, but their work is
incomplete, because all lengthy straps have parts
in which the fibres are less close than at others. A
good method is to knock the edges all along, con-
solidate them as much as possible, and then trim
them round and level with the spokeshave; afterwards run a glass scraper over them and sandpaper.
Finally, a good rubbing with brown paper and bone,
after gumming, will give a fine polished edge to all
brown work.

Black straps and harness are prepared in the same
way for polishing; black dye them, then rub dry
with a rag, and polish with brown paper and bone.
Sometimes, after blacking and rubbing, a coat of
liquid blacking is applied, and rubbed until dry.
Again, some harness-makers employ black-ball and
a burnisher to finish after blacking, rubbing down
well; this is recommended for the best harness. It
should be understood that whenever the word finishing is used here in connection with best harness this
process is referred to for black and brown harness
and single straps.

Common harness and cart gear, especially in
country places, are usually finished by levelling the
edges, scraping with glass, blacking, rubbing with a
rag, and finally, after passing a ball of hard tallow
along the edges, rubbing with a bone or hard knife
handle.

Webs are used for a variety of purposes by saddlers. Girth web for making saddle girths is sold
in 15-yd. pieces. It can be had in cotton, union, or
worsted. Race girth is a superior material for
racing saddles; it is about 5 in. wide. Web for
roller girth is from 4 in. to 6 in. wide and in 12½-yd.
pieces; it is of cotton, union, or worsted. In the
same material is made trace web in 18½-yd. pieces,
1½ in. to 2½ in. wide. Game-bag web is sometimes
required, and is bought by the yard in different

colours. Men's body-belt web is to be had in 18-yd. pieces from 4 in. to 8 in. wide, and in seven or eight colours. Straining-web for saddle seats can be bought by the yard or in the piece. A country saddler finds diaper-web very useful ; this is bought in 15-yd. pieces.

Other requisites, such as bits, spurs, stirrups, and harness furniture are described in Chapter X.

A few reliable recipes for some of the most necessary articles employed in harness making will now be given.

Iron Liquor for Dyeing.—(a) Green copperas, 2 lb. ; vinegar, 2 qt. ; pulverised nutgall, $\frac{1}{4}$ lb. ; and water, 4 qt. Two weeks after mixing add another 2 qt. of water. (b) Bichromate of potash, $\frac{1}{2}$ lb. ; logwood extract, 1 lb. ; copperas, 1 oz. ; and water, 1 gal.

Saddlers' Black Wax.—(a) Pitch, 2 lb. ; resin, $2\frac{1}{2}$ lb. ; seal oil, one pennyworth. In winter add 2 lb. of resin instead of $2\frac{1}{2}$ lb., and never more than $\frac{2}{3}$ of the oil until the stiffness of the wax has been tested. (b) Pitch, 1 lb. ; resin, 1 lb. ; and linseed oil, one pennyworth.

The exact amount of oil to be used in both of the above recipes depends on the season and the weather. A little lampblack may be well mixed in when the wax is required very black. Always melt the pitch and resin together, and then add the oil. Afterwards pour the mixture into cold water, and knead and pull it until it floats. Try a small piece first to ascertain whether there is sufficient oil, and likewise after pulling to see whether it floats.

Brown Wax.—Beeswax, 1 lb. ; pale resin, 3 oz. ; and white-lead, 3 oz. The wax can be softened or hardened by adding more or less beeswax. Melt the mixture, stirring it, and then pour it into water and pull until it floats.

Flour Paste.—Water, 1 qt., and alum 3 oz. Heat until the alum has melted, and when cold add flour to the consistency of cream ; then let the mixture boil, stirring it at the same time. By adding a little powdered resin and a clove or two before boiling, the paste will keep for a year and can be softened with water when dry.

Brown Stain.—Boil equal parts of pine and alder bark in six times their bulk of water until the colour is extracted, and when cold add a little alcohol.

Yellow Stain.—Boil some fustic berries in alum water and darken the shade by adding powdered brazil, which must be boiled with the berries.

Brown, Russet, and Yellow Stain.—Boil a given amount of saffron in water until the colour is extracted, cut a quantity of annatto, putting it into urine, and mix the urine and extract, the proportion of each determining the shade; the greater the amount of annatto the darker the colour.

Stain for Riding Saddles, etc.—Saffron, three pennyworth; annatto, one pennyworth; soft soap, one pennyworth; and boiling water, 1 qt. Mix and let the whole stand until ready.

Reviver for Patent Leather.—Mix warm linseed oil 1 pt., and cream 1 pt. Apply with a sponge and polish with a soft flannel or rag.

Harness Composition.—(*a*) Glue, 4 oz.; gum arabic, 3 oz.; water, $\frac{3}{4}$ pt. Dissolve all by heat and add 6 oz. of treacle and 5 oz. of very finely powdered ivory black, and slowly evaporate with constant trituration until the composition is of the proper consistency when cold. When nearly cold, bottle and cork; if necessary the bottle can be warmed before use. (*b*) Mutton suet 2 oz., and pure beeswax 6 oz. Melt this mixture and then add finely powdered sugar candy, 6 oz.; soft soap, 2 oz.; lampblack, 2oz.; and finely powdered indigo, $\frac{1}{2}$ oz. When perfectly incorporated add $\frac{1}{4}$ pt. of oil of turpentine. Keep the composition in pots or tins. (*c*) Beeswax, 1 lb.; soft soap, 6 oz.; ivory black, $\frac{1}{4}$ lb.; Prussian blue (ground in), 1 oz.; linseed oil, 2 oz.; and oil of turpentine, $\frac{1}{2}$ pt. Mix well together and pot. Put a thin layer of one of the above on the leather and polish gently with a brush or rubber.

Harness Jet.—Molasses, 8 parts ; lampblack, 1 part ; sweet oil, 1 part ; gum arabic, 1 part ; isinglass, 1 part ; and water, 32 parts. Mix well together and add 1 pt. of turpentine. Apply the mixture with a sponge. If it is hard, place the bottle in hot water to soften the mixture. One ounce of spirit of wine can also be added when cool.

Waterproof Paste for Carriage Harness.—(*a*) Dissolve three sticks of black sealing wax in ½ pt. of alcohol, or dissolve lac in alcohol and colour with sufficient lampblack. (*b*) Melt 2 oz. of black resin in a glazed vessel over the fire, and then add 3 oz. of bees-wax, and as soon as all is melted remove from the fire and add ½ oz. of fine lampblack and ½ oz. of Prussian blue in powder. Stir all well and add enough turpentine to form a thin paste. Cool and apply with a sponge ; polish with a soft brush.

Oil for Farm and Team Harness.—Melt 3 lb. of pure tallow without letting it boil, and gently add 1 lb. of pure neatsfoot oil. Stir continually until cold, so that it will be perfectly mixed, otherwise the tallow will harden in lumps. To colour, add a little bone black or lampblack.

Brass Polishing Paste.—(*a*) Dissolve 3 parts of oxalic acid in 40 of water, with 100 of pumicestone powdered, 2 of oil of turpentine, 12 of soft soap, and 12 of any fat oil. (*b*) Beat equal weights of soft soap and rottenstone into a paste.

Plate Powder.—Take as much sulphate of iron as will fill a clay pipe, keep it on the fire for a quarter of an hour, and mix with powdered chalk.

Leather Preserver.—To preserve harness from the effect of ammonia in stables add a little glycerine to the oil employed.

Leather Cement.—(*a*) Dissolve guttapercha in bisulphate of carbon until of the consistency of treacle. Shave well the parts to be cemented and then spread a little cement evenly over them. Warm them for about half a minute, apply one against the other quickly, and press hard. Keep the bottle well corked and in a cool place. (*b*) Melt gutta-percha, 16 parts ; pure rubber, 4 parts ; yellow pitch, 2 parts ; shellac, 1 part ; and linseed oil, 2 parts, and apply as above. (*c*) Guttapercha, 1 lb. ; indiarubber, 4 oz. ; pitch, 1 oz. ; shellac, 1 oz. ; and linseed oil, 2 oz. Melt all together. The composition will harden when kept, and must be melted for use.

Bronzing for Leather.—A small amount of so-called insoluble aniline violet is dissolved in a little water and the solution brushed over the article ; it will dry quickly. If the result is not satisfactory, repeat the process.

To Gild Calf- or Sheepskin.—Wet the leather with some egg albumen, and, when dry, rub it with the hands damped with a little olive oil. Then apply the gold leaf, and pass a hot iron over it.

CHAPTER III.

STRAP MAKING AND STITCHING.

INSTRUCTIONS have been given on making threads and cutting leather, and now a simple exercise in stitching may be given in the putting together of small straps.

In making a box strap, cut with the round knife or plough from the back of the hide a good piece of leather, which should be 6 ft. long, and 1½ in. wide. Turn down about 2 in. of one end, cut a hole within about ¼ in. of the bend, and slit the part out with two cuts. Neatly shave down the point of the under piece with the round knife, and slant the other end a bit at each side to make a neat point to enter the buckle easily. Run the No. 1 edge tool along the sharp edges of the two sides and of the top and bottom ; this takes a small strip off, rounds the edges, and produces a better finish. If brown leather is used, wipe the edges with a damp sponge ; instead of pure water, a very thin solution of gum may be used. Then rub the edges with a rag or with a piece of brown paper until they are smooth and polished.

Adjust the screw-crease so that it marks a line about ⅛ in. inside the edges, warm the crease in a gas or candle flame, and rub it sharply all along the edge, guiding the crease mark on the strap by keeping the other side of the crease close up to the strap. Rub backwards and forwards until there is a deep polished mark on the strap, then mark across the point in the same way. This operation is known as creasing.

Two crease marks instead of one may be made after turning the thumb-screw to widen the points of the tool. Then cut a piece to form a loop about

O

$\frac{3}{4}$ in. wide and long enough to go round any part of the strap and make the ends meet. Edge this in the same way as the strap, polish with dye or water according to colour, and then crease.

For a running loop—one that runs loosely along the strap—the leather about $\frac{1}{2}$ in. longer than twice the width of the strap so as to overlap; shave one end on the top or grain side, and the other on the bottom or flesh side, so that when jointed the pieces will make an even thickness. Allow sufficient length for the two thicknesses of strap to go through, and mark where it is to overlap. Put one side of the doubled part in the clamp and stitch the side opposite, then reverse it and stitch the other; all running loops are made in this way except for very common straps, when the strips are simply brought end to end and a stitch or two is made from side of the doubled part in the clamp and stitch the buckle, put the tongue point of the latter through the hole made for it in the strap, and having marked the stitches eight or ten to the inch with the wheel-pricker on the short underpart, put the loop in between the two leathers deep enough for the stitches to hold firmly. Begin stitching by the buckle, putting a cross stitch downwards close to it. Stitch the straight row along the line of marks close to the buckle end, and have a stitch over; do not pull the thread up at the last stitch, but have both the ends underneath. Put two or three stitches in the centre at the point; here also the last stitch is downwards. Then begin stitching the other side. With the awl put the first hole close to the point and pull the thread through; make the next hole and put the other thread up and the top one down, and so on until the loop is reached. See that the loop is of the right length; if too long, cut a bit off. Put the point in between the two leathers, deep enough to catch the stitches, and put one or two stitches in the side next to the thread, slanting the awl a little outwards at the point. Put the upper needle through the loop so that the stitching will not be over it, and have a stitch or two in the side of the loop next to the worker; finish it up to the buckle. Put a cross stitch at the finish, the same as on the other side, and cut the thread. Put a loop stick of the same width and thickness as the strap through both loops, hammer them lightly to shape, and run the warm single crease along the edges. With a punch of the right size cut the required number of buckle holes, beginning about 5 in. from the point; make the distance between the holes a little more than the width of the strap. This is always the rule in punching single straps, such as garters, cart hame straps, dog muzzle straps, luggage straps, etc.

With regard to threading the needles, a properly made thread will have a nice point, which must be well waxed, and pulled between the finger and thumb two or three times to warm the wax so that it will stick. Pass the end through the eye of the needle for from 1 in. to 2 in., according to the fineness of the point, and holding the thread between the finger and the thumb of the left hand, spin it from you with the finger and thumb of the right hand. Afterwards draw the thread from the needle downwards at the point between the fingers so as to stick the point together well and make it smooth. Take care not to put it too far through the eye, or it will be too thick to go through the holes in the leather, while if it is not pulled through far enough the thread is liable to break. Be careful also to get needles of proper size; light thread for light work and strong thread for thick and heavy work; and a fine awl for fine thread, and a coarse and strong one for coarser thread, and so on.

In making the first hole in stitching, put the needle and thread up from underneath, and draw exactly half of the thread through. Put both

needles together and adjust the lengths of the two
portions of threads, and with the awl cut the second
hole, and stitch on. Always put the lower thread in
each hole first and draw it up about 3 in., then put
the other needle in and pull, always keeping the
thread from below lowest in the hole and the top
thread above. This is managed by pulling with the
upper hand a bit downwards, and with the hand at
the back of the work a bit upwards, thus tending
to keep the stitches in position. It may be noticed
that the hole is not round, but square and elon-
gated, and tends to help the manipulation of the
thread. Do not make a practice of pushing the awl
through the work at right angles to the face, but on
the slant ; the holes made by the wheel-pricker are
all on the slant. The above instructions also apply
to double-thread stitching, the kind mostly used in
harness making, though many things, such as the
straps, described above, are stitched with single
thread.

In back stitching, use one thread only ; begin by
putting it up from below ; put it down backwards in
the next hole to the one last made, and then pull it
tightly from below. There is not much difference
on the top side, but the stitches on the underside
are twice as long and cross each other in chain
fashion. Sometimes it is convenient to adopt this
method to use up waste points, etc., but such things
as traces, surcingles, waist-belts of web, saddle
girths, etc., are always stitched with single thread.
When repairing inferior harness, single thread can
sometimes be used without stitching backwards, by
doing what is called spotting, that is, always going
forward thus / / /, and only up and down forward,
the stitching appearing like spots, and not as an
unbroken chain.

Stitching with white lace in cart work is done in
this manner :—Put the holes on the upper side very
close together, but underneath ; the distance apart

may vary with the fineness of the work. This kind
of lace stitching is not much in vogue now, but it
looks well when across the end of breechings for
cart purposes, across the openings in cart cruppers,
etc. Lace needles and white skin will be necessary
for this work.

Riding bridles and almost all light brown work
are stitched single thread and backwards, with
either white linen, cotton, or silk beeswaxed, or
sometimes with yellow fine hemp thread beeswaxed.

Dog-collars are made in a similar way to the
straps previously mentioned, only the bend is made
a little longer underneath to allow sufficient lining
under the D to which the chain may be fastened.

Now that an insight into stitching has been obtained, the making of a waist-belt, Figs. 64 to 66,

Fig. 64.—Plain Waist Belt.

may be described. Cut the web so that its ends
meet together round the waist, and also cut pieces
of very thin belly brown leather or basil, for binding
the ends ; the latter should be about 1¼ in. wide, and
as long as the webbing is wide. Turn down the
binding along the centre lengthways, hammer it
lightly, and with the screw-crease mark along one
side ; then slip it in both sides of the ends of the
web, and either put a tack or two in it, to keep it
in place, or paste it down. Allow the paste to dry
before proceeding further. With the wheel pricker
along the crease mark the stitches, about ten to the
inch, then put the web in the clamp, the latter
being between the knees, and begin stitching at the
end farthest from the worker. Use one yellow or

white linen thread dressed with beeswax. On
coming to the end, cut the thread ; also cut the binding square with the edge of the web and stitch both
ends across at some distance from the edge.

Prepare the pieces to be put over the straps and
chapes ; cut them about 3 in. wide, and straight on
one side, making any fancy cut on the other ; two
of these pieces are wanted, one at each end. Then
cut the straps and chapes, and use light tinned
bridle buckles or brown covered buckles ⅞ in. wide.
With the compasses set to the right width, mark out
the straps on a close piece of brown shoulder or
belly leather. Cut the straps about 6 in. long and
the chapes about 2½ in. long. They may be cut in
long strips, being afterwards divided into the re-

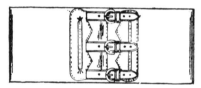

Fig. 65.—Fancy Waist Belt.

quired lengths. Form the strap, point one end a
little, and shave the other end to go under the pieces
above mentioned ; rub the edges either with water
or solution, and crease them about $\frac{1}{16}$ in. from the
edge. Then turn down the chapes for the buckles,
shave down both ends thin, and let the lower one
be a little shorter than the other. Punch a small
hole about ¼ in. from the end, cut the hole clean out
at the bend, and the piece is then ready for the
buckle.

Use thin brown waste to make the loops ; with the
compasses mark a width of this about ⅜ in., cut to
the right length ; then rub and crease the chapes.
Place the buckles in the leather, put in the loops
about half the width of the chape between the two

points of the chape, and close to the buckle, and
put two or three stitches in each end. The pieces
to hold up the belt firmly at the small of the back
should be about 1 in. wide. Rub the edges and
crease them as well as the two pieces for the front,
and mark stitches with the pricker in all of them
Three of these back supports will be needed, one
right across the centre of the belt and one on each
side, 3 in. from the centre at the top and slanting
inwards to within 1½ in. from the centre at the
bottom.

To determine which is the lower and which is the
upper side of the belt, bear in mind that, when being
worn, the buckles will be on the left-hand side and
the straps on the right. Put one of the 3-in. wide

Fig. 66.—Waist Belt with Pockets.

pieces flat on the belt, within about 3 in. of the end,
and either paste or tack it in its place from the
lower side. Put the straps in about ¾ in., all three
exactly alike, one in the centre, and the others one
on each side within ⅛ in. of the edge. Place the
other piece in the other end so near the edge that,
in putting the buckle chapes up to the loops under
the edge of the piece, the outer edge of the buckle
is flush with the end of the belt. Fasten the chapes
in position exactly opposite the straps in the other
end. Then backstitch the pieces in each end all
round, in the same way as the binding was treated.
Put a second row of stitches farther in than the first,
through the strap ends and through the end of the
chapes; leave about ½ in. between two rows, and
then lay on the back straps. Having pricked them,
stitch them in the same way as the others. If

pasted on, they can be kept more easily in their
place ; if pasting is not convenient, pencil on their
positions and keep them to the mark in stitching.

It is usual to put a piece of whalebone or good
hard cane inside these to keep them up ; thin the
bone or cane and push it in between the leather and
webbing from one end, and then stitch both ends
across. Put four or six holes in the straps and see
that they work easily in the loops, when the belt is
finished.

CHAPTER IV.

Some hints on looping will be given in this chapter. The loops are pieces of leather placed crosswise on all straps, which have buckles, to keep the point of the strap in its proper position. Sometimes also loops are employed merely to hold the straps in place, as for example in the case of shaft tugs. Loops are common to all kinds of straps in general and to harness and cart gear in particular.

Straps made to exact length with only one hole are cut long enough beyond the hole to go through the loop, and so give the work a neat finish. When the unused part of the strap varies considerably in length, the part run through the buckle being sometimes 6 in. long and sometimes 3 ft. long, a runner loop must be made to hold the point of the strap.

A runner is a loop which runs loosely along the strap to any required part. To make it, one end is laid on the other, overlapping it more or less according to the size of the loop, and the material is then stitched; it must be made loose enough for two thicknesses of the strap to pass easily.

The width of the loops, except in the case of pipe or box loops (defined later) must always be in proportion with that of the strap; the broader the strap, the broader is the loop. Taste and a due sense of proportion are necessary here as elsewhere. The loop must never be placed too near the buckle, particularly when the strap running through is stiff. Both ends of the loop should be placed so that they can be firmly stitched; the first end is stitched easily, but the second requires more practice. The ends of the loop should be made to meet in the centre of the strap, care being taken to catch it at the first stitch, for then it will not easily slip from its place. Two stitches on each side may suffice, but a very wide loop will need four or five on both sides of the ends. Slant the awl with every stitch, using the end of the awl to drive the loop a little out of the way.

It must not be taken for granted that a firm hold of the loop has been obtained until it is completely stitched; but make sure of the work at the first stitch, as otherwise it may be necessary to

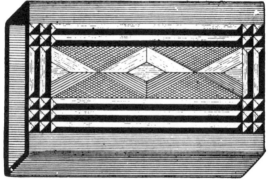

Fig. 67.—Box Creased Loop.

unstitch the work and do it again. Care must be taken also to ascertain that the loop is straight in its place at the first stitch, and that one side of the same end is not farther in than the other. A crooked loop spoils the appearance of the whole of the work.

Box loops (Figs. 67 to 70) or, as they are styled, pipe loops, are long loops like those on bridle cheeks, bearers of gig breechings, hame tugs, etc. To make them, measure the length and width of the loop required; for example, a bridle cheek $\frac{3}{4}$ in. wide and 8 in. long will need a loop $1\frac{3}{8}$ in. wide and $7\frac{1}{4}$ in. long.

Before making the loop, crease a line along the place to be stitched, about $\frac{1}{8}$ in. from the edge, and cut a groove along the line to about half the depth ; then open the groove well with the blunt point of a compass, passing it backwards and forwards. The stitching is done along this groove, which is finally closed.

The groove is necessary on account of the coarse stitches, about four to the inch, which are thus kept out of sight and prevented from being worn away by friction. Another method is to slit the leather about

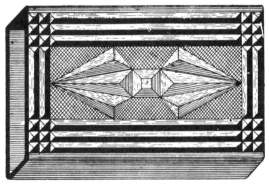

Fig. 68.—Box Creased Loops.

$\frac{3}{16}$ in. from the side ; then to raise it and stitch under it. When finished, apply a litle paste or gum to hold it firm, and smooth it down over the stitches.

Mark a line on the loop at about half the width of the strap and run a writing pen along it to keep the mark visible ; the loop, being of brown leather, will retain the mark of the ink, whereas the compass mark alone would be obliterated by damping. This mark is essential as a guide in fixing the loop and stitching. Mark the inside of the loop first time and the outer side the second. Damp the loop well first. Stitch the first side with black wax three-cord

thread about ¼ in. apart; this is an easy job, the
difficult point being the blind-stitching. Put the
loop between the winker. and the cheek as far as

Fig. 69.   Fig. 70.

Figs. 69 and 70.—Box Creased Loops.

the mark and put a tack in each end and one in the
centre.

The first stitches are simple enough, but when it
becomes impossible to see and reach the hole the

awl must be put right through the loop to the other thread about $\frac{1}{4}$ in. apart; this is an easy job, the side, the needle and thread being passed afterwards. Take the needles off both threads, and by means of a wire hook pull the inside thread out through the loop until it is 3 in. from the hole it entered. Now put the awl through the thread close to the loop, run the end of the other thread through for about 2 in., and pull it through the hole by the aid of the first thread to the side being stitched. Take out the end of the thread, put through and pull both extremities until tight, one in the groove and the other inside the loop. Repeat this operation with every stitch, but when about half-way through the loop, the thread inside must be run through to the other end, the work being continued from that end until finished.

Another method of making box loops, though it is not recommended, is as follows: Put an iron loopstick inside and fasten the loop down by driving small tacks into the groove, this groove being then closed by rubbing the edges well. A third method consists in running the threads through with a bristle, or twisting the threads together and thus running them through.

CHAPTER V.

CART HARNESS.

THE make and pattern of cart gear are very varied
in all parts of the kingdom, and there is often a
local name for each particular style; but the only
gear which can claim special favour is one that
combines proper strength with minimum weight.

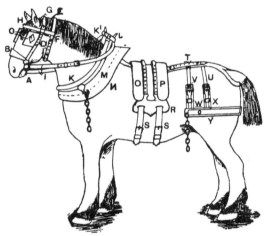

Fig. 71.—Horse in Cart Gear.

A typical shaft gear is shown by Fig. 71, in which
A is the bit ring, B the noseband, C winkers, D
cheeks, E ear-pieces, F throat-lash, G head-strap,
H forehead band, I reins, K collar forewale, K' hame
straps, L hame or jambles, M collar body and side-
piece, N collar draught, O forecart saddle housing,
P back housing, R cart saddle skirt, S girth and

girth straps, T crupper, U and V hip and loin straps,
W and X fore and aft breeching tugs, and Y breeching.

The ornaments used are brass buckles (Figs. 72 to

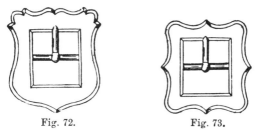

Fig. 72.   Fig. 73.

Figs. 72 and 73.—Scotch Brass Gear Buckles.

75) instead of tinned or japanned buckles, with brass
face-pieces (Figs. 76 to 78) on the bridle to hang on
the horse's forehead, brass bells for the bridle (Fig.
79), hame plates (Figs. 80 and 81) at the top of the
collar between the two points of the hames or
jambles, with a strap across from one hame point
to the other to hold it in position, brass squares,

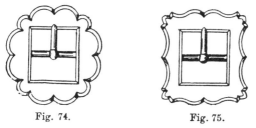

Fig. 74.   Fig. 75.

Figs. 74 and 75.—Scotch Brass Gear Buckles.

ovals (Fig. 82), octagons (Figs. 83 to 85), hearts
(Fig. 86) on bridle winker or saddle housing corners,
and brass beading instead of nails over the top of
the housing where attached to the tree. When

making gears this must be remembered. Other details of cart ornaments are shown in Figs. 87 to 92.

Cart and leading gear made according to the following directions will be useful anywhere, and when this method has been learned any other style can be made.

The winkers c (Fig. 71) must be prepared first; blocked winkers with fancy pattern raised against the eye are little used nowadays. Plain winkers are just as safe for the eyes if well made. Special winker leather must be obtained either from a middling in

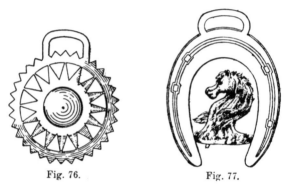

Fig. 76.   Fig. 77.

Figs. 76 and 77.—Brass Face-pieces.

stock, or, cut to pattern, from any currier or leather-seller.

Cut the pieces straight 7 in. by 7½ in., and mark three rows all round the long side and across one of the shorter sides with the race compass or racer, making the groove deep; edge them above and below with the edge tool and black the edges. After soaking them well in water, bend them along the centre of the longer width into something that is nearly, though not quite, a semicircle. Nail them down in any convenient way, with the raised part above, on a flat board and let them dry in this shape; drive in the nails near the edges only at the side that will be covered and stitched over with the cheek. They can be put to dry near a stove or fire.

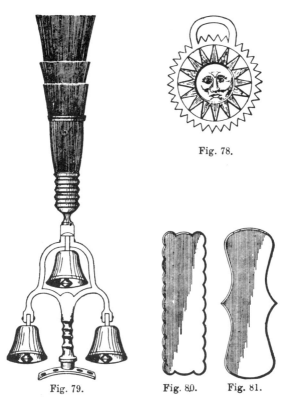

Fig. 78.

Fig. 79.

Fig. 80.   Fig. 81.

Fig. 78.—Brass Face-piece. Fig. 79.—Bells and Brush.
Figs. 80 and 81.—Brass Hame Plates.

Then run a big hot beveller round the edges and along the lines made until the groove looks deep and polished. Having two ¾-in. roller tinned buckles, or

P

brass Scotch buckles, cut two chapes to the same width. Chapes are pieces to hold on the buckles; the name is also applied to the part going round buckles on any length of strap. The chapes are

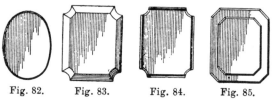

Fig. 82.   Fig. 83.   Fig. 84.   Fig. 85.

Fig. 82.—Brass Oval.   Figs. 83 to 85.—Brass Octagons.

made 3½ in. long and turned down 2 in. from one end; make the short end very thin and the other end slightly so, then point the piece. Cut a buckle hole at the bend, edge, crease, and prick for stitching; then put the chapes in the buckles and make the tops of these last flush with edge and front of winkers, working as follows:—

Tack the chape down in its place in the front corner where the creasing on the edges meets, and

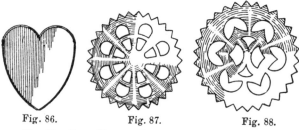

Fig. 86.   Fig. 87.   Fig. 88.

Fig. 86.—Brass Heart.   Figs. 87 and 88.—Brass Stars.

stitch. With tinned buckles put on a loop; Scotch buckles, as Figs. 72 to 75, do not need any; place the other chape and buckle on the corner of the other winker and stitch likewise, taking care to put it on the reverse corner to the other to make the winkers pair.

Now cut the cheeks D, or the pieces that run down

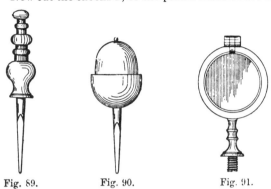

Fig. 89. Fig. 90. Fig. 91.

Figs. 89 and 90.—Brass Hame Knobs. Fig. 91.—
Brass Swing.

the side of the head, making them 2 ft. 2 in. by 1¼ in. ; turn them down so as to make both ends

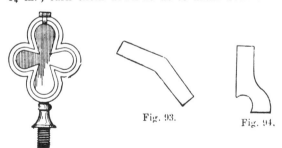

Fig. 92.

Fig. 93.

Fig. 94.

Fig. 92.—Brass Swing. Fig. 93.—Ear-piece. Fig. 94.—
Corner-piece.

meet underneath in the centre, and give the bends in each end a slight tap with the hammer. It is

better to draw in the underpart a little so as to have
the top somewhat longer, because as there is a bend
in the winker outwards the lower side should be a
little shorter. Cut a hole for the buckle in one end
and another in the centre of the bend, which is also
the centre of the strap, at the other end ; from this
hole cut straight out to each side and shave the
edges of the cut. Edge the cheek on the outside
only and race it along the top part with the race
compass ; the second race must be made close to the
other, care being taken not to run them into one
another. Make another line a little more than $\frac{1}{8}$ in.
from the last, blacken the edges and lines with
black dye, and rub them with a rag ; then prick the
two inner rows with the pricker, eight per inch, put
the buckle in its place and the bit ring A in the other
end, and stitch both ends of the cheek together.
There are two bit rings on each side, fastened
together by a small link ; one ring, that placed in
the cheek, is larger than the other. The smaller
ring must be kept for the bit after the completion
of the bridle. Both cheeks are made in the same
way, but the slit from the centre hole in the bend
must be reversed, otherwise the cheeks will not
pair.

The winkers C and cheeks D (Fig. 71) being ready,
cut the nose-band B about 2 ft. long and 2 in. wide ;
turn in both ends equally, leaving about 1 ft. 4 in
for the noseband ; shave the ends rather thin, and
make a punch-hole in the centre of the bend, then
slit it out straight from both holes on the same side,
and shave the sides of the slit.

Edge both sides of the nose-band where it is not
double, and make two rows along it with the race
compass, deepening and polishing them with the
hot beveller, after which prick the double row on
both sides from the bend to the lined part.

The nose-band is now ready for adjustment at the
proper time. The forehead band H (Fig. 71), or

front, must be cut about 2 ft. 3 in. long and 1½ in.
wide. Edge, crease, black, and rub it and pass a
hot beveller over the grooves. Cut the ear-pieces E
(see also Fig. 93) 1½ in. wide and 9 in. long, and
double and flatten the bend, shaving one end well.
Take a piece of any strap 1¼ in. wide, and put it in
the bend, close up ; mark how far the inner side runs
in the ear-piece, the 1½-in. strap being allowed to
run smooth in the opening between the line and the
bend. Mark two rows of pricking, eight per inch,
on each side from the cross-mark to the point or
end, having previously made a double row of creasing all along. Stitch from the cross line to the point
with three-cord thread ; stitch the cross line coarse,
about two stitches for one of the other stitches. Rub
the edges, making them even by cutting if necessary, then black and rub. Place the forehead band
H in position, and stitch it end to end with the ear-
pieces, and cut a small V-nick in the joint of each
end on the same side.

The object of the nick is to provide space for the
small projection in the tongue of the buckle when
put into position. Some harness-makers cut the end
of the ear-pieces, before joining them to the forehead, in a slightly slanting way in such a manner
that the end with the opening will turn up a little
when in place, but this is not essential. Moreover, if
the forehead band is to be covered with any kind of
fancy cloth or leather, this covering had better be
done before the ear-pieces are stitched, because the
work will be much easier than when the bridle is
completed. Cut the material, red American cloth,
leather, etc., double the width of the forehead, and
allow ½ in. more to go round the edges ; finally,
herring-bone-stitch underneath along the centre,
and stitch on the ear-pieces.

Corner-pieces (Fig. 94) are now required to support the nose-band and to join it and the cheek well
together when complete. They are in one single

piece near the bit ring corner, descending from
cheek to nose-band. To make the chin strap, cut it
1½ in. wide, one piece being made 6 in. long, leaving
2 in. of the original width, and then narrowing the
rest to ¾ in. with a rounded point. The other part
is made 12 in. long, and 2 in. of the original width is
preserved, the rest being narrowed to ¾ in. ; then
turn down a chape and make a hole for the buckle
in the narrow end, after which edge, crease, and
black both, then adjust buckle and loop.

To put the bridle together ready for stitching,
work as follows : With a ring at one end and a
buckle at the other, place the forehead band between the cheeks in such a way that the centre
where the forehead band and ear-pieces join may be
right under the centre of the buckle with the nick
against the tongue. Drive a tack on the inner side,
and put the nose-band in the same ring as the cheek
at the other end, with the slits made in the bends
upwards ; fix the corner-pieces one part in the cheek
and the other in the nose-band, sufficiently low to
catch when stitching the nose-band. The corner-
pieces must, of course, be placed between the two
leathers, both in the cheeks and nose-band : the
inner side of the corner-piece must follow the ring in
the cheek like a half-circle.

The outer part is supposed to have been previously edged and creased. The point of the slits in
the nose-band comes underneath the slits in the
cheeks on both sides in such a way that the edges in
the cheeks may cover and neatly overlap the edges
of the slit in the nose-band and catch them during
work of stitching the cheek. Both winkers are now
adjusted with buckles in the front corners, turned
upwards to meet each other ; place the winkers close
to the ear-pieces and forehead, making the outside
flush with the outer edge of the cheek. Tack down
the winkers, keeping the bend in shape as set after
drying ; thus there is an opening between the two

sides of the cheek from the end of the corner-piece to the bottom of the winker.

Cut a piece of leather as near as possible of the same thickness as the winkers and of the same width as the cheeks. Place it between the two sides of the cheek to fill the hollow, and so have a firm cheek all along; tack the piece down and see that it fits tight; there must be no looseness where it joins the winker and corner-piece.

The chin strap is now adjusted, the wide end of the short piece being placed inside the cheek under the centre filling for a distance of about $\frac{3}{4}$ in. and about $1\frac{1}{2}$ in. from the bottom ring. This is the right-hand side, taking a front view of the bridle. The other piece, with buckle, goes on the other side, and both are tacked down. When two small loops are to be placed on each side near the buckle at the top of the cheek they should be tacked down so that they may be stitched in with the cheek; but for a long loop, adjust beforehand on the cheek, by stitching the ends loosely together. Nail the first side of the long loop and clinch the nails underneath over a loop-stick, leaving this inside while nailing the other side in the same manner, partly running over the ear-piece E (Fig. 71) and forehead band H and partly over the winker.

Stitching may be begun on the near side at the ring, and continued up to the loop on the outside; then begin at the loop on the outside of the other cheek and stitch down to the ring. The outer row on the inner side of the first cheek and of the second cheek is now stitched. When stitching opposite the winkers on the inner line two stitches may be made instead of one by slipping a stitch between each; fine stitching is apt to cut the winkers, and they often fall off before being worn out; consequently slipping a stitch is a good method. A row must now be stitched on each side of the nose-piece in each end, then the inner rows of the cheek, and finally

the inner rows of the nose-band. Level the edges of
the cheeks and nose-band, scrape them, and black
the edges ; then rub them with tallow and bone.

Having creased and finished the loops, make two
basil pads as long as the distance from the buckle
to the bottom of the winkers. For a cheek of 1¼ in.,
cut the pads 1 in. wider than twice the width ; fold
them lengthwise so that the edges will meet in the
centre, and stitch the ends together with the basil
inside out. Now, after turning them inside out,
stitch the edges together like the ends with pointed
needle, thimble, and white linen thread. Run the
stitches from both ends and leave an opening about
1 in. long in the middle, through which ram in the
flock stuffing, but not too hard. Having stitched the
opening, place this side against the cheek of the
bridle under the winker, and as far as the buckle ;
choose three nails having large heads, run small
tufts of flock to the heads of the nails, and fasten
the pads down firmly to the cheek by driving a nail
in each end and one in the centre, taking care that
the points do not appear on the other side ; trim
the flock on the nails with the scissors.

The winker straps are made as follows : Cut a
strap 24 in. long and 1½ in. wide, then slit it exactly
in the centre for 13 in., making a punch hole at the
end of the slit ; shape the points of each slit to go
through the buckles on each winker, and make a
cross line 1½ in. from the end of the slit, marking it
deeply. At a distance of 1½ in. from this line make
a second line, and a third 1⅝ in., making them all
deep ; turn down the strap so that the centre of the
bend will be exactly at the last mark. Knock the
bend flat if the point runs beyond the end of the slit
after turning down ; cut some off and shave it down ;
edge it on both sides except where the parts overlap. Crease all along the edges, and make one or
two rows with the screw-race ; then black, rub, and
finish the creases. Leave an opening from the bend

to the next cross line, then put a piece of leather to fill the space between the cross line and the next to it and wide enough to be stitched through in working across ; then leave the space between the next two lines open, and stitch down the point of the bend from the end to the cross line. Stitch along the pricked part and along the cross lines, the stitches on the latter being twice as coarse as the straight lines.

There should now be two openings, one at the end and the other beyond the next stitched part ; that at the end is for the throat lash F (Fig. 71), and the other for the head strap G. Having rubbed the edges and finished, cut the head strap 1 ft. 10 in. long and 1¼ in. wide ; narrow the ends for the passage of the buckle, crease, black, and finish. Now cut the throat lash 3 ft. 8 in. long and 1¼ in. wide ; turn in 2 in. for the buckle at the best end and narrow the point to enter the buckle at the other end ; crease, black, finish, stitch on the buckle and loop, and then finish the loop.

A rein is now cut 5 ft. long and 1¼ in. wide for the off side, and another 2 ft. 4 in. long for the near side. Turn down the chape for the buckle in the weakest end of the short rein, and 3 in. at the best end of each to fasten to the ring at the bit ; then edge crease, finish, and stitch in the buckle and loop, also making a running loop on the short rein. Now mark four rows of stitching on the double part about to be stitched to the rings ; stitch the shortest part of the rein with the buckle to the ring hanging by a link from the cheek ring on the right hand when looking at the front of the bridle, then stitch the long rein to the ring on the other side. Make three punch holes on each side of the head strap, equidistant from the point and from each other, and then six holes in the throat lash, three in the slits of each winker strap, and nine in the long rein.

The bridle being ready for adjusting, place the

head strap up to its centre in the opening next to the slit in the winker strap ; then fasten each end of the head strap to the cheek buckles through the second holes. Now place the throat lash in the opening in the ear-piece on the off side, running it through the outer opening in the winker strap, down the opening in the other ear-piece, and then through the buckle at the other end.

Buckle the winker strap slits to the winker buckles, pass them through the loop, and buckle the rein in the sixth hole ; this completes the bridle. It it is to be polished, coated with jet, or ornamented, this must be done before putting the parts together.

Cut out all parts according to the dimensions given before beginning to stitch ; this is more workmanlike than cutting the parts as the work proceeds.

CHAPTER VI.

CART COLLARS.

IN making a cart collar (see Fig. 95) the first part to take in hand is the forewale A; the material for this must always be cut 8 in. longer than double the length of the collar when finished, to allow for shrinkage. Supposing the collar is to be 20 in., the leather must be cut 48 in. long. The leather can be cut from the bellies of gear hides, which come in handy when proper hide is not available. Cut it 7½ in. wide and make the length to meet requirements, and then damp it thoroughly. Stretch it on

Fig. 95.—Cart Collar without Side-piece.

a flat board by holding one edge with the hand and pulling the other edge with the pincers. Fold it over 2¾ in. all along; adjust the compass by rule to 2¼ in., and mark from the turned side, so that there will be ¼ in. of leather outside the mark on which to stitch the lining. On the opposite side there will be about 2 in. to draw in the body B and stitch the side-pieces. Tack along the mark here and there to keep it in its place.

Make a ten-strand thread, waxing it before and after twisting. This thread must be long enough to stitch all the length, and at least twice as long as ordinary thread. Use strong needles, making about three stitches to the inch; always leave the stitches slack, merely drawing them home, especially for about a foot on each side of the centre. Thus the forewale will bend easier in working round, and the stitches will tighten enough in stuffing. If the leather has an uneven grain, close here and open there, a piece of calico slack may be put inside the forewale A; take care that both sides of it are caught in stitching. This will help to keep it straight even when being stuffed.

The forewale is now ready for stuffing. Having a bundle of rye straw at hand, pull a few handfuls across the knee until the straw is straight; cut the ears off, and then cut the handful of straw in half, and again divide it with the collar knife until about 9 in. long. Place it neatly in a heap near the working-seat on the right-hand side, with the collar rod and mallet lying close by; there must also be a thick, solid block of wood placed on the firm ground in front of the worker's seat.

The collar-maker must now sit down and mark the centre of the leather with a nick or stitch. The forewale is now placed on the block, and the left foot laid on it, about 2½ in. from the centre, the folded part of the forewale being furthest. Put the other end on the right knee, and, holding the collar rod in the left hand point upwards with the head against the knee, take about half a dozen cut straws, and give them a half twist with both hands. Place the centre of the wisp in the nick of the collar rod and hold it firm with the right hand, the forewale being handled with the left. Put the straw in the forewale and press it down to where the foot is on the block, 2½ in. from the centre; beat the wisp well on the block with the mallet, leather as well, and then put another wisp in from the other end, taking care, when putting in the wisps, that they do not catch those already inside and drive them back ; to avoid this, beat well after each wisp has been put in, and when the iron reaches them raise the point a little. Continue to work in this way, putting in wisps alternately at each end until the forewale is as hard as it can be made. When the straw seems firm enough not to move, the wisps can be knocked in instead of being pushed by hand. See that they go into the centre of the straw. Push the straw and rod down the centre as far as possible ; turn the forewale and the rod with the point upwards, knocking the wisp in firmly against the collar block in front.

Repeat the process from the other side, and so on until all is as hard as a piece of wood. To shape and round the collar it must be continually turned round the knee, turning one side to the right and the other to the left hand. This operation is repeated after every one or two wisps are put inside ; take care that the forewale does not get straight. When turned enough, three or four wisps may be put into each side before changing ; but both sides must be shaped alike.

When approaching the top, shape it inwards a little in the same way as it was turned ; fill with straw until the top is quite firm, and then place it flat on the block, beating it well into shape with the round mallet, and holding it down with both knees at one end while shaping the other. Now damp it, and turn it backwards a little at the top on both sides ; stitch both points firmly together with waxed twine and collar needle and hand iron, cutting a little off when necessary to bring it to the right length.

To make a pipe collar, follow all the above directions and proceed as below. Obtain a piece of iron 9 in. long, $\frac{1}{2}$ in. in diameter, and having a sharp point ; in the middle it must be shaped half-round, with the points turning a little outwards and upwards. Put straw around it, tying it as tightly as

possible to within 2 in. from each point, and let the
straw at each end be of different lengths, a few
inches longer than the points of the iron, so that it
will splice well when stuffing is commenced. Add
straw, and tie again until the straw around the iron
is the right size, then place it in the centre of the
forewale, and stitch as tightly as possible, pulling
the stitches well ; make sure that it fills the forewale
well, but having passed this part, leave the stitches
slack. Now stitch from end to end, and stuff from
each end as in the other case, remembering to splice
them well where the iron ends ; the sharp point will
not be much of a hindrance. Finish as with the
other collar.

In making the body of the collar, cut the lining
to Fig. 96, and in any required size ; 14 in. is about
the average at the draught when the strain of pulling is on the collar. Cut a leather throat-piece
about 2 in. wide at the base, and widening out to
$3\frac{1}{2}$ in. in a sweep to the top. Stitch the narrowest
end of the lining, which is about $4\frac{1}{2}$ in. deep, to the
sweep of the throat-piece, turning in a little of the
linen or woollen check to make the part under the
stitches strong.

The narrowest part of the centre of the throat-
piece must now be tacked to the exact centre of the
collar by the stitches, putting the edge even with
the rim of leather running inside from the stitches.

Add another tack without pulling at the lining,
but leaving it rather slack from the centre, just at
the part where the forewale begins to run straight
upwards. Another tack is now placed within 5 in.
from the top on both sides, and the lining pulled
tightly to there from the bottom, the edges being
turned in all round.

Basil is employed for part of the lining in some
localities ; about 6 in. is measured from the top of
the collar. A pattern of the lining must be cut out
of brown paper, and then the basil can easily be

made to fit the shape of the linen lining; the basil must be whipped in with white linen thread and the linen turned in a little under the stitch, being rubbed flat afterwards. The lining being ready, make a four-cord thread of black-wax, cut it in two, and thread a harness needle with half. Having a suitable awl, whip the lining in all round through the leather rim above the stitches inside the fore-wale; the stitches of course must be inside, and should be well rubbed. Everything is now ready for making the body. Wax some strong twine or make a long beeswax thread, with four or five strands, 3½ yds. long, and have another about 1½ yd. long with six or seven strands.

Now a strong old strap, 1 ft. long, with a buckle is wanted; this is called the throat strap. The hand-iron, a medium-sized collar needle, seat-awl,

Fig. 96.—Cart Collar Lining.

scissors, and collar knife being placed near at hand, get a bundle of rye or wheat straw, preferably rye, and place it straight together by the side of the stool, with a sheet of drummed flock or basket of carded flock all within reach. As during work the legs are placed inside the collar, making it awkward for the operator to move, it is well to have handy a flat-headed mallet besides the collar mallet. Thread the collar needle with the shortest thread and hang it close by, and having pulled a big handful of straw from the bundle, sit down and put the right leg through the collar lining, the throat being placed upwards.

Place the middle of the handful of straw exactly

in the centre of the throat-piece, between it and the forewale; then take the needle and thread it, the handiron being in the right hand. Make a stitch from the centre of the throat over the straw to the big margin of leather on the other side; make another stitch at the same place to keep the throat in the centre, and more stitches, about $1\frac{1}{2}$ in. apart, for about 6 in. up one side from the middle towards the left. Fasten the thread and cut it, turn the collar with the other side facing you, and stitch it again on this side exactly like the first, taking great care to make both sides similar in shape and size.

Take the stuffing-stick and fix a wisp of straw on the point, beating it along to the centre of the straw and a little beyond the centre of the throat. Place a similar one on the opposite side, and so continue until the bottom part is firm and hard. Now lay it on the block, with the lining on the top, and pull the lining outwards as much as possible. Hold it by the knees, one on each side, and beat the throat outwards as far as possible with the round collar mallet. Put the throat strap round it and the forewale, pulling it as tightly as possible to keep it in position while making the other part. Now take a wisp of straw, large enough to fill the body of the collar pretty well, cut it square at one end, so as to get almost the full bulk at the section, and see that it is long enough to go the full length of the collar body.

Wrap a piece of hemp five or six times round the part just cut, making it firm for about 6 in. along, and somewhat pointed. Run the long thread through the needle, and put both knees through the collar with the lining towards you. Open the lining flat as it lies on the knee and raise the straw issuing from the throat so as not to be in the way; then cut a piece of drummed flock to the same size as the lining, to come within an inch or so of the edge. Take care to place it level in all parts, reaching well down towards the throat and forewale. Cut another handful of straw and put it over the flock opposite the draught and as near as possible to the forewale.

Open the straw running from the throat in the centre, and put the long tied wisp inside, ramming it as near as possible to the throat; pull the lining over the straw from the top to the bottom, and then pass the seat-awl through the lining and leather to fasten the top. Turn the collar the other way about, put both legs in again, and begin to draw in the lining where the bottom stitching left off.

Now lace it from bottom to top, running the needle from lining to leather and leather to lining till finished. Draw the stitches as tightly as possible, pulling each to tighten the other, as in lacing a boot. So far, the collar is neither hard enough nor shapely enough; the straw must therefore be beaten down between the lacing. To do this, the mallet must be grasped round the handle close to the head, and the straw struck as hard as possible with the handle.

Having improved the shape of the collar, begin to tighten the lacing again from end to end, keeping the desired shape constantly in mind. If the collar is not firm enough, begin work at the bottom, ramming down some wisps towards the throat from between the stitches, and continue this until the draught is reached, shaping as well as stuffing. It may be hardened, from the draught up to the top, by driving some wisps from the extreme top, and shaped by tightening or slackening the lacing, as the work demands.

Great attention must be given to shaping, for a well-shaped body is very important from the point of view of both utility and appearance; it should be graceful and rounded at the bottom and somewhat flat at the draught, gradually growing narrow towards the top. At the extreme tip, however, the collar should be rather full, with extra flock to ease the neck. Work in the same manner with the other side, using as nearly as possible the same amount of flock and straw ; take care to obtain the same shape and size.

If any lumps can be felt in the flock, loosen and level it with the seat-awl by stuffing it off or on as required ; beat it slightly all round to give it a smooth appearance. Cut the straw at the top, turning the lining down out of the way ; beginning close to the forewale, cut it slanting upwards a little towards the back. Make two or three long stitches in each side through the lining on both sides and the straw to pull the linings together. Then stitch together the two sides, drawing the lining over the outer side ; run the stitches through from side to side and cut the spare lining at the top ; this completes the work. Trim the points of the forewale previously stitched, and cut them into a neat point, which should be neither long nor sharp.

Having cut a piece of soft leather, form it into a cap reaching low enough to cover the stitches that join the point on each side ; stitch the front with a welt between the edges long enough to reach the back under the forewale, so that a stitch can be put through it there when stitching the cap. This last must be long enough to come over the point of the body behind ; damp the cap and put it in its place. Take a lace and the collar needle, draw it down tightly into the hollow between the body and the forewale, then stitch through it, burying the welt underneath to fasten the cap in front by a stitch.

The other part must be stitched with a lace all round over the top of the body ; make the point of the forewale very prominent to hold the hame strap.

Two 1½-in. straps, 18 in. long, must now be cut ; race the edges and blacken them, point them for the buckle, and punch four holes in each, and another hole in each corner at the opposite end and one in the centre 2½ in. from the end. The four holes in the forepart are to fasten the buckles to the crupper or cart-saddle and the others to stitch to the collar. Place one on each side of the collar down to the forewale 5 in. from the top. Fasten them with lace by stitching through the hollow between the forewale and collar body, putting two stitches through and through to the other side ; then send the collar needle in the direction of the other hole in the centre of the strap, and make one stitch from each side of the strap through this hole ; fasten the lace well and cut it.

Pieces of leather of the shape shown by Fig. 97 are now required to cover the side of the body. The pattern can be cut out of brown paper according to the made body and kept for other work. Cut the

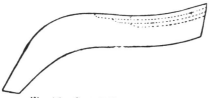

Fig. 97.—Cart Collar Side-piece.

paper close to the rim all round to cover the body full in all parts outside, but a little wider and pointed at the top to keep rain-water off and give a good appearance. Cut one side only at a time, and, as the two sides join in the centre at the top and bottom, cut the top slanting downwards towards the forewale to the same shape as the body, and line the top for about 1 ft. downwards on each side with firm leather ; shave it on the inner side and bottom.

The pieces need not be so wide as the side-piece ; half its width or a little more will do. Make three rows of stitching, and join them together at the lower part along the lined part ; the distance between the rows should be about 1 in., with nine

stitches per inch. Rub the side-pieces and blacken
them; crease two rows with a screw-crease all
round the outer side not stitched. When cutting,
take care to have the best part under draught.
Join the two sides together at the top with stitch
after stitch from one to the other, thus drawing
them close end to end.

Crease and prick a 1¼-in. piece of leather, cutting
it to the same length as the joint, and thinning it
towards the collar end; the other outer end must
be shaped to the point of the joint. Now tack the
piece and stitch, keeping it quite over the centre of
the joint, and making the stitches exactly at the
same distance on both sides; it is well to put a bit
of thin lining underneath the stitches. Damp the
side-pieces well in water, and have a long lace ready
to run the side-piece in; damp and grease it, and
have it long enough to go all round the collar if
possible, with sufficient to spare for fastening.

Take out the side-pieces, beat the water from the
leather, and fasten the pieces to the centre on top
with a big strong awl or seat-awl. Pull them together as tightly as possible from top to bottom;
let them overlap about 3 in. at the bottom, shave
the leather down a little here, and fix the pieces in
place with the awl. Then see that they are in the
right position, not too near nor too far from the
forewale; put an awl on each side near the draught
to keep them in position there.

Begin lacing them in at the throat-piece, making
the stitches 2 in. or 2½ in. apart, at about the same
distance from the edge all round; be sure to catch
the lining underneath with each stitch. Then take
another long lace and pull it in at the throat; draw
it close to the forewale all round till the point of
commencement is reached, running a stitch over the
edge of the side-piece, and catching the leather
everywhere by the forewale; the stitches should be
about 1½ in. apart.

Some harness makers run a piece of leather about 13 in. under the draught, fasten it with a few stitches to the collar body in the lower part, and spot with lace to the side-piece all round the top part; coarse flock, or anything which will keep the chains from the horse's shoulder when pulling, being employed for stuffing; but this will not be necessary if the body of the collar is well made. Others make the side-piece without lining, using instead a round piece of leather with canes round the rim, covering them with leather stitched on both sides to protect the shoulders and collar from wet. They are stitched with lace to the collar.

Experience, however, has demonstrated that neither the horse nor the collar is any the worse without such a device. In other localities the housing and side-piece are cut in one piece—a poor imitation of a Scotch collar—and stiffened all round with cane; this involves a great waste of leather, and is unnecessary.

CHAPTER VII.

CART SADDLES, REINS, ETC.

The saddle is another important part of cart harness. To make a saddle for a horse about 15½ hands high will need a tree (Fig. 98) measuring 14 in. across the board right through the centre. It may have an iron plate for the back chain covering entirely the top of the tree, or only partially covering it, but with plates at the point and one in the centre of the groove. The plate can be removed from the first kind of tree when making the saddle, but the partial plates are permanently riveted with an iron pin. If the board across the tree is very long it may be sawn off at each end, but never at one end only. Saw off the same length at each end; a 1-ft. board is always long enough.

The tree can be obtained also in the pattern required for nailing housings (leather covers) on the bridge of the tree at the top, or with a projection running along both sides lower down for nailing. If the housings are nailed at the side, the width need not be so great as when nailed on the top; the part of the tree above must be covered with thin leather, nailed under the housing at the lower edge, damped and rubbed down close to the tree and nailed at the very top.

The panel (Fig. 99) can be made when the tree is ready. From the middle of each side cut the panel-back about ½ in. longer than the boards and 2 in. wider than the central width of the board. Leave the space between the middle lines of stitches about 2 in. wider in front than at the back to prevent the shoulder-bone of the horse being caught when carrying a weight. Cut both sides alike, reversing the pattern to pair them. Then whip them together

along the centre and shorten the panel-back in front
by cutting from the point, slanting inwards and
upwards in the fore part.

When the sides are joined, rub the stitches flat
and put pieces of leather, about 3 in. square, at
each end at the positions of the boards when the
panel is in position ; mark the back of the panel on
the spot to which the boards reach and then adjust
the pieces of leather, stitching them across, the
marks being nailed as nearly as possible in the
centre of the board. These pieces are for nailing
the panel in place when completed.

The panel must now be laid flat on the flannel
check or linen lining, which is cut about ½ in. larger
than the back. As the panel is wider in front, the
lining must be slit in the centre of the front as far

Fig. 98.—Cart Saddle Tree.

as the point where the panel begins to widen ; then
cut a piece of the same material of the necessary
width in front and narrowing towards the back.
Whip this piece to the lining, turning down the
edges of both while stitching. The extra ½ in.
beyond the size of the back is now turned in, and a
coarse stitch run all round.

The leather basil facing for the panel is now cut
about 2¾ in. wide, then whipped in all round the
lining, being joined and stitched in the centre of
each side. Rub the stitches flat, and cut the lining
down round the back to about 2 in. wide, from the
centre on each side. Then, when stuffed, the panel
will be somewhat thicker in the front than at the
back, and will not sink down and press on the
shoulder-bones under a load. Now cut about 1¼ in.

from the front part of the facing opposite the widening piece stitched to the lining; cut it about 4½ in.
long, gradually slanting it out towards the ends,
and cut about 2 in. at the back in a similar style.
Tack the facing round the back, centre to centre,
and both inside out; run it with coarse stitches,
about three to the inch, keeping the edges together;
it can be either spotted or stitched double. Now
well damp the back of the panel and the basil facing with sponge and water.

With scissors cut an opening in the lining exactly
in the centre of the panel and just large enough to
allow it to be turned inside out; the cut must run
along the panel, not across. This opening can be
utilised for stuffing, but if it is necessary to make
the cut longer than is required for this, let the opening be made a little shorter at each end so that the
slit will be in the centre of the length. Put a line
on each side of the stitches in the joining of the
back, about 1½ in. on each side at the back, and then
gradually widen from halfway to the front until it
is about 2¼ in. on each side of the stitches. Tack the
lining underneath, making it tight and flat between
the two lines and keep the slit in the centre, so as
to have the lining distributed equally on both sides
of the centre of the joining in the back.

Now take a wisp of straw, about 9 in. long, and
wrap it round with hemp, making it firm and slightly
thicker than a finger; tie the centre of the wisp
for about 5 in. and place its centre against that of
the panel in the gullet at the front, and draw the
facing tight for the distance between the two lines
just made. Stitch it from above tightly round the
wisp with a spot stitch to keep the gullet open and
from the shoulder.

The lining must now be spot-stitched on the back
along the two lines which have been marked, the
needle being passed up and down through both.
Leave an opening of the same length as the slit, and

carry the thread on the leather si͘ n end to end
of the slit so that the panel can be stuffed through.

To stuff the panel, place it on the bench in front,
with the lining uppermost. Drive a stout clout nail
with a head into each corner, and one into each end
of the stitches in the side opposite the outer corners,
the other side of the panel being allowed to hang
over the bench, and the slit in the lining running
along the edge of the bench. Having a heap of
straw cut to the same length as the panel close by,
and grasping the stuffing stick in the right hand, lay
a wisp across the front and push it to its position
with the stick. Lay another across the back, and
work it through the hole with the fingers ; then use
the stick to drive it against the facing inside.

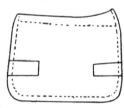

Fig. 99.—Cart Saddle Panel.

A third wisp must now be placed in the side
farthest from the operator, and worked into place
with the right hand and stick, the left hand being
employed to keep the straw in position. Wisp after
wisp can now be added along the front until the
side is filled, but no more straw is put in the ends
after the first wisp.

Beat the panel level and flat with the collar
mallet, and run a piece of leather of the same width
as the opening and about 9 in. long inside the slit
for about half the length between the straw and the
lining ; this will clear the opening for the flock.
Have a hamper full of carded flock, and put a thick,
even layer over the straw, and press it down with a

stick or seat iron to the edges and corners, making it as smooth as possible ; then beat it again with the mallet, and use a seat awl to level the surface, feeling for lumps with the left hand. Work in the same way on the other side to complete the panel.

A dock to fasten the crupper to the saddle is placed across from board to board at the back. Two 1¾-in. tinned rings are needed, and the leather must be cut 1½ in. wide, and doubled to reach on each side as far as half the width of the board. It is better to make the dock in four thicknesses, running double through the rings. Insert these, one at each end, and drive a clout nail through each extremity and clinch it on a piece of iron ; put one or two nails in the centre, the points being shaved to make a good joint in the leather. Spot it with white lace, or stitch it coarse with strong thread, a row on each side. Trim the edges, and black and rub it with tallow.

Take two fine-pointed staples, and, with the dock in its place, mark the position with the points of the staples. Make holes for these with a gimlet half-way between the tree and the end of the board. Run the staples through the ring and knock them down in the holes until about ¾ in. shows on the other side ; turn the points and knock them against the iron level with the board, turning in the tips a little to enter the board. The dock must be slack, with at least the same sweep from board to board as there is in the tree. Some harness makers nail to the centre of the tree a 2-in. strap, about 10 in. long, for fastening the crupper. This device can be adopted instead of the dock, and a buckle put on the crupper ; with a dock the crupper goes round it.

The flaps to protect the horse's side from the back trace reach from end to end of the boards on each side of the saddle. Cut them 9 in. deep more or less, according to needs, making them ½ in. longer at each end at the top than the boards. Swell them out at the sides from the top and round the corners at the bottom, and cut a fancy point in the centre of the lower side.

Now hold them against the board with the same length exactly over each end, and mark the width of the tree on both sides on the flaps. At the marks cut a slit about $\frac{3}{4}$ in. deep towards the near edge, and turn the leather inwards between the cuts in the centre. Knock it down between the slits, and cut a hole to admit the $1\frac{1}{2}$-in. girth or strap at about the middle of the flap on each side just opposite the junction of the boards and the tree; as there will be two girths, a strap will run from each end of the board. Edge the flaps and holes all round on both sides, and make two or three rows round them with the race compass; finish them with a hot iron after having blacked the edges. Reverse the cuts in cutting the flap to catch at the top on the boards, as these may not be the same length, back and front, over the trees, and there may be a difference in the positions of the holes for the girth.

The girths and straps must be made from good leather, the fore girth being 4 ft. 10 in. and the hind 5 ft. 2 in. long, an allowance of 2 in. being made to turn down for the chape. The fore strap must be 1 ft. 6 in. long and the hind 1 ft. 8 in.; the width of girth and straps is $1\frac{1}{4}$ in. to $1\frac{3}{4}$ in. Edge the girths along both sides, and turn down the chapes and shape the points of the straps. Leave the best end of each girth and strap for nailing to the tree; put two rows along the edge with a race compass and bevel with a hot iron. Stitch the buckles and make the loops, adding two running loops; finish the loops with a loop-stick, and then crease them. Black the edges before using a hot beveller and cut four or five holes in the straps.

Now take the flaps and place the slit in the centre opposite the tree, and turn down the part below, thus having about an inch of leather on the board

under the slit. Drive a saddler's tack in each end
of the board ; do this gently to avoid splitting. Put
the shorter strap in front and the longer behind into
the flap hole from above so as to bring the square
end out at the top between the flap and the board.
Adjust both in the same manner, and put four or
five nails along the edge of the flap and board,
taking care to drive two of them through the straps
and flap ; finally put another nail in the centre of
the strap above the edge of the flap. Add the girths
on the other side in the same way, and see that the
straps are on the near side and the girths on the
off, and that the longer of each set is behind.

It is not difficult to determine which is the front
of the tree because in this part the boards rise a
little and converge towards each other. Sometimes,
instead of cutting a hole, a leather loop is stitched
on the flap with an opening wide enough to admit
straps and girths.

The girths, flaps, and dock are now put in position. Then place the front of the panel against that
of the tree, and press it in the centre just against
the top of the tree. Having the pieces to be nailed
on the centre of the board stitched to the panel,
fasten them to this part with four or five small
tacks, making sure that the panel lies close. Deal
with the hind part of the panel in the same manner.
Some harness makers always run a piece of lace
from the centre of the panel to the centre of the
tree in front, where it is nailed close to the tree.

The next operation is to cut the housings (Figs
100 and 101) or cover for the saddle top ; the width
must be 5 in. to 7 in., and the length sufficient to
reach from end to end over the tree by the side of
the groove on each side. The length can be measured with string. Do not cut the ends square to
the measurement, but bulge and round them so that
they are 3 in. more along the centre. Narrow the
front housing (Fig. 101) slightly for about 10 in. in

the centre so that it will rise there, and cut the part
to be nailed at the back as before, namely about
6 in. wide on each side from the centre, narrowing to
a sharp point at the lower end. The back housing
(Fig. 100) being straight on the outside, begin to
cut on the side about to be nailed from the corners
upwards, narrowing an inch from the corner until
it comes to a point in the middle. This improves
the appearance and lifts the front from the shoulder,
the back being thus made to match the entire piece.
Make three rows around the edges with a race compass and run the lines deep with a beveller.

A brass oval or octagon may be placed on each
corner of the housings at equal distances from the
edge and end. Put these pieces in position and nail
them to the tree through the centre; then tighten

Fig. 100.—Cart Saddle Hind Housing.

them at each end with the seat awl or other strong
awl, pulling down hard from the centre and driving
in a nail on each side while tightening. Drive nails
all along about 2 in. apart, being careful to make
the edge of the housing quite flush with the edge of
the tree so as to obtain the proper shape. The nails
can then be covered with brass beading $\frac{7}{8}$ in. wide,
or a welt of the same width may be nailed down
with brass or japanned head nails. Seven or eight
stitches, nine per inch, must now be put in the
lower part of the housing at the four ends through
the flap, and will thus bind all neatly and firmly.

For the cart-saddle crupper, the body must be
cut 2 ft. 6 in. or 2 ft. 8 in. long and $3\frac{1}{2}$ in. to 4 in.
wide; cut a semicircle in the centre from the weak
end, a point about $\frac{3}{4}$ in. wide being left at each side

of the semicircle, and then cut an 8-in. piece to line
with this end. Next cut a piece of leather $\frac{7}{8}$ in. wide
and $8\frac{1}{2}$ in. long, shaving the ends thin. Stitch it
with the edges together so as to make it round to
within $1\frac{1}{2}$ in. from each end. A cord or bit of leather
may be placed in the centre to reinforce this; then
rub it round and blacken it, and flatten both ends
out with a hammer; this is for hanging the saddle
on a peg.

The body that was cut first must now be pointed
at the square end, the width being reduced to about
2 in., the same cut being made on each side. Race
it along the sides and ends, then edge, black, and
run a hot iron over the creases. Now prick it,
about nine per inch, as far as the termination of the
lining from the semicircle.

The ends of the round piece lately made are
brought together and put under the points, one on
each side; place the lining under them, and stitch it
all round and across the points from side to side
with a three-cord black wax thread, and trim, black,
and rub the edges. Cut the lay 1 in. narrower than
the body and 3 ft. long; turn it in 10 in. at the strong
end and beat it flat. Turn it down 2 in. at the other
end, and cut it slanting down to $1\frac{1}{2}$ in. wide for a
buckle of the same width; cut a hole for the buckle
and run a line across the broad end 2 in. from the
point, another in the same direction $\frac{1}{4}$ in. from the
end of the bend underneath, and a third $2\frac{1}{2}$ in. from
this part towards the buckle. Edge only the top,
just reaching over the end of the broad bend; then
make two lines of creasing and run a hot iron over
them.

Inner lines are made about $\frac{1}{4}$ in. from the innermost line, from the first cross line to the second, and
from the third to the buckle. Two spaces are left
for openings for the hip straps, one in the bend and
the other in the middle; black and prick the parts
to be stitched, four lines between the two openings

and four lines from the other side of the second opening in the direction of the buckle. Fix the buckle in place and lay it flat in the centre of the body, the extremity of the broad end of the lay reaching the edge of the semicircle ; tack it down and stitch, keeping it well in position while working. Stitch coarse or spot along the three marked lines near the openings. The body is now finished.

A pad or panel is next needed. Cut some thick felt to the same width as the body, and long enough to reach from the point of the semicircle to 2 in. beyond the cross line near the buckle ; cover it with basil, and coarse-stitch it with a pointed needle along the centre. Turn the ends neatly over the felt and fasten ; then with stitches put it in place next the crupper body. Tack down each end, and run

Fig. 101.—Cart Saddle Front Housing.

four or five stitches here and there through the body and panel ; make sure that the work is well secured at each corner. Cut a hole through the body exactly opposite the buckle 1½ in. wide and broad enough to pass the strap ; this is made 9 in. long, pointing one end and shaving the other. Crease and black it, and stitch the shaved end against the narrowed end of the body. When finished and punched, this will go round the dock in the saddle and fasten to the buckle on the lay, running down through the hole made in the body.

Sometimes, instead of the opening in the bend, an iron dee is employed for the crupper, and the hip straps are fastened thereto, a strap about 20 in. long being used on each side of the dee. This is a matter of taste, but care must be taken that the measurement from the second cross line to the extreme end of the dee, when the lay is turned down, equals what it would be to the extreme end of the bend.

To make the breeching, cut the body, if possible, 7 ft. 4 in. long and about 4 in. wide. Turn it down to 4 ft. 10 in. long, the strong end less than the weak; edge and black, and crease two rows along the edges. Shave the ends, and mark a cross line about 1½ in. from the centre of the bend on both sides and at each end of the body.

Now cut some pieces 1 ft. long for lining between the two marks in the bend and shave their ends; bend them flesh outwards, leaving one end about 1 in. shorter than the other; otherwise it will be bulky when inside the breeching. Put it inside the bend after pricking the second row along the part having the leather doubled, and across the bend from one cross line to the other. When this lining has been tacked in the bend, stitch from row to row; this is the eye for the bridgeband pin used for fastening the chain. Trim the edges of the bend, blacken, and rub them with tallow and a bone; then tack down the double part as far as it goes. If, after being lined, the bend is rather hard, beat it with a wooden mallet and stitch the double part along both the ends and sides; then trim, black, and rub the edges.

The body is now ready for the lay, which must be of the same length and 1 in. narrower; edge, crease, and black it all along, and make another line with the compass ¼ in. from the inner line of the crease. Prick the two innermost lines nine to the inch, and turn down the lay at both ends to the same extent as the body. Shave the ends and tack the lay in the centre of the body, the light end of the lay being placed against the heavy end of the body and inversely; pull it down close over the ends of the body and tack it in place.

Stitch all along the pricked part from end to end

to the cross lines, and spot or stitch cross lines, making the stitching bulge inwards at the middle to the extent of about 1 in. Make a hole with a large punch exactly in the centre where the stitches bulge inwards, and then, holding the round knife firmly in the hand, cut out straight at each side to remove a piece that allows the chain to enter and catch the pin. Cut another hole in the centre 1 ft. 4 in. from the ends by punching a hole 1½ in. farther on ; then remove the part between the holes by two cuts, allowing space for the 1½-in. tug to go through.

Prepare the two bridgeband pins and four 1½-in. buckles to match those on the saddle and crupper. The pins have a dee at one end, and at the other a screw-thread with nut and washer to fix it in place. Two hind tugs 1 ft. 8 in. long must be cut from the leather, 6 in. being turned down at each end to meet the point ; make a buckle hole in the weak end of each, and black, crease, and rub them. Prick the tugs from where the chapes leave the bridgeband to the loop or to the part which will have the loop. Place the strong end in the hole in the centre of the bridgeband from underneath, so that the joint will be in the front under the loop, and put a buckle on the other end. Make a loop about 2½ in. long and sufficiently wide to go round the two thicknesses of the strap. Make two rows of creasing, one at each end, and stitch the sides loosely together ; then put the loop on the tug and stitch the end of the tug. Pull the loop over the joint and keep this and the stitches out of sight in the centre of the strap.

A safe must now be cut sufficiently long to run from the body of the bridgeband to an inch beyond the end of the buckle at the top and ½ in. wider on each side of the tug. Narrow the bottom to the width of the tug and shave it : round the other end, putting a loop on its extreme point in the centre, both the ends meeting. Stitch it for about 1½ in. along both sides through the safe ; put the 1½-in.

R

loop-stick in it, and black, crease, and finish. In the next place put the 1½-in. iron loop-stick in the long loop on the tug and beat it gently until it is quite flat and square. Fasten it securely from underneath with about five nails on each side, clinching them against the iron loop-stick inside. Crease this again with a hot iron and put a fancy stamp with the maker's name or a neat creasing in the centre. Then put the safes in their places, fixing the loops on their ends just against the buckle at the top, and stitch the safe along the part pricked from the loop to the body of the bridgeband. Make two or four rows and strong cross-stitch the tug at the bottom. Now run a row of stitches across the top of the tug through the safe between the buckle and the loop.

Make both the tugs alike, and to prepare the tugs for the pins the loop is made as before, but it must be shorter because the tug with the dee-pin should have the same length from the body of the bridgeband as the hind tugs. Join the ends and make the safes similar, creasing the loops to a similar pattern ; in fastening the safe to the tug, however, stitch a row only across the bottom and top of the tug, as it will be too short for more. Two loin straps 3 ft. 8 in. long by 1½ in. wide must be cut to fasten to the tugs and pass through openings in the crupper ; point at each end, crease double at each side, edge, black, pass a hot iron along the creases, and make six or seven holes in each end to complete them.

The parts next to be made are a leading rein, a 1-in. strap with a billet and buckle at one end and a chain with a spring hook, called a cheek, at the other. Black and crease the rein, and then stitch on the buckles, billet, and chain.

The billet is the piece of leather stitched under or behind the buckle for fastening this particular end to any object. Make the billet 1 ft. long. The full length of the rein must be about 8 ft. 6 in. ; the chain by which it is fastened to the horse's mouth is put through the near ring and secured with a spring hook to the opposite ring. The billet end is fastened to the crupper of the leader or the shaft horse. This is very useful when horses take fright, as the driver may then be able to catch the rein and pull them in, though unable to reach their heads.

The 1¼-in. hame straps are simple straps with a buckle and loop at one extremity, the other end being pointed with holes. Their length is about 1 ft. 8 in.; they are employed to secure the hames at the top.

Some harness-makers, for the purpose of ornament, make, for cart horses, a breast-plate which extends from the bottom of the hames and collar to the fore girth of the saddle or to the belly-band of a leader. It is made of leather, bound with red or yellow leather or American cloth, and the sides are scalloped, and have two or three face-pieces placed opposite the swell in the scallop, these face-pieces being a litle narrower than the leather. A narrow strap runs from underneath through a hole, catching a loop at the top of the face-piece, and then down through another hole, and so on to the next.

When the strap is run all along, fasten the end at the bottom, the other extremity being secured by the billet, and buckle to the hames at the top. Run a strap about 2 ft. long from the base of this scalloped part, and furnish it with a buckle. Put it on the reverse way and bring the other end through the buckle, fastening it thereto; stitch the end to the bottom of the scalloped part, the other end being furnished with a loop through which the girth may pass. The part underneath the face-pieces may, before being bound, be covered with coloured leather to give it a good appearance.

Now cut the cart belly-band 3 in. wide and 3 ft. 8 in. long; narrow it down to 2 in. along a length of 6 in. at both ends, and, without bending the band, cut a buckle hole about 3 in. from the point. Make two billets 2 ft. 2 in. long and 2 in. wide, and edge, crease, and black everything. Two loops must also be made about 1¾ in. wide. Prick the billet, six per inch, for about 6 in. from the shaved end, and adjust the buckle and billet, making the latter lap over the buckle for 3 in. lower down. Place the loop about 1 in. from the buckle, tack all down, and stitch with a six-cord black wax thread, twice waxed; then make two or three stitches in the centre of each end. Having opened and creased the loops, make four holes in the billets; finally, give them a coat of Harris's liquid or composition.

CHAPTER VIII.

FORE GEAR OR LEADER HARNESS.

THE bridle and collar for a fore gear or leader harness must be made in the way described in the previous chapters, and will require no further explanation here.

The back-band A (Fig. 102), long crupper F, and belly-band D, still need description, however. Cut the crupper from good leather 3 ft. 8 in. long and 5 in. wide, and make a split 9 in. long at the light end and another, 7 in. long, at the tail end, leaving the points of the slits in front of the full width, merely cutting a little out of the corners. Narrow the points at the tail end gradually to about 1½ in., and cut a little from the sides of each slit. A piece of leather must be cut to line a foot or so of the tail end, and a piece of soft leather 16 in. by 3½ in. for a dock. Damp the dock well and turn down both edges in such a manner as to overlap deeply along the centre, the ends having been previously shaved thin.

Now bring both ends together, making both sides meet flat, but not with the flat sides together; then, taking hold of the piece on the flat in the centre, turn the lower edge inwards and upwards, still keeping the points together with the other hand. Nail each point to a board and keep all parts in shape until dry, when the dock will be firm. Edge, crease, and black the body, making two rows all round, rubbing the edges well and hot-creasing the lines. At the tail end prick the second line as far as the double runs; if the dock is dry, put it between the lining and body at each end of the slit. Tack it down around the lining, and stitch.

A few egg-shaped stitches can be put inside the
outer stitches through the body and points of the
dock to keep the last in place ; trim the edges, and
black, rub, and tallow them, and do the same inside
the edges of the slits.

Cut two chapes to hold the buckles in front for
fastening the crupper to the collar straps ; bend the
chapes down about 4 in., shave one end and point
the other. Cut a hole for the buckle and prepare
the chapes for stitching ; then, having two loops
ready, about 1½ in. wide, tack them in their places,
keeping the outside of the buckle exactly level with
the end of each slit and the chapes right in the
centre. Stitch them down, put a cross stitch on
each side of the buckle, and shape and crease the
loops. Now cut the crupper lay 1 ft. 3 in. by 3 in.,
and turn it down for about 1 ft. at the good end ;
shave the end of the short turn thin, and round the
other end ; then edge, crease, and black the lay.

Cut two hip straps H (Fig. 102) 2 ft. by 1½ in., and
turn them down for 3 in. at the heavy end ; then
shave the turn down, point the buckle end, and
crease and black the straps. Attach them to a
3-in. japanned or tinned dee, one strap on each
side ; stitch four rows in the double of each, and
rub and finish the edge. Prepare two more straps
in the same manner, each 2 ft. 10 in. by 1¼ in., and
stitch them in the middle round part of the dee
between the two other straps. These are the carrier straps L (Fig. 102) for the stretcher ; the hip
straps are for carrying the traces.

The straight part of the dee is now put in the
bend of the lay and placed on the centre of the
crupper body at the same distance from each side,
the extreme point of the dee being within 8 in. from
the points of the tail slits. Tack down and stitch
two rows ¼ in. apart all round, eight per inch, with
three-cord thread ; then stitch the lay coarse, or
spot it across just to the dee. Some makers put a

pad under the crupper as with the cart-saddle
crupper, running it from the end of the tail slit to
1 in. beyond the point of the lay.

Hip-strap tugs K, must be made to buckle to the
hip straps running from the dee, and for hooking
in the traces. Having a pair of 1½-in. hip-strap
chains (Figs. 103 and 104), cut the tugs 10 in. by
1½ in.; bend them so that the points meet in the
centre, and cut a hole for the buckle in one end.
Stitch the points together and put in two narrow

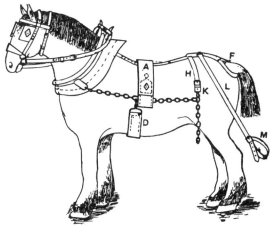

Fig. 102.—Set of Leader Gear.

loops, one to be used to hide the joint, or have one
single broad loop for the same purpose. Place a
safe underneath the same as on the bridgeband
fore tugs, but stitch it instead of nailing.

In the next place make the tugs for the stretcher
carrier strap M (Fig. 102), and a strap 1¼ in. by
1 ft. 2 in., and in the last bend a chape, and cut
a hole for the buckle. Stitch the buckle on with a
loop and make a running loop and a hole 1 in. from
the point of the strap.

When placing the carrier straps in position, fix a loop on each end of the stretcher and nail the ends of the latter, leaving space for the strap to pass. Run the strap down through this loop, the runner loop having previously been put on the strap; then pass it through the runner loop to the buckle, where it is fastened. Secure the carrier straps to the same buckle over the carrier straps, bringing their points down into the loop. Keep the runner loop down by the stretcher to tighten the tug and to produce a neat finish.

The hip straps must now be buckled in the tug buckles, the hook fastened to chain traces, and the collar straps buckled in the fore-slit buckles. Whether the dock is put under the tail is optional, because the hip straps, when fastened in the dee, suffice to keep the crupper in place.

The back-band A, to carry the traces, is the next part of the harness to be made. It must measure about 4 ft. 4 in. from tip to tip, including the terminal chains or the eye, to which the traces are hooked. If pipe, the leather must be made 6 ft. 4 in. by 5 in. Mark a cross-line 1 ft. from each extremity, and another 6 in. from each line, so that there will be 3 ft. 4 in. between the two middle marks. A piece of lining is required for the part between the two lines at each end; this should be of the same width as the back-band and 1 ft. 3 in. long. Shave thin both tips of the lining and also the ends of the turn-in of the back-band; crease, black, and rub the back-band, the crease being made from the extreme lines right along. Prick the piece from the outer cross-line at each end as far as the double will run, making five rows with two on each side; then put the lining under the space between the two lines so that it is 6 in. over one and 3 in. over the other.

A narrow piece, shaved at the inner edge and about 6 in. long, is now placed on both ends at each side of the 6-in. space to strengthen the eye. Stitch the four rows in the 6-in. space, between the two lines, with three-cord thread, eight per inch; turn the edges of this part and black and rub them. Now turn down the ends, bringing the cross-lines dividing the eye exactly opposite each other; flatten the eye so as to bring the parts with the lines close together, and tack it in this position. Take two 1-in. dees and place a piece of leather inside them, on the flat side, for about half their width. Put both on each side of the back-band, one in each end between the double close to the eye and low enough to stitch through the piece of leather inside, when stitching the outer row.

Fig 103.   Fig. 104.

Figs. 103 and 104.—Hip-strap Chains.

The dees must be tacked down as well as the double; fasten it right along both sides. The four rows at both ends and sides are stitched to the top of the double from the cross rows. If desired, a fancy wave or pattern can be made instead of the two inner lines of stitching. Then stitch or spot with lace across the back-band along the cross-lines near the eye; open out the last by placing a thick piece of wood, etc., inside.

Two straps must be cut 10 in. by ¾ in., a buckle and loop being adjusted to one end, and four or five punch holes made at the other for the dee fixed at the side of the back-band to pass through a link in the trace, and thus secure the back-band.

Some harness-makers line back-bands from one end to the other and stitch them; others line the inner part of the eye with sole leather, and place a safe under the eye. This safe is about 1 in. wider at the bottom, and narrows down to the same width as the back-band at the top; the lower corners are rounded, and then it is stitched in from the eye upwards.

For the belly-band D, a pair of 3-in. chains is required, and the leather must be cut 3 ft. 4 in. by 3 in. Turn in 4 in. at the ends, and shave, edge, black, and crease them; then put the leather into the openings in the chains, stitch four rows along the double part, and spot or stitch across near the chain.

The set of shaft and chain gear, as described in Chapters V. to VIII., is now complete. The chains are attached to the shaft harness or jambles to pull from the shaft, while the leader harness has only a hook for hitching the chain traces.

CHAPTER IX.

In plough gears the ordinary bridle and collar are
employed. The back-band is made in various ways.
The method with hooks is taken first. The eye of the
hook (Fig. 105, p. 109) is 4 in. wide. Cut the leather
3 ft. 9 in. long and 4 in. wide; turn down 3 in. at
each end, and beat the bend slightly with the hammer to keep it down, and crease it with the screw-
race, making two rows on each side; mark the
centre from each end, and draw a line straight
across at this point, then two lines each 5 in. from
the centre, so that the distance between them will
be 10 in.

Cut two pieces of leather 10½ in. long and ¾ in.
wide; dye and crease one side of each piece, having
previously cut a small piece out of each corner of
the side being worked. A line must then be drawn
with the compasses along the centre of this narrow
piece. Make a mark across the centre, and place it
underneath the back-band, centre to centre, as far
as the line just drawn; tack it down for stitching,
and place the other piece in the same manner on
the other side, so that the pieces may be a little
over both lower lines at each end. This piece is
called the facing; the place on the back-band where
the pieces are to be stitched is pricked out before
tacking them down. The work of stitching is now
commenced, care being taken to keep the line close
to the edge of the back-band; make the thread of
three or four cords of coarse hemp.

Having a 1½-in. tinned dee at hand, cut a piece of
leather 1½ in. by 4 in.; shave and point both ends,
then crease, black, and prick them like the side,
with eight or ten marks per inch. Place the dee in

the centre of this piece, and lay it flat on the back-
band in the centre, measured from both sides, or
from the top line to either of the lines below, and
then stitch, having tacked it down. When ploughing is being done, the rein is run through this dee,
and there must be one dee on each back-band on
the opposite side when the horses work in pairs,
but for a single horse there is one on each side of
the same back-band.

The next part to be made is the panel, used for
preventing soreness of the back of the animal when
ploughing, brought about by the constant pressure
in one place. Take a piece of linen, or basil
leather, 14 in. by 7 in., and lay the back-band on it
centre to centre, and evenly over both sides ; make
the spot stitch thus // // // across the back-band,
and through the linen along the middle line. Then
the partition between the two sides will show the
object of these facings, which make the pad slightly
wider than the back-band, and so ease the horse's
back.

Having stitched across the centre, turn in the
lining all round about ½ in. ; if, however, the
material employed is basil, no turning is required.
Make a pleat at each corner of the end of the
facing, making both exactly the same length ; put
another pleat opposite the first, so that the width
may be the same as that of the back-band and
facing combined.

If the panel is basil, the corner is cut off to obtain
the true length, and then stitched together where
the cut was made instead of making a pleat. Now
begin to stitch all round, commencing about 1½ in.
from the centre on one side so as to have an opening for stuffing. Work round along the cross lines
at the bottom until within 1½ in. of the centre of the
other side in a direct line from the starting point.
Spot-stitching is executed in the usual style.

Stuffing is the next operation, the flock being put

through the opening left on each side of the centre line. Lay the back-band flat on the bench and stuff each side rather tightly by the aid of the stuffing-stick; the leather side of the back-band is underneath, whilst the openings are near the edge of the bench. Smooth well towards the sides, and flatten with a mallet, and continue the stitching along the opening to the starting-point; this completes the top.

The hooks must now be put in, an operation which is performed as follows: Cut two saving pieces from a thick, firm face of hide; good, close-grained stuff is wasted on such work as this, the best material, as a rule, being that from the face of a gear hide. Cut the pieces 7 in. long, and if the back-band is to be 4 in. wide, make the pieces 5 in wide. Cut one end slanting to 4 in., of the same width as the back-band, and shave it. Round off the corners of the other end, leaving it the full width; black and crease the edges.

Fig. 105.—Plough Back-band Hook.

Put the hooks in their places and the saving pieces under them about 1½ in. lower down than the extremity of the hook; tack them down exactly in the centre. Having marked and pricked the back-band with four rows running from the hook upwards to the end of the saving pieces, stitch with a four-cord thread, nine or ten stitches per inch, and then stitch a line across close to the hook to bind all together. Now the back-band is in working order.

The plough back-band, with chains instead of hooks, is made in exactly the same manner, but when there is only one chain and a bar across in the bend to hold it, a hole must be cut in the centre of the bend for the passage of the chain. For two chains and a bar make two holes; the saving pieces can be made a little narrower with chains, and the body of the back-band need not be so long in proportion to the length of the chains. As a guide in determining the length of the body, whatever may be the length of the chains or hooks, it should be remembered that the length of the back-band over all must be about 4 ft. 4 in.

Couplings are also a necessary part of plough gear. In some localities only cross-straps are employed from mouth to mouth when ploughing in pairs. Cut the strap 1 in. wide and 28 in. to 30 in. long, turn it in about 1 in. at each end, and make a hole for the buckle, and shave the points. Take two billets of the same width, 1 ft. long, and trim them to a point at one end, shaving the other; then edge back, and crease them; place the buckle in, and then the thin end, 2 in. down at the back of the buckle. Put a loop between the chape by the buckle and stitch one billet and buckle at each end; punch two holes in each billet.

Sometimes two coupling straps are employed for a pair: the straps cross each other from the hames of each horse to the mouth of the other. They are made to the first style, but longer, being 38 in. in length, each with 12-in. billets; in some cases they are made a foot longer than this, the coupling being cut into two, one end 15 in. long with a buckle and loop, and the other made to buckle on, with numerous holes for adjusting the length. This is a very convenient method, for when a young horse is coupled with an old one, the coupling must be shortened on the side of the former animal to keep it back until it has learned the ordinary working pace.

CHAPTER X.

BITS, SPURS, STIRRUPS, AND HARNESS FURNITURE.

BITS, their patterns and materials, will now be considered. Bits are made in polished iron, tinned iron, in steel of various qualities, and in nickel. Nickel is as expensive as good steel, but does not

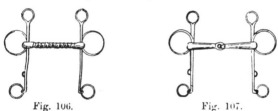

Fig. 106.   Fig. 107.

Figs. 106 and 107.—Pelham Bits.

tarnish so soon, and when worn still continues to take a good polish.

Some of the more expensive kinds of bits have

Fig. 110.

Fig. 108.   Fig. 109.

Fig. 108.—Pelham Bit.   Fig. 109.—Hackney Bit.
Fig. 110.—Bridoon.

ornamented and silver-plated cheeks ; this is especially the case with carriage, military, and riding bits.

Riding bits are snaffles for a single head bridle and rein, hence their name snaffle bridles. Pelham bits (Figs. 106 to 108) are used for single head bridle and double rein, this bridle being known as the

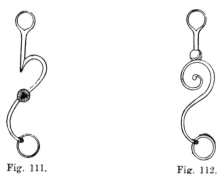

Fig. 111.　　　　　　　　Fig. 112.

Figs. 111 and 112.—Ladies' Horse Bits.

Pelham. The Hackney bit (Fig. 109) has a bridoon (Fig. 110), that is, the bit has only a mouthpiece and a ring at each end with a jointed bar. This bit is used for the Weymouth bridle, which has a

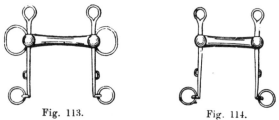

Fig. 113.　　　　　　　　Fig. 114.

Fig. 113.—Pelham Snaffle with Indiarubber Mouth.
Fig. 114.—Hackney Bit with Indiarubber Mouth.

double head and a double rein. Curbs are used with the two bits last mentioned.

Bits for horses to be ridden by ladies are shown by Figs. 111 and 112. They are on the same principle as those previously mentioned, but are lighter and more fanciful, many of them being ornamented about the cheeks. The Pelham snaffle (Fig. 113) and the Hackney bit (Fig. 114), with indiarubber

Fig. 115.   Fig. 116.

Fig. 115.—Gig Snaffle.   Fig. 116.—Wilson Snaffle.

mouths, can be had for tender-mouthed horses, and double or twisted or smooth-mouthed bits can be had for vicious or quiet horses as required.

Driving bits are commonly gig snaffles (Fig. 115); Wilson snaffles (Fig. 116) have rings at each end and two loose rings on the mouthpiece, one of which is

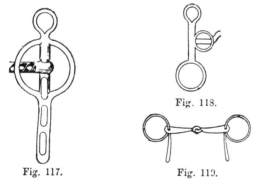

Fig. 117.   Fig. 118.

Fig. 117.—Liverpool Bit. Fig. 118.—Globe Cheek Curb
Bit.   Fig. 119.—One-horn Bridoon Bit.

buckled to the bridle cheek; the outer ring on each side is for the driving rein, but sometimes the rein billet is put through both rings at the same time. Wilson snaffles can be obtained bar jointed, twisted, or smooth-mouth. The Liverpool bit (Fig. 117) has a curb cheek, and a straight or solid bar

Fig. 120.—One-horned Bridoon with Indiarubber Mouth.

Fig. 121.—Gig Curb Bit.

mouth with the mouth bar loose on the cheek. The Globe cheek curb bit (Fig. 118) has a ring at the bottom of the cheek to which the mouthpiece is attached instead of being loose as in the Liverpool

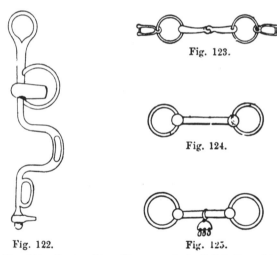

Fig. 122.   Fig. 125.

Fig. 123.

Fig. 124.

Fig. 122.—Buxton Bit. Fig. 123.—Swivelled Bridoon Bit. Figs. 124 and 125.—Breaking Bits.

bit. A " one-horn bridoon " (Fig. 119), with one ring at each side and either a solid or a jointed mouth, sometimes has a leather or indiarubber mouth (see Fig. 120).

Gig curb bits (Fig. 121) have the billet of the

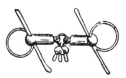

Fig. 126.—Breaking
Bit.

Fig. 127.—Snaffle with
Indiarubber Mouth.

bridle fastened to the top of the cheek, with cheeks on the lower side to which the reins are fastened.

The carriage bit most in use is the Buxton bit (Fig. 122), which has a bend in the cheek below the

Fig. 128.

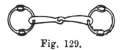

Fig. 129.

Figs. 128 and 129.—Exercising Bits.

mouthpiece, and a bar across at the bottom from one side of the cheek to the other, the solid mouthpiece having a port in the centre; this is a smart and very powerful curb bit, but it is being super-

Fig. 130.—Show or Stallion Bit.

seded by the Liverpool bit. A swivelled bridoon (Fig. 123), as sometimes used with the ordinary driving bit, has the bearing rein running from the hames down through the swivel and up to a strap stitched between the two slit straps of the head-

strap. Breaking bits (Figs. 124 to 126) are special
kinds of patent bits. Fig. 127 is an indiarubber
mouth snaffle ; Figs. 128 and 129 are exercising
bits ; Fig. 130 is a show or stallion bit ; and Fig. 131
is a double-mouthed snaffle.

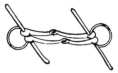

Fig. 131.—Double-mouthed Snaffle.

On the subject of spurs, very little need be said.
Besides ordinary pattern spurs (Fig. 132), there are
officers' regulation spurs (Fig. 133), dress spurs
(Fig. 134), ladies' spurs (Fig. 135), trousers spurs
(Fig. 136), and box spurs. The last-named are

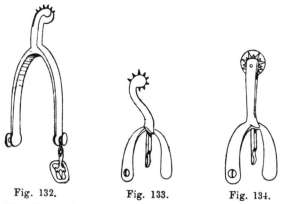

Fig. 132.   Fig. 133.   Fig. 134.

Fig. 132.—Ordinary Spur. Fig. 133.—Officer's Regulation
Spur. Fig. 134.—Dress Spur.

fastened to the heel of the boot by a spring inserted
in a steel box inside the heel. Like screw spurs,
which screw into a hole in the heel, they may be
taken off at will. Spurs are made in polished steel

and brass, some being silver-plated. The saddler must have a supply of spur rowels for repairing spurs.

Stirrups may be solid (Fig. 137), three bar or open

Fig. 135.   Fig. 136.   Fig. 137.

Fig. 135.—Lady's Spur.   Fig. 136.—Trousers Spur.
Fig. 137.—Solid Stirrup.

bottom (Fig. 138), or they may be of the waving bar pattern (Fig. 139). They vary greatly in weight according to the purpose for which they are required, and are made of polished steel and of plated brass or silver. Ladies' stirrups (Fig. 140) are of various patterns, some having pads to protect the

Fig. 138.   Fig. 139.   Fig. 140.

Fig. 138.—Open Bottom Stirrup.   Fig. 139.—Waving Bar
Stirrup.   Fig. 140.—Lady's Stirrup.

foot, others having foot plates of the same shape as the foot ; others, again, have slippers (Fig. 141). Safety stirrups (Fig. 142) both for ladies and gentlemen are made so that if the rider falls or is thrown off the horse the stirrups spring open and release the rider's feet. Thus the danger of being dragged along the ground by the horse is obviated.

Fig. 141.—Stirrup Slipper.

Fig. 142.—Safety Stirrup.

Some particulars will now be given of harness furniture. First the material will be touched upon.

Japanned iron furniture is strong and durable, and has a fairly good appearance when new, but the japan soon wears off and allows the iron to get rusty. Common iron buckles, covered with leather, are also used, but not so extensively as they were formerly The iron soon rusts, and the rust affects the leather and causes it to crumble off, giving a

Fig. 143.

Fig. 144.

Fig. 145.

Fig. 146.

Fig. 143.—Flat Side Wire Front Buckle. Fig. 144.—Wire Front Bevelled Buckle. Fig. 145.—Bevelled Flat Top Buckle. Fig. 146.—West End Bevelled Flat Top Buckle.

very shabby appearance to the rest of the set of harness.

Brass furniture is largely used, and it is got up in many qualities and styles of finish. The best brass does not tarnish nearly so soon as common brass, and, of course, has a good appearance when clean. Partly covered brass or plated furniture is also sometimes used, the buckles being covered with

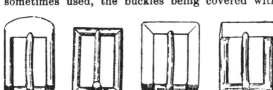

Fig. 147.   Fig. 148.   Fig. 149.   Fig. 150.

Fig. 147.—Spade Buckle.   Fig. 148.—Square Wire Buckle.
Fig. 149.—Chatham Buckle.   Fig. 150.—Flat Top
Turned-up Buckle.

leather about half-way up the sides, leaving the top and a little of the side bare. This looks very well, and is more durable than iron-covered buckles, as the brass- or silver-plate does not destroy the leather so soon as iron; partly covered furniture is, however, very awkward to clean.

Buckles are occasionally covered with celluloid; sometimes this only partly covers the brass, alu-

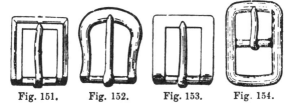

Fig. 151.   Fig. 152.   Fig. 153.   Fig. 154.

Fig. 151.—Fluted Buckle.   Fig. 152.—Swelled Front Bent-
leg Buckle.   Fig. 153.—Flat Top Cab Buckle.   Fig. 154.
—West End Whole Buckle.

minium, or gold-plated buckle, and it then looks very rich. The celluloid-covered article is made in imitation of the leather-covered buckle; it is dur-able, and does not require much cleaning, the occa-

sional application of a wet sponge being sufficient.
Celluloid is more commonly used in America than
in this country. It is a very inflammable material,
and will break if given a hard knock or if allowed
to fall.

  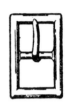

Fig. 155.   Fig. 156.   Fig. 157.

Fig. 155.—Chased Buckle. Fig. 156.—Melbourne Buckle.
Fig. 157.—West End Square Buckle.

Nickel furniture looks well, but costs a little more
than brass. Nickoline, white metal, or Victoria
metal furniture costs about the same as brass; all
three look well when cleaned, but quickly tarnish.
Plated furniture is used on superior harness; it can
be bought in different qualities, being plated with
silver, white metal, German silver, or nickel.

Of course, the hames and the buckle tongues are

Fig. 158.   Fig. 159.   Fig. 160.   Fig. 161.

Figs. 158 and 159.—Covered Buckles. Figs. 160 and 161.—
Part-covered Buckles.

of iron, plated in whatever metal the rest of the
furniture is made; they have to be of iron to with-
stand the strain to which they are subjected. In
ordering, it is necessary to state whether plated

hames are required of the same material as the
furniture, and whether the latter is brass, silver-
plated, etc. The pattern of buckle required will

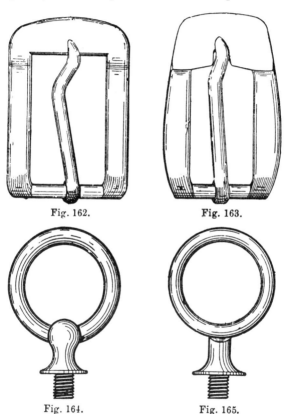

Fig. 162.   Fig. 163.

Fig. 164.   Fig. 165.

Fig. 162.—Shaft Tug Buckle. Fig. 163.—Burgess's Buckle.
Fig. 164.—Ball Terret. Fig. 165.—Plain Terret.

make a little difference in the price; the wire-
shaped pattern is the one mostly used.

There are so many patterns in gig and carriage furniture that it is impossible to mention them all.

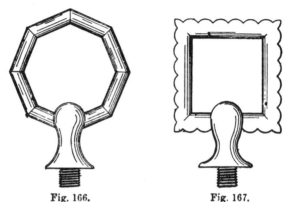

Fig. 166.   Fig. 167.

Figs. 166 and 167.—Ball Terrets.

Attention will be directed, however, to some of the most useful patterns of buckles. The flat side wire front (Fig. 143, p. 118), the wire front bevelled (Fig.

Fig. 168.—Ball Terret.

144), the bevelled flat top (Fig. 145), the West End flat top wire (Fig. 146), and the spade pattern (Fig.

147, p. 119) are all very neat buckles. Square wire
buckles (Fig. 148) on light gig harness look very
well. The Chatham (Fig. 149), flat top turned up

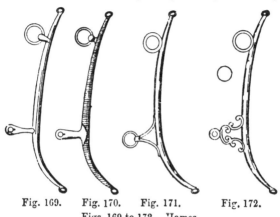

Fig. 169.   Fig. 170.   Fig. 171.   Fig. 172.

Figs. 169 to 172.—James.

(Fig. 150), and fluted (Fig. 151), are very strong
buckles for cab harness, as are also the swelled
front bent leg (Fig. 152), and side and flat top cab

Fig. 173.   Fig. 174.

Figs. 173 and 174.—Bearing-rein Swivels.

(Fig. 153) buckles. The West End whole buckle is
shown by Fig. 154; it looks very neat for any fancy
harness. "Chased" (Fig. 155, p. 120), "Melbourne"

(Fig. 156), or " West End square," or " square wire "
(Fig. 157) whole buckles, are all very showy and
smart when worked up. Figs. 158 and 159 are covered buckles, and Figs. 160 and 161 part-covered
buckles.

There are many different kinds of shaft tug
buckles; that shown by Fig. 162 (p. 121) is a good
pattern, as is also Burgess's patent buckle (Fig. 163).

The terrets (Figs. 164 to 168) for the reins to
run through on the saddle and hames (Figs. 169 to
172), as well as the bearing-rein swivels (Figs. 173
and 174) and all parts of the set of furniture, are of
a pattern conforming with that of the buckles.

Fig. 175.   Fig. 176.

Figs. 175 and 176.—Roller Buckles.

Cart-harness furniture may be of galvanised or
japanned iron, with buckles of brass or white metal.
All the brass patterns illustrated are known as
Scotch gear buckles. Cart fancy-brass breeching
loops may be used instead of leather ones for
bridgeband carriers and bridle cheeks.

Fly-terrets are much used as ornaments on the
top of the bridle between the ears of the horse,
being either screwed down into a socket or riveted
in place. Brass face-pieces for the front of the
bridles on the forehead can be obtained in numerous
patterns.

Hame plates, to be put between the two points of
the hames or jambles above the collar, look very

well with a strap across from side to side as a fastening.

Cart hames are either wholly or partly covered with iron, and generally take their names from the district in which the particular pattern is mostly used. Thus there are the Manchester, Lancashire, Irish, and Yorkshire hames. Cart bits, together with their fittings, are always firmly attached to the bridle, and are made either of tinned or japanned

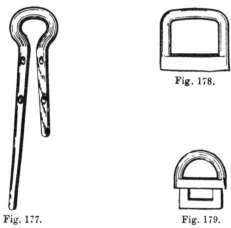

Fig. 178.

Fig. 177.   Fig. 179.

Fig. 177.—Hame Clip.   Figs. 178 and 179.—Breeching Dees.

iron. They may be straight and jointed, or twisted.

Chains, such as backband, crupper, or hip strap chains, and watering chains for bridle reins, and plough backband hooks or chains, are all wanted in making up a set. Others necessary are:—Leader backband chains, cheek chains for the end of leading rein, bridgeband chains, and chains for the bellyband, instead of billets, to go round the shafts.

Riding bridle buckles range in width from ⅜ in. to 1 in. Stirrup leather buckles are also a special

line, being from 1¼ in. to 1½ in. in width. Saddle
girth buckles are 1 in. wide. Roller buckles (Figs.
175 and 176, p. 124) vary in size from ⅝ in. to 1¾ in.,
and are largely used on all kinds of leather work.
Head-stall or head-collar buckles range in size from
1¼ in. to 1½ in. ; some have the collar attached, to
which is fastened the throat lash.

The following buckles must also be kept ready to
hand :— D-buckles for use on small straps ; and
japanned legging buckles, in sizes ranging from ½ in.
to ¾ in.   Head-collar stop squares, for making
and repairing head-collars, must also be stocked, as
well as tinned and brass rings of different sizes, for
making head-collars and for miscellaneous repairs.
Brass, tin, and plated dees will be necessary for
making and repairing dog collars, and for holding
coat straps on riding saddles, etc. They range in
size from ⅝ in. to 1½ in.

Belt, brace, and garter buckles may often be
wanted, and 2 lb. or 3 lb. of buckle tongues for repairing old buckles should also be obtained in all
sizes and strengths. Strong double-pronged buckles
may be wanted from 1½ in. to 2 in.   There may also
be occasion to use harness buckles of all sizes,
patterns, and material, saddle terrets, hame clips
(Fig. 177), various kinds of nails, breeching and
bearing-rein rings, breeching dees (Figs. 178 and
179), and rivets for clips. etc.

CHAPTER XI.

VAN AND CAB HARNESS.

THE making of a set of gig harness is described in the companion volume "Saddlery." Van harness for heavy work requires a set of furniture, including buckles, hames, and chains, and a van saddle-tree. The furniture should be of brass, nickel, or silver. Burgess's patent tug buckles (Fig. 163, p. 121) can be recommended for shaft tugs.

A pair of winker plates of any pattern (see Figs. 180 and 181) are necessary to make the winkers. Beginning with the winkers, cut the leather about ¼ in. wider than the plate all round, except at the back, where it must be ⅞ in. wider. If patent leather is used, make a line all round the edge, and another about ½ in. from it, and race a line across, 1½ in. from the back part, from one end of the inner line to the end of the other; of course, the other lines must not be brought nearer than this to the back. Prick along the lines, about eleven per inch, and single stitch the inner line all round the four sides, through the leather, employing black linen thread double, with two needles.

Cut the lining to the same size as the top, but lightly stuffed and with little oil in; put the top on it and stitch all round three sides, leaving the back open. Put the leather in water and wet it thoroughly, and then, having opened out the two leathers with the hand, put a good coat of paste on both of the inner sides by the aid of a spoon or other convenient implement.

Push in the winker plate front to front; but if the front is round cornered, it must, of course, be put in first. Push in the pieces until they lie square in the leather and close to the front stitches; then rub the top and the lining down to the sheet iron, being careful to make the lining stick well to the sheet.

Place the winker on a board, lining underneath, and tack down each of the hind corners, and if necessary, the middle; then put some paper or rags between the winker and the board so as to keep the lining up to the sheet. When quite dry and perfectly adhering, remove them from the board, trim the edges, finish and polish well.

The collar is made practically in the same way as a cart collar. The forewale must be turned down 2 in., that is 4 in. altogether, and instead of whipping the basil lining in as previously described, cut it a little smaller, and stitch it in at the same time as the forewale; tack it down in such a manner that when the lining is turned over to stuff the body, the stitches will not be visible. Take a pattern (see Fig. 96, p. 79) and let the lining overlap in the centre of the forewale for quite 2 in. Stitching is done as for a cart collar, both for the forewale and the drawing in the body, but the last must not be so big and clumsy.

In making and setting the top piece, no stitches should appear in front other than the cross row; the top piece must not be joined downwards as in the other. Turn in the bottom of the top piece for $\frac{1}{2}$ in. across, and stitch a line with black linen thread $\frac{1}{4}$ in. from the edge to keep the turn in its place. Damp the top piece, put it across the front, and draw it tight, putting a tack in both sides; then make it overlap at the top centre of the back so as to obtain a good point to hold the hame strap in place; then stitch all round the hollow.

Cut the side piece close along the sides of the body to fit tight by the forewale. Then take a piece of soft thin leather binding $1\frac{1}{4}$ in. wide, damp it, and place it edge to edge with the outside of the side piece, tacking it down. Having stitched the side piece, putting a small welt at the joint at the bottom, and shaving a little round the edges, stitch the binding and side piece together around the edge with black linen thread, about seven stitches per inch. Run a piece of twine along the stitches round the rim, and turn down the binding over the twine towards the inside, being careful to keep the twine in place. Mark a line and prick it, about eight per inch, and ⅜ in. from the edge; then stitch the binding down below the twine. The last must be in one piece with 4 in. or 5 in. to spare at each end.

Damp the side piece and adjust it; tack it with

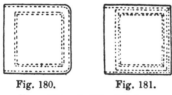

Fig. 180.　　　Fig. 181.

Figs. 180 and 181.—Winkers.

an awl at the bottom and draw it tight at the top. Now wax a piece of collar twine, about 18 in. longer than is necessary to pass round the collar, and begin to stitch the side piece in at the top on the off side, running the stitches through the binding close to the stitching and through the lining at every other stitch. The stitches may be about 2 in. long; draw them tight while working, and be careful that the side piece is in its proper position, with both sides equally level. Fasten the thread after stitching the side piece all round. Take hold of the hanging ends of the twine which has been run along the binding inside, and pull them well to draw down the edges of the side-piece along the side of the body; then knot and fasten them to-

gether. Draw in the side piece at the forewale as
with the cart collar, using only thread or very fine
white lace.

A layer of old carpet may be placed on the
stitches next to the body under the side piece to
give the sides smoothness and roundness. Fasten
the two side pieces together at the top by stitching over from one to the other with the collar
needle.

A small housing to cover the top of the collar
must be cut, almost half-round in shape, but with
slightly widening points and a V-shaped notch on
the side next the collar for the points to pass, one
on each side of the top piece ; bring it down close
to the forewale. It may be bound in the same
style as the side piece, stitched fast edge to edge
with the binding, the latter being then turned and
a line stitched round a short distance from the
edges ; about ¾ in. below that another row of
stitches is made all round. The point on the outside of the body must not project more than about
¼ in.

Plain or patent leather can be employed to
make the collar and winkers ; patent leather must
always be marked for stitching with the race compass, and a groove cut so that the patent will be
raced off and the line quite visible. This kind of
leather, when used to make the collar forewale,
must be lined with calico to prevent it cracking.

The van saddle (Fig. 182) is the next part to be
made. The tree is a miniature cart-saddle tree,
with similar boards and groove. The plates to be
put in the point of the groove where the backband
runs through may be nickel or brass to match the
furniture. Begin work by fixing the terrets and
bearing-rein stand hook on the tree. Take off the
sockets which are attached to the screws, and see
that they are of the proper length to reach over
the groove of the tree from side to side ; file them

down to the width of the tree if they are too long. Place the stand-hook socket exactly in the centre at the top, and mark its position on each side and end.

Cut out a hollow at the mark deep enough for the socket to enter and lie flush with the surface, and drive a small screw through each socket into the tree. The terret sockets are fixed in the same manner, being sunk level and screwed down, about $3\frac{1}{2}$ in. lower than the stand hook on each side.

Cut two pieces of thin leather, either plain or patent, to the same shape as each side of the tree

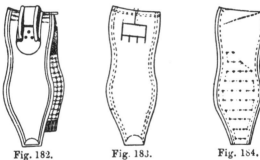

Fig. 182. Fig. 183. Fig. 184.

Fig. 182.—Van Saddle. Fig. 183.—Van Saddle Flap.
Fig. 184.—Van Saddle Panel.

and about 1 in. larger each way. Damp them and make a nick at the top of the boards in the leather so that the centre of the piece will turn down underneath. Tack each end of the leather to the board close to the tree, then pull it tightly along the entire surface of the side over the top, nailing it here and there. Level it down on the surface of the tree, and tack the centre part between the boards underneath the tree, pulling it tight and flat over all parts.

To make the flaps, cut out a paper pattern as a guide (see Fig. 183), making it wider at the top than at the other parts and slightly raised in front. The flaps must reach down from the lower part of the groove in the centre for about 15 in., swelling slightly at the sides and gradually narrowing to about 2 in. at the bottom. The patterns may also be cut straight without the swelling sides, but in both styles they must rise in front more than at the back; as they are cut in two pieces, one for each side, this can easily be managed, because when they are joined at the top this part will stand out prominently in front.

Some flaps are made with stout firm leather, others are lined. In the first case, make two rows along the sides with the race compass and bevel deep with a hot bevel; but patent leather, instead of needing the race compass, has tallow rubbed along the part to be creased and the lines are marked with the compass; then run a warm beveller deep along the marks, being careful that it does not cut the leather.

When patent or plain leather is lined, use the race compass and prick the grooves for stitching. When stitched (or made without lining), cut and polish the edges well and join them with a stitch at the top; place a piece of leather over the joint at the front about 1¼ in. wide, and stitch it on both sides of the joint and across the front; then shave it thin at the side next the tree. A dee, of brass or other metal, is placed on the outside for fastening the crupper. Cover the joint at the back with another piece of leather, turning it down on the outside and shaving the other end thin. These pieces should be long enough on both sides to pass under the tree when the flaps are nailed. On these the tree is placed centre to centre and front to front, and a line is marked along the sides of the tree from board to board on the leather.

Make a mark at the lower side of the board to indicate the width of the tree there, and the width

of the wood on both sides of the groove. Note
that this must be marked at the bottom side of the
boards, four marks being made at each end of the
tree, outside and inside the wood on each side of
the groove.

At this point take away the tree, and cut a slit
from the outer lower mark to the point of the one
running along the side of the tree ; there will then
be two slits of the width of the board, one on each
side of the tree. Now cut upwards from each of
the two inner marks at the bottom, for the length
of the other cuts and equal in width to the wood,
on both sides of the groove. Then cut across the
top of each incision from side to side ; there will
now be one cross cut and four cuts upward, and a
portion along the centre. Cut the middle piece
between the four slits at each end about 1½ in. from
the bottom, and shave the points ; now cut the two
narrow strips at each end to the same length.

The middle piece, unless there are plates, is
nailed along the groove with the narrow cuts underneath. Place flaps over the top and make the
edges of the centre slit meet at the centre of the
tree below. Nail the flaps down along the edge
of the tree, putting four or five extra nails opposite
the crupper loop in its chape. When there is no
plate, nail the centre piece in the bottom along the
groove ; put the narrow pieces down and nail them
with the brass beading, making sure that the part
of the flaps over the boards runs close to the tree ;
fasten it to the boards with four or five tacks.
Turn the centre piece down like the narrow ones,
and nail it to the board at each end.

Cut a top cover of strong leather of the same
width as the tree and to reach to within 2½ in. from
the bottom, so that there will be an opening for the
backband ; crease it across both ends and bevel the
creases with a hot iron, or line both ends for about
2 in. and shave the inner side ; then make two rows

of stitching across the points. Place it on the tree
in its proper position, and give two or three light
taps with a hammer opposite the three openings
for the terrets and stand hooks in the sockets ; thus
the size and position of the holes is marked on the
cover.

Holes, of the same dimensions as the socket
holes, must now be cut in the cover, and this nailed
down on both sides of the tree, keeping the holes
in the leather exactly opposite those for the
sockets. A strong nail must be driven into each
corner so that it will not be prized up by the back-
band. Take a piece of beading long enough to run
along the top on each side and go down underneath
through the opening opposite the narrow cuts in
the bottom ; nail the beading on the side of the
boards or under them, securing in the same way
the narrow turned-down strip. The beading should
lie close to the leather along the top of the tree ;
drive the nails for the beading with a wooden
mallet.

The saddle is now ready for the panel (Fig. 184,
p. 131), the back of which must be cut to the same
size as the flaps ; it must not reach quite to the bottom ; let it end, say, 2 in. from it. Basil can be
employed as material, and if this is light, a piece of
linen can be pasted inside, or a narrow slip may be
pasted along the edges. When dry, see again that
it is of the same size and shape. The facing must
be cut about 1⅛ in. wide, and of the same length as
the sides of the panel ; it may be in patent or plain
leather to match the flaps.

When the material is not long enough it may be
cut into two parts and joined at the centre ; it is
then tacked along the edges and stitched for about
six inches. Rub the joint down as flat as possible.
Take some blue serge lining or collar lining and lay
it out smooth on the bench, and place the panel
back on it inside out ; with hemp, tack it along

the sides to the lining, cutting the latter to the
same shape as the back, but wider by 1¾ in. or more
on both sides at the top. The lining then tapers
to exactly the same width as the base at the extreme point. Narrow the lining at the gullet and,
just at the back in the centre opposite the opening
to be left, turn it in about ¼ in. ; run a stitch to
keep it down, and then whip it in with the facing
from end to end and across the bottom, employing
black linen thread and a pointed needle and
thimble. No facing is placed across the bottom.

Now turn the panel inside out through the opening at the top ; the joint is not stitched right across,
only two or three stitches being used at each end.
Some piping is now needed to run round the facing
to make both sides of the panel front stand out
round and straight.

Sometimes the facing is made of straw whipped
round with hemp until it is hard and round ; sometimes with damp brown paper rolled with both
hands on the bench ; or a simple cord of light twist
may be employed, and, in America, cane. In harness of this description, cord will suffice ; it may be
covered with brown paper to about ⅝ in. in diameter. Place it in the facing through the opening
at the top, making it reach to the bottom at each
side but not across. Turn the facing tightly over
it and begin to spot from the back, the stitches
being small and even on the lined side.

While working, the panel should be kept flat on
the bench, the lining being uppermost and being
stitched close to the facing with a quilting needle
and thimble. Then place the lining flat and even
at the top, parting it alike on both sides and running a line of cross stitches from side to side on
both sides of the joining at the back, to about 1½ in.
apart at the back and about 4 in. in the front.

The panel is now in two compartments. Cut
two openings across it, one on each side, below the

line of stitches just made, and one to cross them ;
then stuff the panel with carded flock through
these openings, the stuffing-stick being employed
for the purpose. Fill it level from top to bottom,
but not too full.

Next mark, say, six cross lines, about 1½ in.
apart, from the bottom of the panel towards the
top, a rule being used as a guide. Take a long
three-cord black hemp thread made with beeswax
and quilt it, making four stitches or so in each line ;
use a thimble and quilting needle. Keep the
stitches in a straight line both downwards and
crosswise, and when the last line is reached, make
two stitches from back to front, thus leaving the
last line half finished. Now flatten it over the
stitches and stuff the top to the requisite thickness,
taking care to make it firm, though not hard, otherwise it will become very thin when pressure bears
on it. Place the panel to the centre of the tree and
flaps, and put a tack on each side at the top to
retain it in this position. Some harness makers
run five or six stitches through the flap and panel
here and there, others spot them all the way along ;
but the best method is to put the panel in with
copper wire.

Stitching or spotting might do for common
work, small stitches being put in spotting on the
flap side and about 1¼ in. apart below. The
stitches, whether spotting or stitching double-
handed, should run out in the hollow between the
facing and stuffing below. Keep the facing even
along the edge of the flap a little outside rather
than underneath.

To fasten a panel, cut the wire into pieces about
5 in. long, and with a bent awl cut holes underneath
the flaps close by the outer row of stitches, all at
the same distance from the outside. Then place a
piece of wire in each, and, if for a gig or cab saddle,
nail the panel in the centre on both sides ; but in

the case of a van saddle, nails need not be employed; simply wire it all round. Keep the panel right in the centre and fasten a wire in the top, on each side, by cutting a hole with the bent awl for each point of the wire just below the facing. Put one wire in each hole and push the panel close to the flap; then twist the wire on the panel side with a pair of pincers till the panel is pulled tight to the flap. Give the wire a sharp twist with its points together, and cut them within $\frac{1}{4}$ in. of the panel; turn down the points and press them out of sight into the hollow between the panel and the facing, repeating the process along both sides with the wire about $2\frac{1}{2}$ in. apart.

A strap and a girth are needed to fasten to the bottom of the flaps. Cut the girth 2 ft. long and 2 in. wide, and have a lay to put on about 9 in. by $1\frac{1}{4}$ in. Make a buckle hole in the lay so that the edge of the buckle will be level with the end of the girth, as the chape is not to be turned down, but is stitched on the flat.

A strong strap must now be cut 18 in. by $1\frac{1}{4}$ in., rounded at one end and shaved at the other, and another piece of leather 2 in. by $4\frac{1}{2}$ in., with one end shaved and the other narrowed to $1\frac{1}{4}$ in.; edge, black, and crease both. Tack the lay on the girth with the buckle level to the end, and narrow the girth to the width of the lay at the point; then place two loops beyond the buckle and stitch the lay. In the next place, the shaved end of the strap must be stitched to the $4\frac{1}{2}$-in. piece, the strap being placed within 1 in. of the broad end. Finish the loops, punch the straps, and stitch them, the strap on the near side and the girth on the off side at the base of the flaps, the stitches running across and in a half circle from corner to corner.

The winkers by this time will be dry and fit to work as part of the bridle. Straighten the outside —that is, the part to be stitched—if it has got a

little out of shape in wetting and nailing. Rub
the other edges with sandpaper and give them a fine
polish; then shave the side for the cheek.

Having got four ¾-in. buckles ready for the
cheeks, cut the latter 2 ft. 9 in. by ¾ in. and measure
1 ft. from the better end, marking it across for a
billet. Now round its point and measure 8 in. from
the first mark; turn it down there, and again turn
it down 8 in. from the bend. Make a buckle hole
in each bend, and edge, black, and crease along the
billet part. Make a groove with a round knife or
grooving tool underneath on the billet side from
the cross mark to within ¼ in. of the top bend, the
depth of the groove being about half the thickness
of the leather; open it out with the point of a
blunt compass or anything suitable.

The buckles can now be fixed, one in each bend,
and the winkers can also be placed between the
cheek up to the buckles at the top bend and level
with the outside. Cut a small nick just opposite
the projection of the buckle tongue so that the
winker will ascend on the top end close to the
buckle. See that the point of the turn-down running from the base bend is cut level with the
bottom of the winker, and run a stitch through
both, making the point fit tightly in the hollow
between the lower buckle and the winker.

Place three tacks on the outer side to keep the
edges together in their places. Make one loop for
each from medium heavy winker brown loop
leather about 7 in. by 1⅜ in.; damp it well and place
it in half the width of the cheek on the inner side
and stitch along the groove. Adjust the two sides
in the same manner, reversing the winker to pair
them.

The loops having been damped before being attached, place a loop-stick ¾ in. wide in each loop;
then knock them square and level to shape. Black
them with soda and dye, dry partially with rag, and

rub and polish well with a bone, making them shine brightly. Now trim the underside of the cheek, round the square edges, and polish. Apply a coat of Harris's harness liquid both to the loops and to the edges; rub them well with the palm of the hand and then with a little tallow, after which they must be again rubbed with a rag.

The loops are now ready for creasing and checking, but in the first place make sure that the loops are in condition; if too dry, they cannot be creased deeply enough, and if too wet the bevels and marks cannot be polished. Test with a hot crease and then hold them near the fire a little while; finally rub with the hand until they are dry enough. Attention must also be given to the temperature of the tools when heated in the fire, candle, or gas. Therefore, keep on the bench a small quantity of water into which to dip the heated tools; if the beveller or checker hisses in the water it must be kept there until this ceases.

Now with the screw crease or compass make two or three lines across each end of the loop, and two rows near each other along the edges on the face. Trace out the design on the surface between the outer lines, namely diamonds, single arrow point, or double arrow points, etc. Having warmed the beveller, mark deeply the cross and outside lines, polish them, and then mark the outer lines of the design with the beveller on the surface of the loop.

The space between the outer lines of the design and the straight lines at the edge and sides must now be marked with the warm checker, which may be fine or coarse, according to the style of work; the design also will vary with the fineness or coarseness of the work. The checking being finished, run the beveller along all the outer lines in the design and the straight line, to smooth down the checker marks running to the bevelled lines and to give boldness to the work.

The noseband is made by cutting the leather
2 ft. 8 in. long by 1 in.; it must then be marked 5 in.
from the point and again at a distance of $\frac{7}{8}$ in. from
this mark; then a third mark is made 13 in. farther
on, and a fourth $\frac{7}{8}$ in. from the last mark. Turn
down 2 in. of the end marked last for the buckle;
take $\frac{1}{8}$ in. from each end and each side as far as
the cross mark nearest the ends. Make a buckle
hole and shave, bend, and round the other end for
the point. Cut another piece for a lining, taking
the first as a pattern, and then thin the edges of
both, slanting from the middle of the strap on both
sides, but do not thin the $\frac{7}{8}$-in. space in either
piece.

The first piece of leather that was cut with a
buckle hole can now be damped; then with a groov-

Fig. 185.—Chain and Leather Gig Front.

ing board and hammer handle a groove is made
along the full length, not including the two $\frac{7}{8}$-in.
spaces. Now cut a hole in the outer side of each
of the cross lines, marking two spaces, and cut two
loops about $\frac{3}{8}$ in. by 2 in. Shave the points, damp,
and put one end in each hole over the $\frac{7}{8}$-in. space;
beat the points a little to flatten them to the
leather, and leave sufficient space for the billet to
pass between the loops and the noseband.

Crease the noseband on both sides from end to
end, $\frac{1}{8}$ in. from the edge, and, if required, another
line can be made at the same distance farther in
from opening to opening in the centre only. Prick
the lines all along except opposite the openings,
fine or coarse, according to the style of work, and
then put the lining underneath and the buckle in
its place. Tack it here and there with fine tacks,

and with three-cord fine hemp stitch from end to end, around the point, and across at the end of the centre loops to fasten the loops near the openings.

Stitch a second line if needed, and then the buckle chape from underneath, and put in one or two loops. Trim the edges, sandpaper, black them, and polish; then place sticks in the loops and finish, making four holes in the short end.

The next part of the harness to be described is the front or forehead band. Begin work by cutting it 21 in. by 1 in., bend it down to pass easily round a 1½-in. strap, and then mark it across the length of the required opening. See that there are 13 in. between the two cross marks in the centre and sufficient to stitch down the ends beyond the

Fig. 186.—Chain and Leather Gig Front.

openings; shave the points and stitch down the ends from the cross lines to the points.

It can be covered with fancy coloured or striped cloth or leather and herring-bone stitched along the centre underneath, making a cross at each end; or a chain front (Figs. 185 to 187) can be employed. In the last case a piece of patent leather must be cut of the same length as the front from one cross line to the other and of the same width as the forehead band; adjust the chain and stitch along its centre, taking the thread out at one side of the chain, and running it through the link and down on the other side close by the chain, and so on through every link; at each end through the link joint make a little chape and stitch double through it when the patent leather is being adjusted to the forehead band.

Now mark a line along the edges of the patent leather outside the chain and prick it fine, laying on the patent leather from opening to opening, and stitching double with beeswaxed linen thread and a fine awl. Stitch the patent leather across also at the ends, catching the above-mentioned little chapes. Then pare, sandpaper, black, and well polish the edges.

To make the head-piece, cut the leather 1½ in. wide and 1 ft. 10 in. long; slit it 6 in. at each end, and edge, black, and rub it well, and then crease it with a hot creaser close to the edge and at both sides of the slits. Now cut a ¾-in. chape, long enough to clasp the buckle and the headpiece and to reach no farther than the far side. Make a buckle hole in it, and edge, black, crease, and finally prick it.

Cut a loop ½ in. wide, trim it and place the chape in the buckle, tacking it exactly in the centre of the head-piece, after having cut a small nick exactly in the centre for the projecting tongue to enter. Stitch it in place, running a line across at the end opposite the buckle ; then make four holes in each of the slits.

The winker strap is made as follows: Cut it from stiff leather 1½ in. by 13 in. long and remove the centre piece with a punch at the top of the slit, the last being 7½ in. by ½ in. Beginning at the slit, gradually narrow the other part to ¾ in. wide to run to the head-piece buckle at the top. Crease, black, and rub well with a hot iron and make three punch holes at the pointed end. Take the winkers and open a small slit by cutting the stitches between the leather at the top corner in the front ; put a ½-in. length of the slit in each winker and stitch the points there firmly.

All that is now required to complete the bridle is the throat lash ; make it 2 ft. 3 in. by ¾ in. and turn it down at each end to 1 ft. 8 in. ; then make buckle holes in the bend and shave the points. Edge, black, crease and rub well, prick the bend, and put in the buckles with the bearing-rein swivels, one at each extremity. Having made a loop or two between the buckles and swivels, stitch down the chapes, going below the swivel sufficiently to keep it in place.

Put the bridle together by passing the ends of the front piece into the rosette loops, and placing one slit of the head strap on each side of the rosette loops at both ends of the front piece, the centre buckle at the top pointing in the same direction as the front. Secure the winker strap at the top buckle, and both inner slits of the head strap in the top buckle of the cheeks; then pass the billet through the noseband opening. Make sure that the noseband is buckled on the near side, and then

Fig. 187.—Chain and Leather Gig Front.

put the billets through the cheek of the bit and up again through the loops on the outside of the noseband and cheek buckle.

The throat lash must now be buckled on the off side and the strap passed through the loop on the near side; the noseband being buckled, the bridle is finished. It may be coated with liquid blacking or composition before it is put together, and the buckles and rosettes can be cleaned with paste and washleather or a clean soft rag.

To make a bearing rein a middle piece must be cut 6 ft. by $\frac{3}{4}$ in.; finish it and bend 2 in., making it ready for a buckle. Shave the end thin and cut it to a point; if two buckles are employed both ends must be prepared alike, but with only one buckle one end must be pricked for stitching to the

ring of the round part. Cut the round parts 1⅜ in.
wide and 2 ft. long; turn them down and narrow
them to ¾ in. at one end, the turned-down part
being 2 in. long. Turn down about 1 in. at the
other end and prepare it for a buckle, shaving the
point thin; then damp round the central part,
bring the edges together, and cut a groove on each
side to sink the stitches.

With a blunt point, open the groove before
stitching and have a piece of cord thick enough to
fill the inside and 1 in. longer at each end; unravel
it at the ends and thin the strands by pulling off
some of the material with an awl. Run one end
of the cord through the bearing-rein ring for an
inch and whip it round with waxed hemp so that it
will be secured there.

Open the strands at the other end and put half
of them on each side of the buckle tongue at the
part which will be in the leather; whip this again
fast to the buckle and see that it is of the right
length inside the round to reach tightly from the
buckle to the ring when in its place. It is now
necessary to put the ring in the long bend and the
buckle in the short one.

Now cut a billet 9 in. by ¾ in., and after shaving
one end thin, round the other and prepare and
crease it. Put it in the billet and a loop, and stitch
the other end fine in the ring; stitch the round
along the groove, being careful to have the thread
in the centre of the groove at both sides and to
catch the points of the turn-down at the ring and
the point of the billet in the other end, between
the edges of the round part, making two or three
stitches in each, thus joining them firmly with the
round part. Then with the spokeshave trim them
round and neat, rub with coarse glasspaper, and
finish with fine; close the edges of the groove well
over the stitches and try to make it look as much as
possible like one round, solid piece.

After well blacking and polishing the bearing rein, give it a coat of liquid blacking, polishing by sharp rubbing; finish neatly around the ring and buckle, crease the loops, and make one or two holes in the billets.

Now prepare the middle part. When there are two buckles, begin by punching a dozen holes within 9 in. of each end; with one buckle of course only one end is punched. Five running loops large enough to pass over the strap double must now be made, as explained. When they are finished and polished, put the two points together through one of the loops and pull that loop to within 2 in. from the top; fix a buckle on each side and two loops after each buckle with the right side out. Now run the points through the rings to the buckle and put a chape in place, fastening the buckle in about the sixth hole from the end and leaving the chape unstitched. Then pull one loop over the chape close to the buckle and the other loop down to the ring on each side.

To make the crupper, cut out the body 2 ft. by $1\frac{3}{4}$ in. and slit it for 8 in. at the strongest end; taper the other end to $1\frac{1}{4}$ in. wide and cut a $1\frac{1}{4}$-in. billet 3 ft. 9 in. long. Shave the strong end thin and round the other; cut the lay 16 in. by $1\frac{1}{4}$ in. and shave one end, rounding the other. The points of the slits and the end of the body must also be shaved, the slit points being tapered. Black and crease them all, only the top of the lay being edged.

Place the round end of the lay close to the slit end, in the centre of the body, and 4 in. from the round end make a deep cross line followed by three other lines at intervals of 2 in., and at the same distance from the fourth line cut a hole for the buckle; then put an awl at each corner formed by the cross lines into both lay and body so as to make a mark visible below; there will thus be a guide for

U

use when stitching underneath to indicate where to begin and end.

Cut a groove from the shaved end of the body as far as the first awl mark below, then from the second to the third, and finally from the fourth to a distance of about 1 in. towards the point of the lay ; this groove must be made on the under-side. Cut through one half the thickness of the leather at a sufficient distance from the edge to catch the lay on both sides in stitching.   Now adjust the buckle and lay once again, and then trim four loops about ⅝ in. wide and place one before the buckle, a second on the other side before reaching the first opening, another between the two openings, and, finally, the fourth beyond the lash.

The lay must be stitched in from the underside with double waxed thread, a cross stitch being made at the corners of each opening and the thread being brought straight over the opening to the opposite corner without cutting.   Stitch over the loop at the slit end, but no farther, the remainder being stitched fine round the end from above.   It is better to stitch the crupper lay from below because it will then be smoother and the stitches will not be so likely to rub the hair off as when they are on the surface, there being much friction at this part. Having placed the stick in the loops, finish with the hot iron, making a running loop for the billet.

The dock (Fig. 188) that is placed under the tail is made of soft close-grained leather, 1 ft. 3 in. in length, and tapered from the centre on each side to about ⅞ in. when doubled over at the points. Groove it carefully along the edges at a slight distance therefrom, and stitch it loosely with three-cord fine hemp, about six per inch, merely pulling the stitches home ; then damp it well.

Having a pint of whole linseed near at hand, drive a nail through one end to close the opening, and then, placing the linseed on the apron, scoop it in with the open end and ram the dock tight from end to end with a stick or iron rod till it is filled.

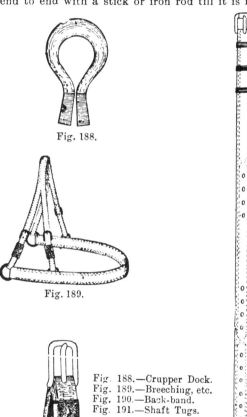

Fig. 188.

Fig. 189.

Fig. 191.

Fig. 190.

Fig. 188.—Crupper Dock.
Fig. 189.—Breeching, etc.
Fig. 190.—Back-band.
Fig. 191.—Shaft Tugs.

Take one end in each hand and twist the piece to a round shape, endeavouring to bring the stitches on

the lower side. Knock the two ends with nails in
them into a flat board, and keeping the centre on
the board, raise both sides and draw them as close
together as possible with a piece of soft leather
tied around them. Then allow them to dry and
trim the stitched part and sand it, rounding it with
the other parts; polish well, thin the top sides of
the points, and knock them flat with the hammer.
Stitch one to each slit of the crupper body for
about ¾ in., finish the edges, and put about a dozen
holes in the billet.

To make the breeching (Fig. 189), cut the leather
7 ft. 6 in. by 1¾ in., and turn it in 4 in. at the better
end, so that it will be 3 ft. 8 in. long when double.
If the lower part is too long, cut it off, allowing
about 2 in. for splicing, and shave both ends. Both
edges must now be shaved on the inside of the top
and bottom so as to slant outwards; damp the top
from one bend to the other. Round it on the large
groove of the grooving board, crease it along both
edges, and prick it eight per inch. If the bend
seems too weak for the rings these can be lined.
Cut a strip of leather or an old rein, 1 in. wide,
and shave it round along the edges and at the
ends; it must be long enough to run from ring to
ring.

Having prepared the rings and breeching dees
(Fig. 178 and 179, p. 125), cut the bearers from
good leather, 10 in. by ¾ in.; turn them down so
that the points will meet, and flatten the bends.
Prepare one end of each for the buckle, and cut a
groove along the lower side, where there is no
joint, and open it. Place the buckles and dees in
two bearers and the rings and buckle in the two
remaining, joining them on the side under the loop.
Stitch the ends together, making them meet exactly in the centre of the bearer.

After edging the end bends, black them, because
this would be troublesome work later; then cut

four loops, 3½ in. by 1⅜ in., blind-stitch them, and
finish them like the others. Make the pattern match,
finish the back of the bearer, and close the groove
well. A ring must now be put in each end of the
breeching, which is then tacked in place for stitching. Place the lining lately cut in the centre to
raise and strengthen it, and then stitch along both
the sides with three-cord coarse hemp; reserve an
opening about 6 in. from the ring for the bearers,
but do not fix these in it until the body has been
stitched and trimmed.

Some fancy style of stitching can be run along
each end from the ring about 6 in. when the straight
lines have been stitched along the sides, or have
two extra straight lines instead of fancy work,
bringing the lines to a point at 6 in. from the ring,
or again make four rows all along the breeching.

The body being well trimmed and finished, put
both bearers in on the same side, one at each end
where the opening was left. Before this, however, put a small piece of leather inside to fill the
hollow square in the breeching dees; stitch this
firmly in place.

For a hip-strap to match the breeching, cut a
strap 4 ft. long and a little more than double the
width of the buckles on the bearers; slit it for 16 in.
at each end, each slit being the width of the bearer
buckles, and if it is altogether too wide, the waste
should come off the centre. Then edge, black, and
crease it neatly and put eight holes in each end.

The breeching straps to go round the shafts
must be cut 3 ft. 3 in. by 1¼ in., and when the light
ends are turned down, are 2 ft. 6 in. long. Round
the point, and shave that of the turn over; then
prepare the bend for the buckle, and edge, black,
and crease.

Cut four strong loops about ⅞ in. wide, and
having neatly finished them, prick along about 3 in.
from the buckle on the lower side. Tack on the

two loops, one near the buckle in the usual position, and the other close to it but in the reverse position to turn under the strap. Stitch them with strong thread, and, having finished them, bend the strap from the loop to the end of the underpiece and run a dozen stitches on each side at the point. Bend it so that when in position in the ring the parts will be even ; if stitched without bending, the lower part will pucker. Finish the loops and put six holes in each strap.

The back-band (Fig. 190, p. 147) may now be cut out, its complete length being 8 ft. The centre piece passing through the saddle is 3 ft. 3 in. long, the strap or buckling end measuring 1 ft. 6 in., and the remainder being for girth. If it is for a van harness it must be in three thicknesses along the centre, but the strap end will be strong enough in two thicknesses ; when the belly-band part is very light it may also be thickened a little. Place the belly-band buckle in the belly-band end, and if necessary line the chape ; then round the point at the strap end. Crease all along and make two rows on each side of the centre, bringing them together in a point at the extremities. Strictly speaking, one row on each side of the belly band and strap will suffice, but four rows are better ; in the last case, crossing the two middle centre lines at the end of the centre part will improve the appearance.

An opening must be left in the stitching about 1½ in. from the buckle, and two openings lower down, 2 in. apart, to receive three loops when the back-band has been completed. Stitch it about eight per inch, with four-cord thread.

For finishing, use a spokeshave, and rub the stitches underneath to level them well ; round the edges well towards the stitches, making the edges neat in appearance. Scrape it with glasspaper, place the buckle on the hook, and black the edges

and stitches; rub vigorously with the rag in the
right hand, holding each side of the back-band
with the other. The hand should be moved briskly
backwards and forwards so as to dry and polish the
edges well. Now pass a ball of tallow along the
edges and again rub well with the rag, after which
the three loops may be placed on the belly band
and stitched from below, the reverse side to the
other stitches. Then punch eight or nine holes in
the strap and three in the centre part at equal
distances from each crossing of the middle row of
stitches, or from the point of the inner rows if the
centre only has four rows of stitching. Leave
about 1 ft. 6 in. in the centre without holes.

The shaft tugs (Fig. 191, p. 147) are made by
cutting a 1 ft. 7¾ in. length of leather to the same
width as the buckles and back-band—that is, 1¾ in.
Overlap this piece 4½ in., the overlap then being
bent together and knocked flat in the centre.
Through both leathers cut a hole for a buckle in
the bend, and shave a little on the sides of the
hole underneath where the tongue enters, so that
the buckle will run close to the leather.

Shave both ends, the inner very thin and the
outer or top one moderately, cutting a little off
each corner. Crease two rows on each side as on
the back-band, and, having pricked the rows seven
per inch, place the brass or nickel loop loose on the
strap and adjust the buckle therein. Draw the two
holes in the centre, where the buckle is placed,
exactly opposite each other, and stitch the top
point of the overlap along the two inner lines for
about 2 in. through the two leathers.

The shape being now obtained, the tug must be
filled and thickened. This is done by cutting a
piece of leather to fit the inside tight from one side
of the buckle to the other, keeping the buckle in
position while working. Cut a nick in the centre
of each end of this piece so that the tongue and

sides may fit close to the buckle, and then cut
another good piece of leather to go round inside
tight and to overlap at the top for about 1½ in.
Now shave each end and cut a groove on each side
for about the length of the loop on the part intended for it, and overlap it on the side opposite
the loop just below the buckle, with the outer point
of the overlap on the top pointing towards the
buckle and not downwards.

If the tug needs more thickening, place another
piece under the inside lining to reach from the
metal loop (placed below the leather loop) round
the bottom and about halfway up the other side,
leaving it with its thickness at the end near the
metal loop; shave the other end thin.

The metal loop must fit tight between the end
of the piece and the leather loop. It must now be
tacked together from the inside, the joint at the
overlap being made firm. The lining should be of
sole leather; damp it well so that it will fit into its
place and be easier to stitch. Begin stitching at
the buckle with four-cord thread and work round
to the metal loop; then begin at this part on the
other side and stitch to the buckle. Continue to
work in this way until four rows are stitched.

Trim the edges, and black and polish them,
paying particular attention to the part about the
buckle.

There is an opening from the metal loop to the
buckle remaining unstitched; this, with a groove
cut underneath on the lower side, is for the loop,
which must be about 2 in. wide. Having inserted
one side for about half the width of the tug, stitch
it with six-cord double waxed thread from the
buckle to the metal loop, being careful to bring the
awl out with each stitch in the centre of the groove.
Stitch the other side as far as the buckle and make
two or three cross stitches on each side of the
buckle.

If there is much unevenness on the part from the end of the loop to the buckle, a little filling may be put in the space. The loop must be longer than usual because the back-band is extra thick. Shape the loop with a thick bent loop-stick big enough to make plenty of room for a back-band. Black and finish the loop, make a pattern or check it if necessary, and then remove all unevenness, close the grooves, and trim neatly about the loop and buckle. Repeat the operation with the second tug, and then all will be ready.

The big loops for a shaft and the hame tugs, etc., must always be made of firm loop leather,

Fig. 193.—Cab Saddle Tree.

Fig. 192.—Four-wheeled
Cab Saddle.

which will grow hard in finishing and retain its firmness and shape in spite of rain and weather.

For the traces, trace end chains will be needed; van and cab traces are stitched to the hames, being shortened by having ten or twelve links of a chain at the other end. The traces may be 4 ft. 9 in. long by 1¾ in., being 1 ft. 1 in. longer with a chain They must be in three thicknesses, but with two thicknesses to go through the chain dee and hame ring (Fig. 171, p. 123).

In putting the upper and lower part together, place the light end of one against the heavy end of the other, thus levelling the trace and making it of equal strength. Shave the points well where one ends and another begins—for example, the lining in the hame ring and chain dee. Having turned the leathers down to the right length, crease and prick them, seven or eight per inch. Tack down with only the chain on and stitch the four rows, but not so far in the hame end as to prevent the hame ring being placed in position when they are finished. When both are stitched, trim, black, and polish them ; then rub down the stitches underneath, and having fixed them to the hame ring, stitch them to it, and finish that end like the other parts.

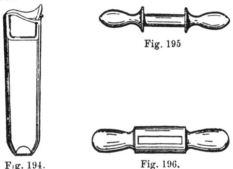

Fig. 195

Fig. 194.   Fig. 196.

Fig. 194.—Hansom Cab Saddle. Figs. 195 and 196.—
Rein Stops.

Make two hame straps ⅞ in. wide, the top strap 1 ft. 10 in. long, and the lower 1 ft. 4 in. Adjust the buckles at the strong ends and make two loops, reversing them as on the breeching straps ; have seven or eight holes in each.

The driving reins are 1 in. wide, and the fore-part near the horse's head is 6 ft. long on each side. Turn down the chapes at the strong ends for the buckles, and shave the point thin ; then cut two billets, 1 ft. long, from a firm piece of leather. Shave one end and round the other, and, having cut two loops, edge and finish them; then rub all and crease them close to the edge with a hot creaser.

Adjust the buckles, prick the part of the billet to be stitched a little inside the outer crease, and stitch the billets in with the loop. When the loops are finished, make a hole in each billet far enough from the point to allow what is over to come through the loop, and cover the stitches on the front.

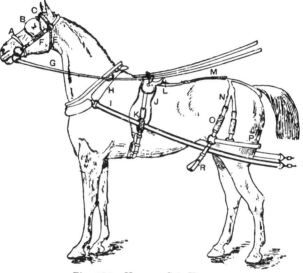

Fig. 197.—Hansom Cab Harness.

Make the brown hand parts 5 ft. 6 in. long, and narrow the light end of one part to pass through into a $\frac{3}{4}$-in. covered buckle; then turn down the other point and narrow it for the buckle chape. Finally, prepare a narrow brown loop. Shave and taper the other end of the hand parts to a point, edge both sides below and under, and damp the edges with gum and water, or with water only.

Polish them well by rubbing, making them even everywhere; brown paper is excellent for polishing either black or brown edges.

After creasing them very near the edge with a screw crease, place the buckle and loop on the end and mark a line a little inside the outer one, about $2\frac{1}{2}$ in. or 3 in. long, on the end to be spliced on the fore-part. Prick it fine and stitch with a fine thread, pointing the stitches in the upper end to the same shape as the others. The hand parts can be obtained ready cut with buckles, and then all that has to be done is to shave the ends and stitch them to the fore-parts.

Four-wheel cab harness can be made in the same way as van harness, except the saddle (Fig. 192), which is made exactly like a gig saddle, but is heavier and has brass or nickel screw studs in each corner of the skirts; Fig. 193 shows the top or tree.

Hansom cab harness is not much different, though the saddle (Fig. 194) is lighter, and some have rollers inside the saddle so that the back-band may run smoothly backwards and forwards through the tree; these trees are made to order. In Fig. 197, A indicates the noseband, B winker, C forehead band, E throatlash, F cheek, G rein, H collar, I trace, J saddle, K shaft tug, L cantle of saddle, M crupper, N tug strap, O bearer, P breeching, and R shaft strap.

The hansom reins must be about 20 ft. long on each side, each brown hand part being about 7 ft. long. They are generally showy and ornamental. Winkers and saddle, hip straps, martingale, and breastplate have ornaments; the reins have ivory rings and stops (Figs. 195 and 196), and there is a face-piece ornament on the bridle.

Both four-wheeler and hansom harness (Fig. 197) are larger and heavier than gig harness, except at the saddle.

INDEX.